Assessing the Capitalist Peace

Researchers have recently reinvigorated the idea that key features associated with a capitalist organization of the economy render nation states internally and externally more peaceful. According to this adage, the contract intensity of capitalist societies and the openness of the economy are among the main attributes that drive these empirical relationships. Studies on the Capitalist Peace supplement the broadly received examinations on the role that economic integration in the form of trade and foreign direct investment play in the pacification of states. Some proponents of the peace-through-capitalism thesis controversially contend that this relationship supersedes prominent explanations like *Democratic Peace* according to which democratic pairs of states face a reduced risk of conflict.

This volume takes stock of this debate. Authors also evaluate the theoretical underpinnings of the relationship and offer an up-to-date idea history and classification of current research. Leading scholars comment on these theoretical propositions and empirical findings.

This book is an extended and revised version of a special issue of *International Interactions*.

Gerald Schneider is Professor of Political Science at the University of Konstanz, Germany, President of the *European Political Science Association*, and Editor of *European Union Politics*. He has published on European Union decision making, the causes and consequences of political violence and various other topics. He is a former Vice President of the International Studies Associates and has advised governments, IGOs and research institutions across the world.

Nils Petter Gleditsch is Research Professor at the Centre for the Study of Civil War at the Peace Research Institute Oslo (PRIO), Professor of Political Science at the Norwegian University of Science and Technology in Trondheim, and Associate Editor of *Journal of Peace Research*. He served as President of the International Studies Association in 2008–09. He has published numerous articles and books on armed conflict, environmental security, the peace dividend, and related issues.

Assessing the Capitalist Peace

Edited by
**Gerald Schneider and
Nils Petter Gleditsch**

LONDON AND NEW YORK

First published 2013
by Routledge
2 Park Square, Milton Park, Abingdon, Oxfordshire OX14 4RN

Simultaneously published in the USA and Canada
by Routledge
711 Third Avenue, New York, NY 10017

First issued in paperback 2015

Routledge is an imprint of the Taylor & Francis Group, an informa business

© 2013 Taylor & Francis

This book is based on a special issue of *International Interactions*, vol. 36, issue 2. The Publisher requests to those authors who may be citing this book to state, also, the bibliographical details of the special issue on which the book was based.

All rights reserved. No part of this book may be reprinted or reproduced or utilised in any form or by any electronic, mechanical, or other means, now known or hereafter invented, including photocopying and recording, or in any information storage or retrieval system, without permission in writing from the publishers.

Trademark notice: Product or corporate names may be trademarks or registered trademarks, and are used only for identification and explanation without intent to infringe.

British Library Cataloguing in Publication Data
A catalogue record for this book is available from the British Library

ISBN 13: 978-1-138-94517-3 (pbk)
ISBN 13: 978-0-415-52989-1 (hbk)

Typeset in Times New Roman
by Taylor & Francis Books

Publisher's Note
The publisher would like to make readers aware that the chapters in this book may be referred to as articles as they are identical to the articles published in the special issue. The publisher accepts responsibility for any inconsistencies that may have arisen in the course of preparing this volume for print.

Contents

Citation Information	vii
1. The Capitalist Peace: The Origins and Prospects of a Liberal Idea *Gerald Schneider and Nils Petter Gleditsch*	1
2. International Crises and the Capitalist Peace *Erik Gartzke and J. Joseph Hewitt*	10
3. Capitalism, Commitment, and Peace *Patrick J. McDonald*	41
4. Capitalism, Peace, and the Historical Movement of Ideas *John Mueller*	64
5a. Capitalism and Peace: It's Keynes, not Hayek *Michael Mousseau, Omer F. Orsun, Jameson Lee Ungerer and Demet Yalcin Mousseau*	80
5b. Does Capitalism Account for the Democratic Peace? The Evidence Still Says No *Allan Dafoe and Bruce Russett*	110
5c. Does the Market-Capitalist Peace Supersede the Democratic Peace? The Evidence Still Says Yes *Michael Mousseau, Omer F. Orsun and Jameson Lee Ungerer*	127
6. Commentaries:	
Coming to Terms with the Capitalist Peace *Michael Mousseau*	137
Capitalist Influences and Peace *Richard Rosecrance*	144
Capitalism *or* Democracy? Not So Fast *Bruce Russett*	150
The Capitalist Peace and the Rise of China: Establishing Global Harmony by Economic Interdependence *Erich Weede*	158
Index	166

Citation Information

The following chapters were originally published in *International Interactions*, volume 36, issue 2 (2010). When citing this material, please use the original page numbering for each article, as follows:

Chapter 2
International Crises and the Capitalist Peace
Erik Gartzke and J. Joseph Hewitt
International Interactions, volume 36, issue 2 (2010) pp. 115-145

Chapter 3
Capitalism, Commitment, and Peace
Patrick J. McDonald
International Interactions, volume 36, issue 2 (2010) pp. 146-168

Chapter 4
Capitalism, Peace, and the Historical Movement of Ideas
John Mueller
International Interactions, volume 36, issue 2 (2010) pp. 169-184

Chapter 6
Commentary section
International Interactions, volume 36, issue 2 (2010) pp. 185-213

The Capitalist Peace: The Origins and Prospects of a Liberal Idea[1]

GERALD SCHNEIDER

University of Konstanz and Centre for the Study of Civil War, Peace Research Institute of Oslo (PRIO), Norway

NILS PETTER GLEDITSCH

Peace Research Institute of Oslo (PRIO), Norway, and the Norwegian University of Science and Technology, Trondheim

Heralding the "end of history," Fukuyama (1992) infamously forecast the total triumph of the twin sisters of liberalism—capitalism and democracy. Twenty years later, over one-third of the world's population live in countries characterized as "not free" (Freedom House 2009) and the economic crisis that a frenzied financial sector has brought over the world has considerably tarnished the public perception of the capitalist organization of markets. History is thus far from over, and the "victory" of the liberal coalition led by the United States seems to have been squandered.

Such developments, however, do not relieve social scientists from the necessity to uncover whether the main attributes of a liberal state—free elections and market economies—have the side effects often attributed to them. One of these hotly debated outcomes is the peace-building effect of democracy and capitalism that Schumpeter (1919) sketched after World War I and that Weede (2003) finally labeled "capitalist peace."[2] Proponents of this variant of the liberal thesis argue that capitalism renders states more status quo oriented and less concerned with traditional security issues. They expect that various facets of capitalism, ranging from increased development to free trade and foreign investment, are positively related to peace. In view

---

[1]Most of the articles assembled in this volume appeared in the special issue of *International Interactions* on the capitalist peace. This introduction offers an updated survey of the main issues in the academic debate on this topic and summarizes the original contributions to the volume plus the three chapters that we have added (Dafoe and Russett 2013, Mousseau et al. 2013a, b). Our work has been supported by the German Research Foundation (DFG) (Schneider) and the Research Council of Norway (Gleditsch).
[2]Outside of the social sciences, the idea has a much older history. In the journals covered by Jstor, the first coinage of the "capitalist peace" is made in a review of a book that questions the role of the USA labor movement during World War I (Simpson 1941). A Google books search dug up an equally critical World War I pamphlet by a presidential candidate of the Socialist Party of America (Benson 1915).

of the continuing controversies over the advantages and disadvantages of capitalism it is not surprising that this view is contested. Drawing on the theory of imperialism, Hilferding (1947 [1910]), Lenin (1921 [1917]), and other Marxist writers, as well as more modern supporters of dependency theory and critical theory see in capitalism one of the key harbingers of crisis and war (see, e.g., Packer 2003).

Despite these controversies, the peace-through-capitalism thesis has only recently received systematic scrutiny by the conflict research community, in the wake of a period where the liberal research agenda was dominated first by the democratic peace (Doyle 1986), then by the Kantian peace (Russett and Oneal 2001). However, Rummel (1979, 1983) wrote of the pacific effects of libertarianism, including economic freedom, long before he switched to the more mainstream term of democracy. He advocated a monadic thesis ("Freedom inhibits violence," Rummel, 1979:292) as well as a dyadic thesis ("Libertarian systems mutually preclude violence," p. 277). He further formulated a "positive peace principle" ("Minimize the power of government," Rummel 1981:266) in direct opposition to the concept of positive peace developed by Galtung (1969), which he saw as a "socialist theory of peace" (p. 83). Early peace researchers (Russett 1967; Wallensteen 1973) had studied some key features of capitalism, notably trade, but capitalism itself generally had a negative image in the founding years of peace research (Gleditsch 2008:707). In his most frequently cited article, Galtung (1971) saw asymmetric trade as an important form of imperialism,[3] views echoed to some extent in the critique of commercial liberalism by Barbieri (2002). Interestingly, the twentieth-century foundations of this argument by Angell (1910) precedes the Schumpeterian vision that capitalist entrepreneurship and democracy go hand in hand as a source of peace. The analytically narrower peace-through-trade literature, which was reinvigorated by Rosecrance (1986) and which Nye (1988) dubbed "commercial liberalism," focuses exclusively on how the international activities of economic actors influence foreign policy choices and, by extension, the bilateral and multilateral relations of states. How other aspects of capitalism such as the protection of property rights or the lack of interventionist economic policies might affect foreign policy decisions remained largely unexplored. Toward the end of the Cold War, Mueller (1989) observed that industrialized countries rarely if ever fought each other, and ten years later he argued that democracy was overrated but that capitalism did not get enough credit (Mueller 1999).

That the capitalist peace argument lay dormant so long in the quantitative literature is astonishing in light of Bremer's (1992) landmark study, which introduced dyads as the standard unit of analysis for research on interstate

---

[3] Although Galtung's reconceptualization of the Marxist theory of imperialism also entailed a critique of capitalism, he did not limit his negative appraisal of imperialism to the capitalist form.

war. He established that joint development strongly decreases the likelihood of conflict. A theoretical basis for a peace based on free trade was sketched by Weede (1995), who undertook one of the first systematic attempts to weave the organization of markets into a more general liberal argument. Nevertheless, it took several years until such claims were further developed and systematically contrasted with the empirical evidence. This first wave of capitalist peace studies highlighted how capitalist markets create peaceful preferences and how the level of development conditions the liberal peace (Hegre 2000; Mousseau 2000; Mousseau, Hegre, and Oneal 2003). Mousseau (2000, 2009), as well as Gartzke (2007, see also Gartzke et al. 2001), were the first to challenge the Kantian peace in econometric studies based on this emerging literature. Gartzke argued that the democratic peace was just an epiphenomenon of capital openness and free trade. McDonald (2009), using similar methods, found the capitalist peace to condition but not to invalidate the democratic peace, while Mousseau (2009) provides an unconditional test of his earlier argument (2000) that capitalism can cause two main components of the Kantian peace, democracy and trade, as well as peace.

This volume explores whether and how such findings alter the liberal research agenda. To this end, we have organized a debate that unites leading capitalist peace scholars as well as some prominent skeptics. In this introduction, we discuss the main research traditions and assess their relative merits before moving on to a presentation of the research articles and the challenges that future research has to confront.

THE CURRENT DEBATE AND THE MAIN CHALLENGES

We can generally distinguish between four main arguments in favor of the capitalist peace. The first one is based on a hedonistic understanding of human nature and argues that capitalism alters human behavior and transforms belligerent individuals residing in interventionist states into peace-loving consumers, traders, and business people. The second set of arguments does not share the naïve optimism of the hedonistic school of thought with regard to an unconditional effect of capitalism on state behavior. Proponents of the more skeptical position only believe in the peacefulness of unregulated markets in certain configurations. A key modifying force, introduced by Schumpeter (1919), is democracy. In his view, the power of the capitalist peace conviction within a country depends on the distribution of power between protectionists and the adherents of the market economy who both are able to voice their wishes within a democratic setting. Another conditionality argument maintains that the pacifying influence of trade grows with the level of development (Hegre 2000; Mousseau 2000; Mousseau et al. 2003). A third line of reasoning refers to the protection of property rights and argues that the contract intensity of capitalist economies renders them more peaceful (Mousseau 2000, 2010).

Drawing on the crisis bargaining literature, a final argument maintains that capitalist economies are better able to signal their resolve than closed economies (Gartzke, Li, and Boehmer 2001; Gartzke 2007).

The contributions to this volume as well as the invited commentaries reflect the whole range of arguments that have been made in favor of the capitalist peace thesis. Extending the argument in Gartzke (2007), Gartzke and Hewitt (2010) rely on the ICB data on crisis behavior, which overlaps only to a limited degree with the data on interstate disputes used in the earlier work. The crisis data allow them to test not only hypotheses about the onset of conflict, but also about the escalation of conflict and the level of severity. The peace-building effects of capitalism, as measured by financial openness, persist.

McDonald (2010) makes use of a different indicator of capitalism and tests the hypothesis that large quantities of public property heighten the risks of being targeted in a military conflict. Using a monadic as well as a dyadic design he concludes that capitalism does indeed promote peace.

Mueller (2010) focuses on three cultural or attitudinal prerequisites of the capitalist peace: that the growth of economic well-being is a dominant goal; that peace is seen as better than war for promoting innovation, progress, and growth; and that wealth is perceived to be best achieved through exchange rather than conquest.

Gartzke and Hewitt conclude that democracy makes no significant independent contribution to peace, McDonald reaches a more limited conclusion: capitalism plays a greater role than democracy in limiting military conflict between states. Russett (2009, 2010), relying to a large extent on Dafoe (2008, see also Dafoe 2011) for the empirics, argues that democracy still counts, and views the contribution of capitalism as supplementary rather than primary. Mueller thinks that a capitalist peace is more likely than a democratic peace, but sees peace and not capitalism as the determining factor in the relationship.

Mousseau et al. (2013a) trace their argument that contract intensive economies are more peaceful to the writings of John Maynard Keynes. Their regressions show that the addition of this concept renders the impact of democracy insignificant. Dafoe and Russett (2013) criticize the reasoning of Mousseau et al. and maintain, based on an altered research design, that liberal scholars should not give up the democratic peace thesis. Referring to the Lakatosian tradition in the philosophy of science, Mousseau and colleagues (2013b) counter this reply and provide some fresh evidence supporting the contract thesis in a debate that will continue elsewhere (Dafoe and Russett 2013).

These contributions and the accompanying comments certainly move us beyond the polarized debate that portrays capitalism either as a source of conflict or as a source of peace. However, the capitalist peace-thesis has to address several challenges if it endeavors to become a real alternative to the Kantian peace or just a qualification of the main liberal arguments. With the exception of the informal arguments advanced by Gartzke (2007), Mousseau (2003, 2009), and McDonald (2009), a key problem of the current capitalist peace literature is its lack of precise micro-foundations that link markets and their main attributes to peace. We do not reject the value of nonformal reasoning. However, the development of the civil war literature has shown that the influence of development on the risk of civil war, for a long time considered to be a key finding of this literature, is based on shaky analytical foundations. According to Fearon's (2008), criticism of rent-seeking models of internal war, higher development makes the bounty for the contending forces more attractive, but it makes conflict also more costly as wages and other compensations for the soldiers simultaneously rise. A similar indeterminacy is likely to hurt models that try to link development to conflict. As nations get richer, they can afford security more cheaply and better protect themselves. However, they also become more attractive targets. Developed aggressors face a similar dilemma. They can use their wealth for their fighting capabilities, but also risk destroying more resources through an attack than less developed attackers. If development as an indicator is linked to peace in any meaningful way, it needs to be based on a more convincing theoretical footing.

A related theoretical limitation of some key contributions to the current capitalist peace literature is the use of the same game-theoretic arguments that have been used as a foundation for the democratic peace. If both democracies and capitalist societies are better able to signal their resolve in an interstate crisis and if the models rely on the same set of actors, we are unable to differentiate between the micro-foundations of these two strands of liberal scholarship. What is particularly lacking is a clear understanding of how "capitalists" as well as "entrepreneurs", and thus the key actors in the Schumpeterian modeling tradition (cf. McCraw 2007), influence public policymaking. The case study evidence assembled by McDonald (2009) is a step in the right direction, but we need more general support for the claim that capitalists lobby for peace in a systematic fashion. Studies on the interactions between international politics and financial markets strongly suggest that investors are rather opportunistic and adapt their behavior surprisingly quickly to the policy decisions of government leaders (cf. Bechtel and Schneider 2010).

Empirically, the literature on the capitalist peace is often hard to distinguish from other research programs in the field. For instance, commercial liberalism, one of the established cornerstones of the Kantian peace tripod, never focused exclusively on trade, but encompassed all sorts of economic bonds between nations. It as a major sign of conceptual progress that McDonald (2009) clearly differentiates between the capitalist and the commercial variant of the liberal peace. This separation is, however, unlikely to solve all conceptual problems. Capitalist economic policies that lead to the deeper integration of an economy into international markets should be considered to be one of the ultimate driving forces of capitalist peace, but the level of development is in the light of some economic growth theorists (Sachs and Warner 1995) endogenous to these policy choices. Therefore, by extension, the capitalist peace could be considered being an epiphenomenon of commercial liberalism. This leads to the question of what attributes of a capitalist economy should be used in empirical applications. At the moment, there are so many indicators that it is hard to see how the "capitalist peace" differs from rival explanations. Some manifestations of the capitalist peace notion that stress a market economy and a strong state border on what could equally well be called a social-democratic peace.

As is often the case with a new research agenda, such theoretical, conceptual, and empirical challenges will be addressed in the next generation of studies on the capitalist peace. With the publication of this volume, replication data become available for the articles by Mousseau et al. as well as by Dafoe and Russett; replication data for McDonald and Gartzke and Hewitt are downloadable at the homepage of *International Interactions*.[4] Skeptics will no doubt examine their data for robustness and debatable interpretations.

In this volume we concentrate on the relationship between capitalism and interstate peace, but similar research is in progress on intrastate peace (de Soysa and Fjelde 2010). We have invited comments from several colleagues who have shaped the earlier discussion on the interface between foreign policy and the liberal vision of the economy. These comments by Michael Mousseau (2010), Richard Rosecrance (2010), Bruce Russett (2010), and Erich Weede (2010) provide sufficient evidence that the controversies over the capitalist peace thesis will considerably shape the liberal research agenda in conflict studies in the years to come.

REFERENCES

Angell, Norman. (1910) *The Great Illusion. A Study of the Relation of Military Power in Nations to Their Economic and Social Advantages.* London: Heinemann.
Barbieri, Katherine. (2002) *The Liberal Illusion. Does Trade Promote Peace?* Ann Arbor, MI: University of Michigan Press.
Bechtel, Michael M., and Gerald Schneider. (2010) Eliciting Substance from "Hot Air": Financial Market Responses to EU Summit Decisions on European Defense. *International Organization* 64(2):199–223.

---

[4]Replication material for the former chapters can be found at http://dvn.iq.harvard.edu/dvn/dv/capitalistpeace, and for the latter ones at http://dvn.iq.harvard.edu/dvn/.

Benson, Allan L. (1915) *A Way to Prevent War*. Girard, KS: Appeal to Reason. Available at http://www.archive.org/stream/awaytopreventwa02bensgoog#page/n12/mode/1up

Bremer, Stuart. (1992) Dangerous Dyads: Conditions Affecting the Likelihood of Interstate War, 1816–1965. *Journal of Conflict Resolution* 36(2):309–341.

Dafoe, Allan. (2008) Democracy Still Matters: The Risks of Sample Censoring, and Cross-Sectional and Temporal Controls. Unpublished manuscript, Department of Political Science, University of California Berkeley.

Dafoe, Allan. (2011) Statistical Critiques of the Democratic Peace: Caveat Emptor. *American Journal of Political Science* 55(2):247–262.

Dafoe, Allan, and Bruce Russett (2013) Does Capitalism Account for the Democratic Peace? The Evidence Still Says No. In *Assessing the Capitalist Peace*, eds. Gerald Schneider and Nils Petter Gleditsch. Abingdon: Routledge, pp.[....].

Dafoe, Allan, and Bruce Russett (2013) Explorations and Challenges to the Democratic Peace: Weighing the Evidence and Cautious Inference. *International Studies Quarterly* (in press).

De Soysa, Indra, and Hanne Fjelde. (2010) Is the Hidden Hand an Iron Fist? Capitalism & Civil Peace, 1970–2005. *Journal of Peace Research* 47(4):287–298.

Doyle, Michael W. (1986) Liberalism and World Politics. *American Political Science Review* 80(4):1151–1169.

Fearon, James D. (2008) Economic Development, Insurgency, and Civil War. In *Institutions and Economic Performance*, ed. Elhanan Helpman. Cambridge, MA: Harvard University Press, pp.292–328.

Freedom House. (2009) *Freedom in the World*. New York: Freedom House. Available at http://www.freedomhouse.org

Fukuyama, Francis. (1992) *The End of History and the Last Man*. New York: Free Press.

Galtung, Johan. (1969) Violence, Peace, and Peace Research. *Journal of Peace Research* 6(3):167–191.

Galtung, Johan. (1971) A Structural Theory of Imperialism. *Journal of Peace Research* 8(2):81–117.

Gartzke, Erik. (2007) The Capitalist Peace. *American Journal of Political Science* 51(1):166–191.

Gartzke, Erik, and J. Joseph Hewitt. (2010) International Crises and the Capitalist Peace. *International Interactions* 36(2):115–145.

Gartzke, Erik, Quan Li, and Charles Boehmer. (2001) Investing in the Peace: Economic Interdependence and International Conflict. *International Organization* 55(2):391–438.

Gleditsch, Nils Petter. (2008) The Liberal Moment Fifteen Years On. *International Studies Quarterly* 52(4):691–712.

Hegre, Håvard. (2000) Development and the Liberal Peace: What Does It Take to Be a Trading State? *Journal of Peace Research* 37(1):5–30.

Hilferding, Rudolf. (1947 [1910]) *Das Finanzkapital. Eine Studie über die jüngste Entwicklung des Kapitalismus* (*Finance Capital. A Study of the Latest Phase of Capitalist Development*). Berlin: Dietz. (English version Abingdon: Routledge, 1981.)

Lenin, Vladimir I. (1921 [1917]) *Der Imperialismus als jüngste Etappe des Kapitalismus* [Imperialism: The Highest Stage of Capitalism]. Hamburg: Cahnbley. (Originally published as *Imperializm kak novejsij etap kapitalizma*. Petrograd: Shisn i Snanije.)

McCraw, Thomas K. (2007) *Prophet of Innovation. Joseph Schumpeter and Creative Destruction*. Cambridge, MA: Harvard University Press.

McDonald, Patrick J. (2009) *The Invisible Hand of Peace: Capitalism, the War Machine, and International Relations Theory*. New York: Cambridge University Press.

McDonald, Patrick J. (2010) Capitalism, Commitment, and Peace. *International Interactions* 36(2):146–168.

Mousseau, Michael. (2000) Market Prosperity, Democratic Consolidation, and Democratic Peace. *Journal of Conflict Resolution* 44(4):472–507.

Mousseau, Michael. (2003) The Nexus of Market Society, Liberal Preferences, and Democratic Peace: Interdisciplinary Theory and Evidence. *International Studies Quarterly* 47(4):483–510.

Mousseau, Michael. (2009) The Social Market Roots of the Democratic Peace. *International Security* 33(4):52–86.

Mousseau, Michael. (2010) Coming to Terms with the Capitalist Peace. *International Interactions* 36(2):185–192.

Mousseau, Michael, Håvard Hegre, and John R. Oneal. (2003) How the Wealth of Nations Conditions the Liberal Peace. *European Journal of International Relations* 9(2):277–314.

Mousseau, Michael, Omer F. Orsun, Jameson Lee Ungerer, and Demet Yalcin Mousseau. (2013a) "Capitalism and Peace: It's Keynes, not Hayek." In *Assessing the Capitalist Peace*, eds. Gerald Schneider and Nils Petter Gleditsch. Abingdon: Routledge, pp.[….].

Mousseau, Michael, Omer F. Orsu, and James Lee Ungerer (2013b). "Does the Market-Capitalist Peace Supersde the Democratic Peace? The Evidence Stilly Says Yes". In *Assessing the Capitalist Peace*, eds. Gerald Schneider and Nils Petter Gleditsch, Abingdon: Routledge, pp.[….]

Mueller, John. (1989) *Retreat from Doomsday: The Obsolescence of Major War*. New York: Basic Books.

Mueller, John. (1999) *Capitalism, Democracy & Ralph's Pretty Good Grocery*. Princeton, NJ: Princeton University Press.

Mueller, John. (2010) Capitalism, Peace, and the Historical Movement of Ideas. *International Interactions* 36(2):169–184.

Nye, Joseph S., Jr. (1988) Neorealism and Neoliberalism. *World Politics* 40(2):235–251.

Packer, Dave. (2003) Capitalism Means War. *Socialist Outlook* (01). Available at http://www.isg-fi.org.uk/spip.php?article10

Rosecrance, Richard. (1986) *The Rise of the Trading State: Conquest and Commerce in the Modern World*. New York: Basic Books.

Rosecrance, Richard. (2010). Capitalist Influences and Peace. *International Interactions* 36(2):192–198.

Rummel, Rudolph J. (1979) *Understanding Conflict and War, Volume 4: War, Power, Peace*. Beverly Hills, CA: Sage.

Rummel, Rudolph J. (1981) *Understanding Conflict and War, Volume 5: The Just Peace*. Beverly Hills, CA: Sage.

Rummel, Rudolph J. (1983) Libertarianism and International Violence. *Journal of Conflict Resolution* 27(1):27–71.

Russett, Bruce (1967) *International Regions and the International System: A Study in Political Ecology*. Chicago, IL: Rand McNally.

Russett, Bruce. (2009) Democracy, War, and Expansion through Historical Lenses. *European Journal of International Relations* 15(1):9–36.

Russett, Bruce. (2010) Capitalism *or* Democracy? Not so Fast. *International Interactions* 36(2):198–205.

Russett, Bruce, and John R. Oneal. (2001) *Triangulating Peace: Democracy, Interdependence, and International Organizations*. New York: Norton.

Sachs, Jeffrey D., and Warner, Andrew M. (1995) Economic Reform and the Process of Global Integration. *Brookings Papers on Economic Activity*, pp.1–118.

Schumpeter, Joseph A. (1919) Zur Soziologie der Imperialismen (Sociology of Imperialisms). *Archiv für Sozialwissenschaft und Sozialpolitik* 46:1–39 and 275–310. English version in Richard Swedberg, ed. (1991) *The Economics and Sociology of Capitalism*. Princeton, NJ: Princeton University Press, pp.141–219.

Simpson, Smith. (1941) Review of *Labor in War-time* by John Steuben, International Publishers. *American Political Science Review* 35(2):380.

Wallensteen, Peter. (1973) *Structure and War: On International Relations 1920–1968.* Stockholm: Raben & Sjögren.

Weede, Erich. (1995) Economic Policy and International Security: Rent-Seeking, Free Trade, and Democratic Peace. *European Journal of International Relations* 1(4):519–537.

Weede, Erich. (2003) Globalization: Creative Destruction and the Prospect of a Capitalist Peace. In *Globalization and Armed Conflict,* eds Gerald Schneider, Katherine Barbieri, and Nils Petter Gleditsch. Lanham, MD: Rowman & Littlefield, pp.311–323.

Weede, Erich. (2010) The Capitalist Peace and the Rise of China: Establishing Global Harmony by Economic Interdependence. *International Interactions* 36(2):206–213.

International Crises and the Capitalist Peace

ERIK GARTZKE
University of California, San Diego

J. JOSEPH HEWITT
University of Maryland

Recent research suggests that free markets and economic development contribute to a reduction in interstate conflict. This "capitalist peace" has been seen alternately to complement or to supplant the more well-known democratic peace effect. Here, we compare the behavior of democracies and capitalist dyads in the context of the Interstate Crisis Behavior (ICB) dataset. The ICB data offers a number of advantages in assessing the conflict decisions of national leaders, rather than the accidents of subordinates or others. In particular, we explore as yet untested implications of each perspective, examining the effect of regime type and economic and interest variables on escalation and crisis intensity. Our findings provide new evidence that free markets, economic development, and similar interests account for the special peace in liberal dyads.

For much of the second half of the twentieth century, in the aftermath of World War II, mainstream international relations dismissed out-of-hand any notion that peace could be perpetual. It was not until the introduction of

---

We thank Nils Petter Gleditsch, Gerald Schneider, and Wolfgang Wagner for helpful comments. Earlier drafts of this paper were presented at the annual meeting of the American Economic Association, January 6–8, 2006, Boston, and at the Jan Tinbergen Peace Science Conference, June 27–29, Amsterdam. Data and a STATA.do file capable of replicating all of the results will be available from the authors upon request, and will also be available on the journal's dataverse page at http://dvn.iq.harvard.edu/dvn/dv/internationalinteractions.

statistical techniques that scholars began to demonstrate that peace had in fact broken out in the midst of the cold war. Conventional scholarly wisdom was being overturned, even as "people power" toppled the Iron Curtain and overturned autocrats around the world. Though no less warlike than other states in general, democracies appeared less prone to fight each other. Researchers naturally assumed that democracy caused this special peace. Faith in the democratic peace was based on induction and the normative appeal of the "lawlike" observation, even while the theoretical underpinnings of the relationship lagged behind. As one observer quipped "We know it works in practice. Now we have to see if it works in theory!" (Lipson 2005:1).

Making the democratic peace work in theory has proven surprisingly difficult. Problems in the fabrication of a canonical explanation for democratic peace may simply reflect the inherent complexity of the contingent observation. Accounting for peace using democracy requires that polities modify their foreign policies in response to regime characteristics of particular opponents. Most connections between foreign policy and international relations had been abandoned on the advice of realists like Kenneth Waltz. Though domestic political origins of international relations are now being explored with renewed vigor, it will take time before researchers have made up for generations of inattention. It is also possible that problems encountered in shoehorning democracy into the democratic peace indicate the need for critical inquiry. There are other plausible causes of peace among prosperous, liberal societies that until recently had received little scholarly attention.

The liberal tradition actually consists of two schools of thought on the causes of peace, one emphasizing representative government and international deliberative bodies and the other advocating global markets and economic development. Research on the democratic peace has chosen to pursue the liberal political school, with a particular focus on Kant's *Perpetual Peace*. Attention to regime type is certainly not unreasonable, but much of the available scholarship can be faulted for ignoring or largely discounting the contributions of liberal political economy.[1] Montesquieu, Bastiat, Cobden, Angell, and others offered insights that were considered comparable to Kant at the dawn of the last century. While both schools fell out of favor in the wake of two world wars, only Kant has received significant scholarly attention, and an intellectual makeover, in recent years.

An increasing number of contemporary scholars are beginning to return to the idea that markets hold the potential for interstate cooperation. Still, many questions remain, even as skepticism about the capitalist peace persists. We use the Interstate Crisis Behavior (ICB) dataset to evaluate new

---

[1] Studies of the democratic peace often include a variable for trade dependence, but measuring markets in this way is no more representative of capitalism than coding democracy as the presence or absence of a constitution, or the nominal practice of voting. Trade may be the least effective component of the capitalist peace (Gartzke, Li, and Boehmer 2001).

hypotheses about the effects of democracy and capitalism on crisis intensity and escalation. Critical comparisons are essential in refining our understanding of the liberal peace. We also replicate work by Gartzke (2007), making a few corrections to this study and demonstrating consistent results.

Our analysis builds on a vision of peace involving free markets and economic development. First, development has contrasting consequences for interstate conflict. Technological innovation and industrialization vastly increase the ability of some countries to project power, while modern production systems eventually make it cheaper to purchase, rather than coerce, land and the resources that exist in and on territory. In contrast, the extension of economic and other interests beyond national borders increases incentives to "police" relevant regions and exercise influence, sometimes through force. Second, since advanced industrial nations do not fundamentally disagree on critical aspects of the international system, most fighting now occurs among developing countries or between developed and developing states (Gartzke 2006; Gartzke and Rohner 2009). Third, global financial networks serve as a test of the credibility of leaders' claims and discourage bluffing (Gartzke and Li 2003). Mechanisms that facilitate the transmission of credible information across international boundaries limit bargaining failure, enhancing interstate peace (Fearon 1994; Schultz 1998, 2001).

We find considerable support for this modernized conception of the capitalist peace. Nations that are financially open to the global economy, and that face constrained or interdependent monetary policies, experience fewer interstate crises. Development appears to discourage contiguous states from fighting over territory, while increasing policy-based crises. Policy affinity leads to fewer ICB crises. Democracy, in contrast, appears to have no significant impact on interstate crisis behavior. Results are also consistent with our expectations for crisis intensity and escalation.

LITERATURE: NORMS, INSTITUTIONS, AND INFORMATION

Evidence is the most important disciplining factor in science. Without it, inquiry risks becoming a philosophical exercise, expressing the (hopefully finite) possibilities that could obtain given a particular set of circumstances. At the same time, reason is necessary for any compelling causal account. If the democratic peace agenda can be faulted, it is probably because research has relied too heavily on evidence, and too little on theory. Explanations of dubious deductive coherence could be advanced because their predictions were validated, often by empirical relationships that were already known or were similar to existing evidence. Explanations for the capitalist peace seem to be mimicking the evolution of democratic peace theories. This is not surprising, since both sets of liberal arguments occupy the same, or a very similar, empirical space. In both literatures, theories can be organized around the putative causal mechanism of peace: norms, institutions, or information. Insights gained from the democratic peace research agenda could prove helpful in honing deductive capitalist peace theories. Still, if researchers are to avoid the trap of inductive theorizing, we must come prepared with coherent explanations and more precise hypothetical expectations.

Democratic Peace

Back in the distant days when the quantitative research agenda on the democratic peace was getting its start, adherents debated whether democracies were more peaceful with each other because of "norms" or "institutions." Both arguments involved constraints on executive power. The claim was that authorities in democracies might be willing to fight, but that they were held in check by attributes of liberal domestic politics. Norms are soft constraints; democracies would not use force against one another because that was not the democratic way (Dixon 1993, 1994). Citizens in a democracy are restrained from violence by (internal or external) modes of appropriateness (Risse-Kappen 1995, 1996). If democratic citizens were loath to use force because of an "ought," perhaps so too democracies were reluctant to fight out of a sense of justice or obligation, or out of fear that other states or groups would not see the nation's actions as just (Flynn and Farrell 1999).

Institutions pose an analogous barrier to violence, though here the constraints are imposed by, in effect, a formalization of these same norms (Bueno de Mesquita and Lalman 1992). This hard constraint, it is argued, ensures that democracies do not fight each other because force is not a sanctioned method of competition within the democratic political process. The same institutions that prevent violence within democracies—institutions that sponsor deliberation and debate as conflict resolution mechanisms—might well prevent democracies from pursuing politics through violence abroad, at least when confronted by other democracies (Ray 1995, 1997; Russett 1993).

For several reasons, this first generation of democratic peace theories has lost some of its luster. For one, it has turned out to be very difficult to differentiate the two explanations empirically (Maoz and Russett 1993; Huth and Allee 2002). Others question the logic of constraint arguments (c.f., Bueno de Mesquita et al. 1999). It was never exactly clear why institutions or norms that were so robust in resisting the impetus to war among democracies could so easily be brushed aside when the enemy was an autocracy. Certainly it might be necessary for a democracy to defend itself if suddenly attacked by an autocratic enemy, but democracies are often the initiators of conflict in heterogeneous dyads. Many contests in the post-World War II period pitted a capable democracy against a weak or distant autocratic power. Even in cases where the autocratic state is strong, the use of force by democracies is often deliberate, concerted, and aggressive. Norms and institutions explanations for the democratic peace have also fared poorly in the wake of U.S. actions in the "war on terror," where it appears that few, if any, constraints on the use of force were effective.

Perhaps the greatest logical challenge to constraint theories comes in the form of the security dilemma. Making force more costly, risky, or unappealing for one actor could certainly prevent that actor from preferring force, but it may have the opposite effect on other actors. Insights about strategic interaction emphasize that power or security is zero-sum. If one ties one's dog to a stake in the yard, one can be confident that the dog will not chase the neighbor's cat down the street, but one will also have to pay more attention to the possibility that the cat will now find its way into one's living room. Reducing the ability of an actor to act aggressively increases the appeal of aggression for an opponent. What the net effects of these changes might be is difficult to determine but in general, the more competitive the environment, the less constraints discourage aggression.

What if the constraint is mutual? If one state or actor is constrained, perhaps the security dilemma still applies, but bilateral barriers to conflict might seem to lend themselves to the dyadic democratic peace observation. Schelling (1966) addresses this issue in the parable of the mountain climbers. A pair of climbers tied together set out to scale a steep cliff face. Their fates are entwined by the rope that physically unites them. If one climber is in distress, the other can use the rope to come to the first climber's assistance. As such, the rope is a linkage with attributes of a public good. Some of the benefits or risks imposed by nature and a climber's own actions accrue to one's partner (externalities), while the costs of the ascent can be distributed through bargaining.

In contrast to democratic peace theorists, Schelling's objective was to find ways to allow nations to continue to compete in a world where many thought nuclear war had made conflict unthinkable. Neither climber (or nuclear power) could intentionally send the other to its death, since this was equivalent to suicide. Schelling used the climbers' predicament to illustrate how accident could be manipulated for gain. Nuclear weapons had made direct confrontation impossible. They had literally changed the game of international politics from prisoners' dilemma to chicken. This did not curtail conflict. Instead, what had changed was how actors competed in the shadow of annihilation.

Figure 1 diagrams the situation addressed by Schelling and the constraint theorists. Both take a similar approach, while claiming contradictory outcomes. Imagine two countries (A and B) choosing between two strategies labeled *Make* or *Take*. *Take* is less efficient, involving some deadweight loss for both parties, so that [*Make,Make*] is the socially optimal outcome. The game and individual strategies are defined by players' rankings over outcomes. For example, if A and B both prefer *Take* to *Make* regardless of the other player's strategy, then this is a game of *Prisoners' Dilemma*.

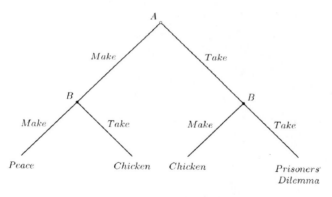

FIGURE 1 Capital and conflict.

Schelling solves his problem (an inability for players to compete) by recognizing that his nuclear protagonists can play *Chicken* rather than *Prisoners' Dilemma*. Neither actor wants to end up at [*Take,Take*] with certainty, but each is willing to play *Take* if the other plays *Make*, or vice versa. More to the point, each player has some willingness to risk the [*Take,Take*] outcome if this increases the chances that it will get to *Take* while its opponent chooses *Make*. Balancing risks and players' valuations for the stakes is central to bargaining and also introduces the question of uncertainty.

What was a solution for Schelling is actually a problem for constraint arguments. Though they want to get to *Peace*, making war mutually unacceptable (if indeed the costs of norms or institutions in deterring conflict are sufficiently grave) fails to preclude the two *Chicken* equilibria. Indeed, precisely because it imposes an upper bound on the intensity of contests, chicken tends to increase the frequency of conflict. A mutual understanding that large-scale war is unthinkable paradoxically makes it safer to consider lower intensity warfare. In the cold war, the two superpowers and their clients engaged in abundant peripheral clashes, proxy wars, and other forms of lesser aggression. Though World War III did not occur, it came close at times as the superpowers struggled to determine who was more resolved on the precipice of nuclear war. The real danger in these contests was thus uncertainty about what would resolve the conflict. Information, available from the "hot line" and satellite reconnaissance, may have helped as much or more than nuclear deterrence.

The U.S./Soviet dyad was among the most, if not the most, disputatious during the cold war. If the vast consequences of nuclear conflagration did not constrain the superpowers from numerous acts of conflict, what cost or constraint are capital or democracy likely to impose to impel peace? Whatever its putative cause, the liberal peace is more than a claim about the reluctant submission of aggressive nations to barriers to war. It is not as if democracies or capitalist countries are chomping at the bit to redress old grievances or to realize ongoing greed. Rather, these nations lack the impetus to war. The most prosperous, developed nations appear largely satisfied with the global status quo. They have few significant differences. They lack the motives for violence, not the ability to act aggressively against one another, should such motives arise. The peace we observe is thus much more about a compatibility of interests or preferences than it is about constraints.

CAPITALIST PEACE

While modest in comparison with the democratic peace research agenda, scholarship on the "capitalist peace" has expanded considerably in recent years. Capitalist peace research involves a range of arguments tied to liberal political economy. Whether as an alternative or complement, there is increasing attention to the role of markets in bringing about the diminution of interstate conflict.

Interestingly, the same set of theoretical frameworks that evolved in democratic peace research now asserts itself in the capitalist peace. Markets may bring about a transformation in accepted modes of interaction. Schumpeter (1955) calls on the culture of economic freedom to raise mankind from the carnage of world war.[2]

Similarly, Polanyi (1957) views the rise of market forces as the critical determinant of the political transformations apparent in modern societies. While not inspired by previous "economic norms" theorists, contemporary scholarship by Mousseau (2000, 2003) reflects the idea that capitalism alters relationships among individuals and between populations and the state in ways that have virtuous consequences for international peace. Mousseau, Hegre, and Oneal (2003) find that peace is exclusive to developed democracies, while poorer liberal states fail to experience any reduction in conflict. The soft constraint of capitalist cultural norms of appropriate competition operates in a manner comparable to normative theories of democratic peace. A "contract rich society" impels leaders to refrain from violence that would harm these relationships (Mousseau 2009).

There are many institutionalist formulations of capitalist peace. Montesquieu, Rousseau, Kant, Paine, Cobden, and Angell all saw market mechanisms as creating conditions that made war more costly, and therefore unacceptable. In recent times, Weede (2003, 2005) has explored the role of globalization in creating incentives for the participants in free markets to

---

[2]Doyle (1986) relies on Schumpeter (1950,1955) as the archetype of the liberal political economy perspective, though he acknowledges that Schumpeter's social/cultural argument is not representative of the core of this school.

cooperate. McDonald (2009), in particular, emphasizes the role of markets as domestic institutions. "The domestic institutional foundations of liberal economic systems promote peace between states" (McDonald 2009:15). There are problems with the assumption that making war more costly or risky leads nations to peace, as we have already suggested. Capitalist institutions must prevent conflict, not just diminish the intensity of conflict that occurs, if in fact contests are to become less likely in an anarchical world. To see why this is so, let us turn next to our version of the capitalist peace.

INTERSTATE CONFLICT AND THE CAPITALIST PEACE

The determinants of political violence can be said to occur in two stages. Peace is more likely if the causes at either stage are interdicted or reduced. War results in this conception from a set of necessary conditions, while the absence of any one condition is sufficient for peace (Fearon 1995).

The first stage of conflict involves motives for competition. National interests or objectives must differ sufficiently for countries even to consider fighting. Realists contend that state interests are essentially always in conflict (Waltz 1959; Claude 1962), but this is both rigid and narrow. States vary both in the intensity of their valuation for material objectives (land, resources), and in the compatibility of their nonmaterial goals (policies, influence). Resource competition has declined among capitalist countries, but these states still use force to seek control of political agendas.

The allocation of resources is strongly zero-sum; states do not share common interests over "who gets what," but mutual incentives exist to avoid costly methods of dispute resolution (such as war). The value of disputed resources may also be insufficient to warrant fighting. Policies often exhibit public goods characteristics; states may (or may not) possess compatible goals over such issues global or regional political, economic, and social institutions, international conventions and norms, cross-border crime, smuggling, piracy or terrorism, as well as the behavior of third-party states. Policy conflict should thus vary as a function of the compatibility of interests (Gartzke 1998).

Classical interpretations of a capitalist peace argue that development and global markets eventually eliminate resource competition as a motive for war. Where early modern technology shocks and productivity increases propelled nations to distant conquest, the maturation of these same factors later led in the opposite direction. Empire was eventually deemed archaic as it became clear that needed raw materials would continue to make their way to industrial centers through free markets, rather than through mercantilist autarkies. Capital-intensive military force structures needed for victory on modern battlefields are poorly suited to the labor-intensive activity of occupation. Developed countries capable of projecting power continue to use force to shape international behavior, but they no longer seek to acquire property. Developing countries covet territory, but they often lack the ability to realize their desires. Territorial conflict is relegated to "tween" states possessing effective militaries, but with economies that have yet to industrialize or diversify.

In contrast, the increasing importance of the global commons for developed countries means that conflict is more likely to arise over policy differences. The distribution of market surpluses, norms and conventions, environmental and humanitarian issues, and nontraditional security concerns such as terrorism and nuclear proliferation all involve influence rather than direct physical control over resources or territory. The same features that make modern armies poorly suited to the labor- and casualty-intensive activities of occupation and resource extraction make them ideal for punitive attacks. Force can be applied quickly, far from home, and with relatively little direct risk to the metropol. Indeed, the increased interdependence of developed countries necessitates more attempts to influence distant states (Keohane and Nye 1989). Even as development expands opportunities to influence other countries' choice of regime type, foreign policies, and other issues, there is little worth fighting about among capitalist countries. A stable consensus within the developed world about major questions of international organization has relegated policy conflicts among the industrialized nations to secondary issues. The motives for conflict, which historically were concentrated among the powerful and their ambitious challengers, are today clustered among the poor, and between the poor and the rich. Peace has broken out among the prosperous precisely because developed states now lack the historic motives that, from time immemorial, fueled conflict, and sometimes war.

The second stage of conflict involves the methods by which differences are addressed and resources or prerogatives are allocated. Under anarchy, these methods are typically diplomacy and war. Diplomacy can preempt fighting, but the two mechanisms are not substitutes, since war is really designed to influence the content of diplomatic bargains, just as diplomacy is widely understood to occur in the shadow of anticipated or ongoing warfare. Even as states compete, they have common incentives to minimize the burden of fighting by seeking to agree on the likely consequences of a contest, should one occur. Bargains are often forged that preempt fighting, just as ongoing contests are eventually resolved through tacit or formal agreements (Hicks 1963; Fearon 1995).

How might capitalism change states' preferences or better inform them about the preferences of others? A considerable literature suggests that trade and other economic activities deter conflict by making fighting expensive (Bliss and Russett 1998; Gasiorowski 1986; Oneal and Russett 1997; Polachek 1980, 1997; Polachek, Robst and Chang 1999). Still, it is difficult to imagine that trade losses would be large relative to the material and subjective costs of fighting. Warfare is already expensive, even among states with autarkic markets. Typically, states at war want to impose costs on an opponent.

A more plausible set of mechanisms can be had by looking at what markets do, and how they alter the interests of participating countries. Capital markets have become the crown jewels of the modern age. Vast wealth is in play each business day. As recent events attest, staggering losses can occur quickly when investors become frightened or skeptical. Any factor that influences the value of securities is salient to investors. Leaders who scare the capital markets pay a high price. Wealth is lost, investors are angered, and the government itself is often affected. The ability of governments in capitalist countries to service their debts depends on investor confidence. If investors and the state have slightly different incentives when it comes to political conflict, then leaders must choose between military aggression and mollifying investors. Rather than deterring conflict, which choice a leader makes informs observers about a leader's resolve and/or capabilities. Ceteris paribus, a leader that is willing to anger the markets to pursue a dispute is more resolved than one who shies away from financial losses. A leader that is unwilling to anger the markets is probably not resolved.

Markets also transform economies by allowing for more efficient allocation and accumulation of capital. As labor becomes relatively scarce and commodities grow cheap, the logic of employing expensive labor to take (versus make or trade) inexpensive inputs to production evaporates. Rich states are unwilling to deploy occupying armies to extract relatively cheap goods and services from other states, preferring instead to purchase these goods and services. If in addition it becomes widely understood that a group of prosperous countries no longer threaten one another directly or indirectly over access to inputs to production, then the security dilemma is no longer a menace.

In contrast, the transition from territorial to globalized commercial nations makes control of international agendas increasingly critical. Capitalist countries continue to contemplate war over policies and politics. However, markets also bring a level of consensus among capitalist states. Letting another country have its way in the realm of policymaking may or may not involve conflict (both nations may "want the same thing"). Adversaries can be allies when facing a common problem. If instead two governments have different agendas, then relations can become fractious. The importance of differences grows with the size of a nation's exposure to the international arena.

Table 1 summarizes the admittedly complex processes discussed above. Three types of dyadic relationships are identified in the left column, developed, developing, and heterogeneous (one developed and one developing state). Each of the remaining columns in the table refers to a type of good over which conflict might occur. Property disputes are unlikely among

TABLE 1 Effects of Markets, Development, and Difference on Interstate Peace

	Property rights	Agenda control	
		Similar interests	Different interests
Developed	PEACE	PEACE	SOME FIGHTING
Value for victory	low	low	high
Cost of fighting	high	high	high
Market signaling	high	high	high
Heterogeneous	PEACE (−)	PEACE	SOME FIGHTING
Value for victory	low	low	high
Cost of fighting	high	high	high
Market signaling	medium	medium	medium
Developing	SOME FIGHTING	PEACE	SOME FIGHTING
Value of victory	high	low	medium
Cost of fighting	low	low	low
Market Signaling	low	low	low

developed states. Developing states mostly fight over property. In heterogeneous dyads, developed states (which can fight aggressive wars against weaker developing nations if they want to) have no desire to acquire more territory, while developing countries (which may covet land or other tangible property assets) are typically too weak or distant to prosecute conflicts against developed countries. Exceptions occur most often in contiguous heterogeneous dyads, and where developing countries are wealthy.

Agenda control can lead to conflict, but only when states disagree about preferred policies. Nations have no reason to fight to gain control of an agenda when victory yields similar policies to those imposed in defeat. Thus, the column for "Similar Interests" contains only PEACE. Fighting is possible when national interests differ, though bargains are still common, as warfare is costly and fighting typically ends in a bargain in any case. Developed states may be more likely to care about policy differences, but they are less likely to have such differences. Conflict resolution among developed countries may also be aided by better information as capital markets create transparency.

INTERNATIONAL CRISIS BEHAVIOR—HYPOTHESES

We examine the capitalist peace using data from the International Crisis Behavior (ICB) project. ICB data ignore "accidental" violence initiated by front line troops without the authorization of central authorities. Liberal peace theories emphasize choices facing heads-of-state, not those of sergeants, sailors, or pilots. The ICB data also code crisis escalation, a critical dimension along which to assess implications of liberal peace. For these reasons and others, the overlap between ICB crises and MIDs is only about 26%.[3] This difference in coding and coverage is a critical advantage of this study, as a statistical artifact is unlikely to migrate across two very different datasets.

Crisis Escalation

ICB data code events in context, making it possible to study elements of the conflict process. Crises are organized in these data so as to allow for testing of hypotheses about escalation. ICB variables identify the initial impetus behind the crisis (TRIGGER), the reaction to the trigger (MAJRES), as well as the goals of the actors (ISSUE, GRAVITY), the crisis management techniques used by participants (CRISMG), and the intensity of any resulting violence (CENVIO, SEVVIO, VIOL).

One or two hypotheses cannot hope to address all existing or possible democratic peace theories. Still, there is consensus in the literature that democracies should be increasingly reluctant to fight each other as crises escalate (Kinsella and Russett 2002). If conflict is proscribed by liberal norms, then the longer a crisis drags on, or the greater the potential for hostility, the more democracies should be inhibited by the norm. Similarly, liberal institutions are said to delay responses to conflict, allowing parties to negotiate and avoid further violence. A crisis that begins among democracies should presumably be resolved more often without escalating to deadly force, especially when force is not used at the outset. Transparency or signaling arguments also imply that democracies are less likely to escalate from initial crises, as audience costs resulting from a crisis increase leader credibility, more often allowing democracies to bargain and avoid additional conflict (Fearon 1994).

H1: Once triggered, a crisis is less likely to escalate among democracies.

Interests and development are "prerequisite" factors in our theoretical model, affecting a state's willingness or ability to compete, but not determining whether states escalate, once a crisis has begun. Market transparency influences conflict in the second stage, facilitating negotiation through signaling after conflict is already at hand. Capitalist countries should be less likely to experience a crisis, even when they are willing and able to fight, but signaling should also impact bargaining even after crisis onset. Market-oriented countries are less likely to escalate after an initial trigger.

---

[3]There are 755 ICB crises and 2155 MIDs in the period 1918–1992. 564 of the MIDs qualify as crises according to the ICB criteria, so that roughly 75% of ICB crises are also defined as MIDs by the Correlates of War criteria.

> *H2: Once triggered, a crisis is less likely to escalate among globally integrated economies.*

Unlike market integration, development and interest affinity have little in the way of residual informational effects. While both processes discourage the initial onset of territorial crises, they should have no effect on escalation once a crisis begins. Development primarily affects whether states possess the basis for conflict, not how conflicts are resolved. Development should thus lead states to experience fewer contiguous crises, and endure more noncontiguous crises (the shift in emphasis from territory to policy), but will have no significant effect on whether crises escalate.

> *H3: Once triggered, a crisis among developed countries is no less likely to escalate.*

As with development, similar policy objectives are likely to discourage the onset of a crisis, but policy affinity will not matter much for how crises are resolved, should they occur. States may disagree on many things to a slight degree, or on a few things intensely. If a crisis occurs in spite of states' general policy affinity, then the precursors of conflict exist. Again, there is nothing about interest similarity that affects the ability of states to negotiate effectively and to end crises quickly.

> *H4: Once triggered, states with similar interests are no less likely to escalate a crisis.*

Crisis Intensity and Specificity

Another set of hypotheses derive from crisis intensity. Democratic peace theories argue that escalation is increasingly less likely at higher levels of crisis intensity. This implies that democratic crises, when they occur, should typically be less violent than crises involving non-democracies.

> *H5: Crises among democracies should exhibit a lower level or intensity of violence.*

Similarly, crises that escalate among integrated states should be less prone to high levels of violence. The signaling argument for integrated economies implies that these states are better able to contain crises that break out, leading to fewer big fights even within the sample of conflicts. Just as economic transparency reduces the need for a crisis, or for escalation, it also reduces the need for extensive fighting to generate sufficient revelation to resolve the contest (Slantchev 2003).

H6: Crises in economically integrated dyads should experience a lower level of violence.

The nature and intensity of crisis behavior should also be affected by economic development. First, developed countries will tend to use more capital, and proportionately less labor, in their military force structures (Gartzke 2001). Contests among developed states should be more expensive, but also less lethal. Here, we focus on the effect of development on the human costs of crises. Second, because development shifts conflict from resource competition to other issues, and because territorial conflict in particular is casualty-intensive (Vasquez 1993; Senese and Vasquez 2003), the shift away from resource competition should reduce the intensity of contests and result in fewer casualties. This shift should be most apparent when censoring the sample of crises (looking precisely at territorial versus non-territorial crises). Thus, we add a hypothesis that identifies the shift from resource competition to crises over policy or other non-resource based differences between states.

H7: Crises in economically developed dyads should result in fewer battlefield casualties.

H8: Crises in economically developed dyads should more often be associated with political-diplomatic or cultural issues and less often involve economic, territorial, or existence issues.

Finally, the intensity of contests that actually occur among states with similar interests should be roughly equivalent to violence levels for states with dissimilar policy interests. The similarity of national policy interests should affect whether states experience crises, but as a component of the "prerequisite" first stage, should not much influence behavior in crises. Unlike development, interests are also unlikely to shift the emphasis between competition over resources and policy.

H9: Crises in dyads with similar policy interests should exhibit about the same level or intensity of violence as crises among states with dissimilar policy interests.

RESEARCH DESIGN

We test our hypotheses on annual observations of dyad years from the post-World War II period (1950–1992). This is conventional practice in democratic peace research. Further, it reflects both data availability and the expectation that this period is most favorable to democratic peace theses.

Dependent Variable

The dependent variable in all of our analyses indicates whether a particular dyad experienced an international crisis in any given year. An individual state satisfies the conditions for crisis when its main foreign policy leaders perceive a heightened likelihood of military hostilities, a threat to basic national values, and a finite time within which to make decisions (Brecher and Wilkenfeld 1997:3). A dyad experiences a crisis whenever at least one of the two states satisfies the ICB conditions and at least one state directs a hostile action against the other during the crisis (Hewitt 2003).

The concept of international crisis is substantially different from a militarized interstate dispute. By definition, ICB crises involve explicit challenges that elicit decisions from a state's highest ranking foreign policy leaders. MIDs, on the other hand, can result from clashes between frontline forces not directly authorized by leading officials. Prominent arguments about liberal peace focus on decisions by the leadership and have little to say about fishing incidents or accidental skirmishes.

The ICB dataset also has important advantages in testing additional implications of liberal peace theories not explored previously. ICB data allow a much closer approximation of the escalation processes of states. Important differences exist in how economic and political liberalism expects states to escalate conflict. The ICB sample also differs substantially from the MIDs, allowing for an independent test. As we point out above, the overlap in the two datasets is about 26%.[4] If testing comparable models in two different domains leads to similar results, we must begin to conclude that the relationships identified have considerable empirical validity. Differences, too, can be instructive.

Independent Variables

Democracy

We use standard Polity IV data to measure regime type (Jaggers and Gurr 1995). We adopt the method recommended in the Polity codebook to minimize the number of missing values by recoding "missing value" of interregnum and transition (Marshall and Jaggers 2002:15–16). The variable DEMOCRACY (LOW) equals the value of the lowest democracy score in the dyad. We also include the variable for the higher democracy score in the dyad, DEMOCRACY (HIGH).

---

[4] MIDs are approximately three times more frequent than crises. About 26% of ICB crises do not qualify as a MID. Roughly 74% of all MIDs do not produce ICB crises. The overlap in the samples represents the extent of convergence between these two conceptions of conflict. However, the area of overlap is not typical. MIDs satisfying ICB conditions have significantly higher hostility levels and fatalities than MIDs that do not qualify as crises (Hewitt 2003).

MARKETS

FIN. OPEN (LOW) is an index of eight variables representing the degree of national economic openness reported by the International Monetary Fund (Gartzke et al. 2001; Gartzke and Li 2003). FIN.OPEN (LOW) is the lower of the two scores in a dyad. When no data are available, we follow the IMF practice of replacing missing values with a zero (missing data tend to be from poor or poorly integrated states). This practice has often been used in other studies of liberal peace (c.f. Gleditsch 2002).[5] We also measure trade interdependence between dyad partners. TRADE DEP is the ratio of total national trade (imports plus exports) to GDP.

DEVELOPMENT

We use GDP per capita (in 1996 constant U.S. dollars) to measure economic development. Development is predicted to have contrasting effects on crisis onset. Increases in GDPPC (LOW) should make international crises more likely in general, while contiguous states that are developed should be less likely to experience an international crisis. Most disputes between contiguous states are territorial. These occur less often as the value of plundering resources declines. We use an interaction variable, GDPPC (LOW) × CONTIG, to measure this contingent effect.

INTEREST SIMILARITY

We use an index of annual voting records in the United Nations General Assembly to measure interest similarity between states. The approach has been applied elsewhere (Gartzke 1998, 2000; Voeten 2000, 2001). The measure ranges from −1 (most dissimilar) to +1 (most similar). States with dissimilar interests are more likely to experience a international crisis.

Additional Variables

We incorporate a set of other variables common to studies of the liberal peace, including a dichotomous indicator of geographic contiguity, interval data on capital-to-capital distance, a dummy variable indicating the presence of a major power, a dichotomous variable for dyadic alliance status, and a variable for the capability ratio of dyad members. Coding of these

---

[5]Imputing zeros for missing values could conceivably bias estimated relationships. Yet, since missing values are nonrandom (poor and poorly globalized states less often report data to the IMF), the missing values themselves introduce bias. We also estimated regressions in which missing values were not replaced with zeros. The financial openness variable remains significant at the 0.001 level, while other estimated coefficients were essentially unchanged.

variables follows Oneal and Russett (1999). Conflict behavior varies by geographic region (Henderson 2002; Bennett and Stam 2003; Lemke 2003). The major oil exporting countries of the Middle East and North Africa also appear developed according to per capita GDP statistics. However, they lack the diversified industrial economies capable of making states prefer commerce to territorial conflict. We include a dummy variable for observations involving two countries in the Middle East or North Africa.[6]

RESULTS

Table A1 in the appendix contains a replication of the basic analysis in Gartzke (2007) of conflict onset, this time using ICB crises rather than MIDs. The results are largely the same, and so we do not dwell on them here. However, before moving on to test the formal hypotheses, it may prove useful to provide a substantive interpretation of the replication findings. The software program CLARIFY (King et al. 2000) allows us to simulate the impact of the key independent variables on the likelihood of crisis involvement.[7] The baseline dyad consists of two unaligned, contiguous, minor powers that have mean values for all other non-dichotomous independent variables. We hold variables at their baseline levels and then simulate incremental changes in one variable of interest. Figure 2 presents four graphs of the estimated relative risk of crisis for different values of the key independent variables. We calculate the relative risk of crisis as the ratio of the predicted probability of crisis to the minimum predicted probability produced by the independent variable. In each of the graphs, we arrange values of the independent variables on the X axis such that the plot of the estimated relative risk of crisis increases from left to right. The vertical gray bars represent 95% confidence interval generated for each estimate at each level of the independent variable.

Graph (A) shows that the relative risk of crisis barely increases at all as the value of Democracy (LOW) decreases from +10 to −10. Graph (B), on the other hand, shows that the relative risk of crisis increases substantially as the level of economic integration decreases in a dyad. At the same time, the graph reveals that the level of uncertainty is relatively higher around the

---

[6]Dafoe (2009) argues that both democracy and capitalist variables matter when dropping the regional dummy variables and adding a "peace years" variable to the spline temporal controls in Gartzke (2007). We replicate all regressions in this study with (and without) the peace years variable, with the Middle East dummy removed, and with regional dummies for North America, South America, Europe, Asia, and Sub-Saharan Africa. These results are substantively the same. He also notes the large number of cases lost to listwise deletion in Gartzke (2007). We have eliminated a large number of missing values for the financial openness and democracy variables through imputation.

[7]We use Model A5, Table A1, but drop the MIDDLE EAST dummy to simplify exposition. Results are comparable.

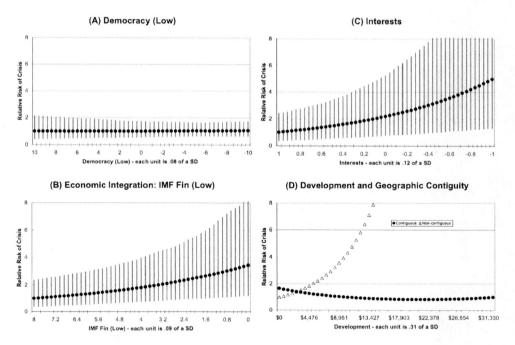

FIGURE 2 Effect of key variables on risk of international crisis (source: Table A1, Model A5).

predicted probabilities of crisis corresponding to low levels of economic integration. While the findings suggest that nonintegrated dyads are clearly more crisis prone, they also point to the higher variability in the probability of crisis for such states. The greater range in crisis propensities for integrated states suggests greater uncertainty about the likely outcomes of challenges with nonintegrated opponents (because, as theorized earlier, signaling is more difficult in such contests), leading to more errors in bargaining and subsequently to higher probabilities of escalation to war (Reed 2003a, 2003b). It should be noted that the apparent heteroskedasticity is not the same as is commonly associated with economic trend data. First, the independent variable in this case is an index, not a metric value. Second, the increase in variance is negatively correlated with values of FIN. OPEN (LOW).

Graph (C) presents the impact of interests on the probability of crisis. The figure shows that as interests change from the maximum of +1 (harmonious interests) to −1 (conflicting interests), the relative risk of crisis increases more than four-fold. Here again, what looks like heteroskedasticity is actually the result of theoretically-relevant uncertainty. States with similar interests almost never experience crises (Pr < 0.004). States with the most dissimilar interests possess a motive for conflict but whether they experience a crisis (or not) still depends on other determinants of bargaining success or failure. These additional determinants, including particularly uncertainty about tangibles (the balance of power) and intangibles (resolve), are only salient if states already possess a grievance (which is also difficult to measure). Thus, as should be the case with a necessary condition, variance in outcomes and the probability of a crisis \emph{both decrease} in policy affinity.

Graph (D) depicts the impact of economic development (we omit the confidence intervals to reduce clutter). The relative risk of crisis for noncontiguous dyads is depicted with a series of triangles. Increases in GDPPC lead to a rapid increase in the likelihood of crisis involvement for noncontiguous states. In contrast, the series of solid circles depicts the impact of GDPPC for contiguous states. This plot reflects the simultaneous effect of two variables, GDPPC (LOW) and GDPPC (LOW) × CONTIG. The plot reveals that as GDP per capita increases for contiguous pairs of states, the predicted probability of crisis onset declines, leading to a reduction in the probability of a crisis across different levels of development. The components of development each have a substantial impact, but since each works in opposite directions, the net effect is modestly negative.

Evaluating Hypotheses about Crisis Escalation

We now turn to testing the hypotheses regarding crisis escalation. Escalation can refer to two types of heightening levels of hostility depending on whether the focus is on pre-crisis interactions or interactions during the crisis. First, at the precrisis stage, interstate interactions can increase in hostility and lead to the initiation of a crisis. That is, if the trigger that initiates a crisis involves the use of force, then the initiating event of the crisis already represents a significant escalation from the precrisis stage. This type of escalation is examined as part of crisis onset in the appendix.

Second, at the crisis stage, escalation can refer to an elevation in the level of hostility between combatants once the initial crisis trigger has occurred. The ICB data is a unique source of information about this type of escalation. However, in the case of triggers involving force, it is difficult to ascertain whether subsequent acts represent an escalation in the second sense of the term or not. When crisis interaction leads to full-scale war, the crisis has clearly escalated (due to the ICB definition of a crisis). In cases in which the crisis did not lead to war, determinations about escalation are more difficult. Noting these limitations, we measure escalation using the ICB coding for each country's major response to the crisis trigger. The dependent variable equals 1 when either dyad member uses military force in response to the trigger, else the escalation variable equals 0.

We test our hypotheses about escalation on dyadic crises during the period 1950–1992. We use moderate thresholds for statistical significance, given the much smaller sample size. In addition to key variables, we also include geographic contiguity, the logged distance between states, alliance and major power status, and the logged capability ratio in the dyad. We add two ICB variables that have proven to be consistent predictors of crisis escalation. First, a dummy variable codes whether the crisis trigger involved force. Wilkenfeld (1991) found that crises exhibit a strong violence-begets-violence dynamic. The trigger intensity variable also addresses the selection problem posed by the discussion above. Second, we add a dummy variable for the perceived crisis threat level.

Table 2 reports the results of five logit regressions of crisis escalation (sampling on crisis onset). We begin with a model equivalent to Model A1 in Table A1 that includes the two democracy variables and trade interdependence, but omits indicators for capital markets, development, or interstate interests (Model 1). As in the replication, we add variables sequentially, first introducing the measure of financial integration (Model 2), then GDP per capita (Model 3), the interaction term between wealth and contiguity (Model 4), and finally the affinity variable (Model 5).

In Model 1, we find that increases in Democracy (Low) and trade dependence have no discernible impact on the likelihood of crisis escalation, a result that persists in each of the subsequent models. Hypothesis 1 summarizing expectations of democratic peace theories is not supported. The estimate for Democracy (High) is positive and significant in Model 1 and remains so in subsequent models. Confrontations between states with dissimilar regime characteristics are more likely to escalate. Crises that begin with the use of force are more likely to feature the use of force as the major response. The estimate for the threat variable is insignificant; escalation does not follow from intimidation. Of the remaining variables, only the alliance dummy is significant, and positive.

Model 2 adds FIN. OPEN (LOW). The estimate is statistically significant ($p = 0.024$) and in the expected direction. The results support hypothesis 2. States that are integrated into global markets are better able to communicate credibly, reducing the need to escalate. Integrated markets facilitate signaling, identifying acceptable bargains that more often make it possible to settle crises short of war. Because learning has follow-on effects, FIN. OPEN (LOW) can be seen to influence crisis escalation even after states have failed to resolve their initial differences peacefully. The variable measuring initial military force in a crisis is also insignificant once we include an indicator of free markets. Military surprise may be less salient, or harder, for economically integrated states.

Regression models 3 and 4 add GDP per capita and the interaction with contiguity, respectively. Hypothesis 3 suggests that development has no effect on escalation, once a crisis occurs. As expected, neither development variable significantly determines the likelihood of escalation. While negative results of this kind cannot be considered definitive (the null is the critical hypothesis), corroboration with the other hypotheses suggests considerable empirical validity. Financial openness continues to discourage escalation. Alliances and Democracy (High) also remain escalation prone.

TABLE 2 Logit Regression of Political and Economic Variables on Crisis Escalation

D.V.: ICB, crisis dyad years	1	2	3	4	5
DEMOCRACY					
Democracy (Low)	−0.010	−0.061	−0.051	−0.045	−0.053
	(0.041)	(0.052)	(0.053)	(0.054)	(0.063)
Democracy (High)	0.042**	0.077**	0.068**	0.068**	0.105**
	(0.022)	(0.030)	(0.031)	(0.031)	(0.048)
MARKETS					
Trade Dep. (Low)	47.599	−0.298	−8.739	−6.586	3.990
	(92.744)	(87.399)	(88.166)	(88.004)	(98.569)
Fin. Open. (Low)		−0.249**	−0.267**	−0.289**	−0.323**
		(0.111)	(0.113)	(0.115)	(0.135)
DEVELOPMENT					
GDP/Capita (Low)			0.294	0.732	0.208
			(0.237)	(0.495)	(0.732)
GDP/Capita × Contig.				−0.569	0.142
				(0.548)	(0.784)
INTERESTS					0.339
					(0.571)
					(0.568)
ADDITIONAL VARIABLES					
ICB: Force in Trigger[1]	0.968***	−0.039	0.063	0.099	0.778*
	(0.264)	(0.371)	(0.383)	(0.384)	(0.451)
ICB: High Threat[1]	−0.127	0.630	0.670*	0.645*	1.159**
	(0.269)	(0.357)	(0.367)	(0.368)	(0.477)
Contiguity[1]	0.345	0.115	0.078	4.058	−1.811
	(0.352)	(0.500)	(0.514)	(3.848)	(5.847)
Distance[2]	0.070	0.250	0.257	0.291*	0.621**
	(0.121)	(0.162)	(0.164)	(0.169)	(0.264)
Major Power[1]	0.433	0.621	0.606	0.496	−0.643
	(0.409)	(0.699)	(0.712)	(0.717)	(0.987)
Alliance[1]	1.231***	1.627***	1.636***	1.572***	1.679***
	(0.357)	(0.462)	(0.474)	(0.480)	(0.569)
Capability Ratio[2]	−0.039	−0.005	−0.031	−0.052	−0.097
	(0.114)	(0.161)	(0.165)	(0.168)	(0.177)
CONSTANT	−0.733	−1.419	−3.471	−6.597***	−4.859
	(1.007)	(1.330)	(2.176)	(3.773)	(5.845)
N	337	235	233	233	176
Log-likelihood	−180.3	−108.0	−106.4	−105.8	−71.3
χ^2 (10,11,12,13,14)	36.4***	32.4***	32.2***	33.3***	35.8***

Significance: *$p < .1$; **$p < .05$; ***$p < .01$. Standard errors appear in parentheses. All p-values based on two-tailed tests.
[1]Dummy variable.
[2]Logged variable.

Model 5 adds the interest variable. As hypothesis 4 predicts, the variable is not statistically significant. While interests have a strong effect on crisis onset, escalation is driven by other factors, such as uncertainty. Adding interests does not alter the estimated effects of financial openness. Also, coefficients for distance and threat level are now significant in the expected direction.

Evaluating Hypotheses about Crisis Intensity

Hypotheses 5, 6, 7, and 9 offer predictions about how democracy, market integration, development, and interstate interests affect the number of fatalities, should a crisis occur. We again estimate five OLS regressions on the number of fatalities (in thousands) suffered by participants during a crisis. Since the dependent variable for the models in Table 3 is a count variable, the more appropriate estimation technique is negative binomial regression. We also estimated the models in Table 3 using negative binomial regression, but since the estimates are essentially the same, we report the OLS estimates to ease interpretation. We retain higher significance thresholds, given robust results.

As Model 6 demonstrates, democracy reduces the intensity of crises, but not in the manner that democratic peace theory predicts. The estimated coefficient for DEMOCRACY (LOW) is insignificant, while DEMOCRACY (HIGH) is associated with *declining* fatalities. The finding is intriguing in light of the finding in Table 2 that DEMOCRACY (HIGH) increases escalation. TRADE DEP. (LOW) also appears to have a strong negative impact (i.e., it reduces fatalities).

With the exception of the variable for major power status, each of the control variables has a significant negative relationship with fatalities. Interestingly, crises between contiguous dyads involve significantly fewer fatalities than noncontiguous states. At the same time, increasing the distance between states also reduces crisis fatalities. Contiguity lowers the "fixed costs" of war. Transport, communications, and other barriers often make it impossible for distant countries to fight. The average level of fatalities in contiguous contests is lower, while the variance in fatalities in contiguous contests is higher. Conversely, distance selects on the middle range of contests. States that only care a little bit about an issue will find the fixed costs of distant warfare unacceptable, while the price of transporting and equipping large numbers of personnel far from home also discourages these contests. Variance in fatalities is reduced, but reduced more often at the low end of fatalities than at the high end. The fact that distant states are slightly more likely to escalate crises in Table 2 reflects the fact that threats of such contests are inherently less credible. Finally, crises between allies produce fewer fatalities, as do crises involving states with disparate capabilities.

Model 7 introduces the financial markets variable. As expected, globalized market economies experience significantly fewer fatalities. A unit increase in the market integration index leads to a decrease of over 40,000 expected battle deaths. At the same time, introducing financial openness leads DEMOCRACY (HIGH) and TRADE DEP. (LOW) to become statistically insignificant. The evidence in Model 7 supports hypothesis 6 but not hypothesis 5. Economically integrated states are better able to contain crises while democracy is largely irrelevant to the scale of bloodletting.

TABLE 3 OLS Regression of Political and Economic Variables on Crisis Intensity

D.V.: ICB fatalities (1000's)	6	7	8	9	10
DEMOCRACY					
Democracy (Low)	3.905	5.424	3.769	1.469	−1.095
	(4.035)	(5.071)	(4.953)	(4.821)	(4.063)
Democracy (High)	−6.471**	−5.844	−3.983	−3.688	−4.348
	(2.258)	(2.978)	(2.987)	(2.888)	(2.789)
MARKETS					
Tirade Dep. $\left(\text{Low}, \frac{coef.}{1000}\right)$	−15.906*	−10.563	−9.501	−9.860	−4.496
	(8.094)	(9.438)	(9.202)	(8.896)	(6.876)
Fin. Open. (Low)		−41.827***	−34.875**	−26.194**	−8.122
		(11.127)	(10.989)	(10.835)	(9.066)
DEVELOPMENT					
GDP/Capita (Low)			−81.248***	−194.614***	39.954
			(21.176)	(34.564)	(35.191)
GDP/Capita × Contig.				173.251***	15.771
				(42.562)	(40.626)
INTERESTS					37.715
					(35.760)
ADDITIONAL VARIABLES					
Contiguity[1]	−186.654***	−200.739***	−178.117***	−1429.573***	−71.255
	(36.484)	(47.735)	(46.952)	(310.772)	(308.115)
Distance[2]	−39.186**	−64.869***	−71.727***	−83.769***	0.976
	(12.757)	(16.730)	(16.410)	(16.137)	(15.541)
Major Power[1]	53.211	38.065	84.203	94.339	−13.493
	(43.106)	(62.188)	(61.899)	(59.888)	(55.371)
Alliance[1]	−142.272***	−135.218***	−138.275***	−110.645**	−70.074*
	(32.233)	(41.117)	(40.263)	(39.508)	(35.379)
Capability Ratio[2]	−38.068***	−33.359*	−32.933*	−22.551	0.700
	(11.187)	(14.678)	(14.300)	(14.057)	(10.980)
CONSTANT	636.684***	879.112***	1459.525***	2298.308***	−278.632***
	(104.181)	(137.230)	(200.899)	(283.154)	(300.319)
N	337	235	233	233	176
F	9.94***	8.73***	9.85***	11.09***	1.95 *
Adj. R^2	0.176	0.229	0.276	0.324	0.061

Significance: *$p < .05$; **$p < .01$; ***$p < .001$. Standard errors appear in parentheses. All p-values based on two-tailed tests.
[1] Dummy variable.
[2] Logged variable.

We add the impact of economic development in Model 8 and find that, unlike with crisis onset or escalation, the estimated coefficient for GDPPC is highly statistically significant (p = 0.000). This result is consistent with hypothesis 7. The size of the hypothesized relationship between development and casualties more than doubles when we add the interaction between GDPPC and contiguity in model 9. For the less developed state in a crisis dyad, a $100 increase in its GDP per capita reduces expected fatalities by approximately 5,200. While crises between economically developed, contiguous neighbors are infrequent, the results suggest that these crises are considerably more deadly. A $100 increase in GDP per capita in the less developed of two contiguous states increases total crisis fatalities by 5,100. Financial openness continues to reduce battlefield fatalities.

Finally, Model 10 adds the impact of interests. Hypothesis 9 anticipates that interest similarity affects incentives to initiate a crisis, but has little impact on the behavior of states once crises are underway. The findings from Model 10 support this line of reasoning. However, since many observations have missing values for the interest variable, our sample has shrunk considerably. The overall model performs poorly in this limited sample, which prevents us from asserting these conclusions with much confidence. While interests are an important determinant of whether crises occur, they are much less relevant to the intensity of crises that are already underway.

The evidence reported here regarding crisis onset, escalation, and intensity appears consistent with signaling by economically integrated crisis actors in ways that avoid, contain, and limit fatalities. Economic development is inversely related to crisis onset and to crisis fatalities, but only in noncontiguous dyads. In contiguous dyads, international crises become increasingly lethal with increases in development, reflecting the potential of developed neighbors to sow destruction. On the other hand, such crises become increasingly rare for developed states. Interests influence whether crises occur, but they do not affect casualties, nor do they matter for escalation. Democracy is not statistically significant in any regression where interests, markets, or development are represented.

CONCLUSION

The democratic peace is important, not just because it is a rare "lawlike" relationship in international relations, but also because of the hope it provides to many that the world can become a more peaceful place. It should not be surprising that the good news of democratic peace has been widely embraced by academic researchers, the policy community, and by interested observers. Nevertheless, the merit of an idea in an empirical science must rest in its observed impact more than its abstract virtue. This study contributes to a small but growing body of literature casting doubt on the robustness of the democratic peace observation. It has been known for some time that democracies are only peaceful in pairs. Other research has shown that the democratic peace is even more exclusive than previously imagined, limiting the finding to developed democracies (Hegre 2000; Mousseau 2000). We take this insight full circle, demonstrating that it is economic development and market freedoms, rather than political liberty, that precipitate interstate peace.

It should be emphasized that the capitalist peace is an equally optimistic discovery. The fact that free markets and prosperity reduce the impetus to war means that the liberal peace still obtains, though with a considerably different causal logic and set of empirical precursors. Indeed, a liberal economic peace may be even more sustainable and transportable to the broader international community than is liberal government. Promoting democracy, even imposing it as some have advocated (or pursued), is not likely to reduce interstate conflict. While democracy is certainly desirable in its own right, democratizing for peace appears to be based on a misconception, and may even lead to a weakening of the actual determinants of liberal peace. If democracy leads to an expression of popular preferences in places where these preferences are incompatible with U.S. or other Western interests, then it should not be surprising to find that democratization can actually increase interstate conflict. The United States may be best advised to focus on promoting economic development and free markets. As we have shown, these are the more proximate causes of cooperation among states in the modern world, and may themselves help to promote democracy.

REFERENCES

Beck, Neal, Jonathan Katz, and Richard Tucker. (1998) Taking Time Seriously: Time Series–Cross-Section Analysis with a Binary Dependent Variable. *American Journal of Peace Research* 42(4):1260–1288.

Bennett, D. Scott. (2006) Towards A Continuous Specification of the Democracy-Autocracy Connection. *International Studies Quarterly* 50(2):513–537.

Bennett, D. Scott, and Allan C. Stam. (2003) *The Behavioral Origins of War*. Ann Arbor, MI: University of Michigan Press.

Bliss, Harry, and Bruce Russett. (1998) Democratic Trading Partners: The Liberal Connection. *Journal of Politics* 60(4):1126–1147.

Brecher, Michael, and Jonathan Wilkenfeld. (1997) *A Study in Crisis*. Ann Arbor: University of Michigan.

Bueno de Mesquita, Bruce and David Lalman. (1992) *War and Reason: Domestic and International Imperatives*. New Haven: Yale University Press.

Bueno de Mesquita, Bruce James D. Morrow, Randolph M. Siverson and Alastair Smith. (1999) An Institutional Explanation for the Democratic Peace. *American Political Science Review* 93(4):791–807.

Claude, Inis L. (1962) *Power and International Relations*. New York: Random House.

Dafoe, Allan. (2009) Democracy Still Matters: Misspecification of Time Underestimates Pacific Effect of Democracy. University of California. Typescript.

Dixon, William J. (1993) Democracy and the Management of International Conflict. *Journal of Conflict Resolution* 37(1):42–68.

Dixon, William J. (1994) Democracy and the Peaceful Settlement of International Conflict. *American Political Science Review* 88(2):14–32.

Doyle, Michael. (1986) Liberalism and World Politics. *American Political Science Review* 80(4):1151–1169.
Fearon, James D. (1994) Domestic Political Audiences and the Escalation of International Disputes. *American Political Science Review* 88(3):577–592.
Fearon, James D. (1995) Rationalist Explanations for War. *International Organization* 49(3):379–414.
Flynn, Gregory, and Henry Farrell. (1999) Piecing Together the Democratic Peace: The CSCE, Norms, and the "Construction" of Security in Post-Cold War Europe. *International Organization* 53(3):505–535.
Gartzke, Erik. (1998) Kant We All Just Get Along?: Motive, Opportunity, and the Origins of the Democratic Peace. *American Journal of Political Science* 42(1):1–27.
Gartzke, Erik. (2000) Preferences and the Democratic Peace. *International Studies Quarterly* 44(2):191–210.
Gartzke, Erik. (2001) Democracy and the Preparation for War: Does Regime Type Affect States' Anticipation of Casualties? *International Studies Quarterly* 45(3):467–484.
Gartzke, Erik. (2006) Globalization, Economic Development, and Territorial Conflict. In *Territoriality and Conflict in an Era of Globalization*, edited by Miles Kahler and Barbara Walter. Cambridge: Cambridge University Press, pp. 156–186.
Gartzke, Erik. (2007) The Capitalist Peace. *American Journal of Political Science* 51(1):166–191.
Gartzke, Erik, and Quan Li. (2003) War, Peace, and the Invisible Hand: Positive Political Externalities of Economic Globalization. *International Studies Quarterly* 47(4):561–586.
Gartzke, Erik, and Dominic Rohner. (2009) To Conquer or Compel: Economic Development and Interstate Conflict. University of California, San Diego and the University of York. Typescript.
Gartzke, Erik, Quan Li, and Charles Boehmer. (2001) Investing in the Peace: Economic Interdependence and International Conflict. *International Organization* 55(2):391–438.
Gasiorowski, Mark J. (1986) Economic Interdependence and International Conflict: Some Cross-National Evidence. *International Studies Quarterly* 30(1):23–38.
Gleditsch, Kristian S. (2002) Expanded Trade and GDP Data. *Journal of Conflict Resolution* 46(5):712–724.
Hegre, Håvard. (2000) Development and the Liberal Peace: What Does it Take to Be a Trading State. *Journal of Peace Research* 37(1):5–30.
Henderson, Errol A. (2002) *Democracy and War: The End of an Illusion*. Boulder, CO: Lynne Rienner.
Hewitt, J. Joseph. (2003) Dyadic Processes and International Crises. *Journal of Conflict Resolution* 47(5):669–692.
Hicks, John R. (1963) *The Theory of Wages*. London: Macmillan.
Huth, Paul K., and Todd L. Allee. (2002) *The Democratic Peace and Territorial Conflict in the Twentieth Century*. Cambridge: Cambridge University Press.
Jaggers, Keith, and Ted R. Gurr. (1995) Transitions to Democracy: Tracking Democracy's "Third Wave" with the Polity III Data. *Journal of Peace Research* 32(4):469–482.

Keohane, Robert O., and Joseph S. Nye. (1989) *Power and Interdependence*. New York: Harper Collins.

King, Gary, Michael Tomz, and Jason Wittenberg. (2000) Making the Most of Statistical Analyses: Improving Interpretation and Presentation. *American Journal of Political Science* 44(2):347–361.

Kinsella, David, and Bruce M. Russett. (2002) Conflict Emergence and Escalation in Interactive International Dyads. *Journal of Politics* 64(1):1045–1068.

Lemke, Douglas. (2003) African Lessons for International Relations Research. *World Politics* 56(1):114–138.

Lipson, Charles. (2005) *Reliable Partners: How Democracies Have Made a Separate Peace*. Princeton, NJ: Princeton University Press.

Maoz, Zeev, and Bruce Russett. (1993) Normative and Structural Causes of the Democratic Peace, 1946–1986. *American Political Science Review* 87(3):624–638.

Marshall, Monty, and Keith Jaggers. (2002) Polity IV Project: Political Regime Characteristics and Transitions, 1800–2002. College Park, MD: University of Maryland.

McDonald, Patrick J. (2009) *The Invisible Hand of Peace*. New York: Cambridge University Press.

Mousseau, Michael. (2000) Market Prosperity, Democratic Consolidation, and Democratic Peace. *Journal of Conflict Resolution* 44(4):472–507.

Mousseau, Michael. (2003) The Nexus of Market Society, Liberal Preferences, and Democratic Peace: Interdisciplinary Theory and Evidence. *International Studies Quarterly* 47(4):483–510.

Mousseau, Michael. (2009) The Social Market Roots of Democratic Peace. *International Security* 33(4):52–86.

Mousseau, Michael, Havard Hegre, and John R. Oneal. (2003) How The Wealth of Nations Conditions the Liberal Peace. *European Journal of International Relations* 9(2):277–314.

Oneal, John R., and Bruce Russett. (1997) The Classical Liberals Were Right: Democracy, Interdependence, and Conflict, 1950–1985. *International Studies Quarterly* 41(2):267–293.

Oneal, John R., and Bruce Russett. (1999) The Kantian Peace: The Pacific Benefits of Democracy, Interdependence, and International Organizations. *World Politics* 52(1):1–37.

Peceny, Mark, Caroline C. Beer, and Shannon Sanchez-Terry. (2002) Dictatorial Peace? *American Political Science Review* 96(1):15–26.

Polachek, Solomon W. (1980) Conflict and Trade. *Journal of Conflict Resolution* 24(1):55–78.

Polachek, Solomon W. (1997) Why Democracies Cooperate More and Fight Less: The Relationship Between International Trade and Cooperation. *Review of International Economics* 5(3):295–309.

Polachek, Solomon W., John Robst, and Yuan-Ching Chang. (1999) Liberalism and Interdependence: Extending the Trade-Conflict Model. *Journal of Peace Research* 36(4):405–422.

Polanyi, Karl. (1957) *The Great Transformation*. New York: Octagon.

Ray, James Lee. (1995) *Democracy and International Conflict: An Evaluation of the Democratic Peace Proposition*. Columbia, SC: University of South Carolina Press.

Ray, James Lee. (1997) The Democratic Path to Peace. *Journal of Democracy* 8(2):49–64.

Reed, William. (2003a) Information and Economic Interdependence. *Journal of Conflict Resolution* 47(1):54–71.

Reed, William. (2003b) Information, Power, and War. *American Political Science Review* 97(4):633–641.

Risse-Kappen, Thomas. (1995) Democratic Peace—Warlike Democracies?: A Social-Constructivist Interpretation of the Liberal Argument. *European Journal of International Relations* 1(4):491–518.

Risse-Kappen, Thomas. (1996) Collective Identity in a Democratic Community. In *The Culture of National Security: Norms and Identity in World Politics*, edited by Peter Katzenstein. New York: Columbia University Press, pp. 357–399.

Russett, Bruce. (1993) *Grasping the Democratic Peace: Principles for a Post-Cold War World*. Princeton, NJ: Princeton University Press.

Schelling, Thomas C. (1966) *Arms and Influence*. New Haven: Yale University Press.

Schultz, Kenneth A. (1998) Domestic Opposition and Signaling in International Crises. *American Political Science Review* 94(4):829–844.

Schultz, Kenneth A. (2001) *Democracy and Coercive Diplomacy*. Cambridge: Cambridge University Press.

Schumpeter, Joseph. (1950) *Capitalism, Socialism, and Democracy*. New York: Harper.

Schumpeter, Joseph. (1955) The Sociology of Imperialism. In *Imperialism and Social Classes*. Cleveland, OH: World Publishing Co.

Senese, Paul D. and John A. Vasquez. (2003) A Unified Explanation of Territorial Conflict: Testing the Impact of Sampling Bias, 1919–1992. *International Studies Quarterly* 47(2):275–298.

Slantchev, Branislav. (2003) The Principle of Convergence in Wartime Negotiations. *American Political Science Review* 97(4):621–632.

Vasquez, John A. (1993) *The War Puzzle*. Cambridge: Cambridge University Press.

Voeten, Erik. (2000) Clashes in the Assembly. *International Organization* 54(2):185–215.

Voeten, Erik. (2001) Outside Options and the Logic of Security Council Action. *American Political Science Review* 95(4):845–858.

Waltz, Kenneth N. (1959) *Man, the State, and War*. New York: Columbia University Press.

Weede, Erich. (2003) Globalization: Creative Destruction and the Prospect of a Capitalist Peace. In *Globalization and Armed Conflict*, edited by Gerald Schneider, Katherine Barbieri, and Nils Petter Gleditsch. Lanham, MD: Rowman & Littlefield, pp. 311–323.

Weede, Erich. (2005) *Balance of Power, Globalization and the Capitalist Peace*. Potsdam: Liberal Institute.

Wilkenfeld, Jonathan. (1991) Trigger-Response Transitions in Foreign Policy Crises, 1929–1985. *Journal of Conflict Resolution* 35(1):143–169.

APPENDIX: REPLICATING TESTS OF THE CAPITALIST PEACE ON CRISIS OCCURRENCE

This appendix offers a series of logit models of ICB crisis onset. We adopt the remedy proposed by Beck, Katz, and Tucker (1998) to control for duration dependence. We begin with a model eqivalent to tests conducted by Oneal and Russett. The model includes DEMOCRACY (LOW), DEMOCRACY (HIGH), TRADE DEP (LOW), and the "control" variables described in the text. Table A1 presents coefficient estimates and standard errors for each model. As expected, the estimated coefficient for DEMOCRACY (LOW) is negative and statistically significant ($p = 0.004$). The estimated coefficient for DEMOCRACY (HIGH) is positive and significant ($p = 0.003$), capturing the impact of regime type difference in a dyad. As this difference increases, the likelihood of an international crisis rises. The estimated coefficient for TRADE DEP (LOW) is also negative and statistically significant ($p = 0.003$). Estimated coefficients for the additional variables generally conform with established findings. Finally, the MIDDLE EAST dummy shows the region is more crisis prone.

Model A2 incorporates FIN. OPEN (LOW). Greater economic openness reduces the likelihood of international crises. However, introducing a measure of economic integration leads DEMOCRACY (LOW) to become statistically insignificant.[8] DEMOCRACY (HIGH) remains significant, perhaps reflecting the "autocratic peace" argument (Peceny et al. 2002; Bennett 2006). The additional variables, including the MIDDLE EAST dummy, remain significant and substantively unchanged.

Model A3 adds the impact of interests. The estimated coefficient for INTERESTS (−0.7419) indicates that pairs of states with similar voting patterns at the United Nations are less likely to become involved in an international crisis. While adding INTERESTS reduces the coefficient on FIN. OPEN (LOW) by about one third, both variables remain highly statistically significant (with $p = 0.008$ and $p = 0.002$, respectively). Observed relationships are in the hypothesized direction.

Model A4 introduces a variable for dyadic economic development. However, variability in economic development has no apparent effect on crisis involvement. This finding is not surprising since the theory in the text anticipates that the impact of economic development on the likelihood of international crises depends on whether conflict is between contiguous or noncontiguous states. Developed countries should be much less likely to

---

[8]Data for FIN. OPEN (LOW) confines the temporal domain to 1966–1992. We estimated Model A1 using only observations from this period and found that DEMOCRACY (LOW) was not statistically significant in this period. The democratic peace result observed in Model A1 depends heavily on the crisis behavior of states in the two decades immediately following World War II. The literature claims a much more general effect for regime type on conflict.

experience crises with their neighbors over borders and territory, but more likely to confront distant countries over ideological or policy differences.

The value of distinguishing between these contrasting effects becomes clearer when we add the interaction term GDPPC (LOW) x CONTIG in Model A5. In Model A5, with the interaction term present, GDP per capita has significant, and opposite, effects. As anticipated, prosperity increases the likelihood of international crises, but decreases the probability of crises among *contiguous* states.

Finally, we offer an additional test that directly assesses the extent to which wealthy dyads engage in crises over policy differences rather than territorial contests. We use two ICB variables to identify crises over territory—GRAVTY (gravity of threats) and ISSUES (primary crisis issue). Taken together, the variables provide information about when the underlying threats and issues in a crisis touch upon territory and the allocation of resources. GRAVTY indicates when crises involve specific territorial threats, threats of grave danger to the population, and threats to existence. ISSUES identifies when crises occur over borders, access to the sea, and natural resources. These variables provide information to identify when underlying issues involve allocation of resources.

We estimate a bivariate logistic regression model using the dichotomous variable for territorial crises as the dependent variable and GDP/Capita (Low) as the sole independent variable.[9] Scaling GDP/Capita (Low) into thousands of dollars to ease interpretation, the estimated coefficient is -0.1964 (z-statistic = -2.94, p = 0.003). For each \$1,000 increase in GDP/Capita (Low), the odds of a territorial crisis between states decreases by approximately 18%. To better appreciate the impact of average national income on the content of crises, consider two hypothetical dyads. In the first dyad, the less wealthy state has a GDP per capita equivalent to the World Bank cutoff between low income and low-middle income states (\$2,262, 1985 dollars). A crisis in this dyad is just about equally likely to involve territory or policy issues (1.015). In the second dyad, the less wealthy state is modestly better off, but not dramatically so, with a GDP per capita in the middle of the range for upper-middle income states (\$6,661, in 1985 dollars). Here, the estimated odds of a territorial crisis declines substantially to 0.428, so that a policy crisis is more than twice as likely.

---

[9] Pr(Territorial_Crisis) = 0.459** − 0.196 [GDP/Capita (Low)]**, N = 444, Log-likelihood = −302.45, χ^2 = 9.09**.

TABLE A1 Logit Regression of Liberal Economic and Political Variables on Crisis Onset

D.V.: ICB, all dyad years	A1	A2	A3	A4	A5
DEMOCRACY					
Democracy (Low)	−0.0582**	−0.0226	0.0044	0.0033	0.0025
	(0.020)	(0.020)	(0.021)	(0.021)	(0.021)
Democracy (High)	0.0325**	0.0393**	0.0036	0.0054	0.0064
	(0.011)	(0.013)	(0.015)	(0.014)	(0.015)
MARKETS					
Trade Dep. (Low)	−188.2158**	−120.8106*	101.5121*	−96.1457*	−78.2747
	(62.623)	(47.902)	(44.438)	(46.422)	(45.334)
Fin. Open. (Low)		−0.2039***	−0.1356**	−0.1314**	−0.1377**
		(0.050)	(0.051)	(0.052)	(0.052)
INTERESTS			−0.7419**	−0.7450**	−0.7368**
			(0.240)	(0.242)	(0.243)
DEVELOPMENT					
GDP/Capita (Low)				−0.0341	0.4852**
				(0.120)	(0.163)
GDP/Capita × Contiguity					−0.7689***
					(0.202)
ADDITIONAL VARIABLES					
Contiguity[1]	2.4989***	2.7079***	2.9025***	2.9308***	8.6213***
	(0.306)	(0.365)	(0.346)	(0.354)	(1.508)
Distance[2]	−0.5654***	−0.5249***	−0.4697***	−0.4577***	−0.4201***
	(0.093)	(0.109)	(0.102)	(0.103)	(0.098)
Major Power[1]	2.2861***	2.0389***	1.7374***	1.7293***	1.7049***
	(0.321)	(0.346)	(0.335)	(0.328)	(0.318)
Alliance[1]	−0.0369	0.2289	0.2574	0.2781	0.2172
	(0.189)	(0.226)	(0.271)	(0.280)	(0.279)
Capability Ratio[2]	−0.3413***	−0.3031***	−.2412***	−0.2339***	−0.2347***
	(0.65)	(0.061)	(0.066)	(0.066)	(0.069)
Middle East[1]	1.1248***	1.0172***	1.2181***	1.2270***	1.3341***
	(0.228)	(0.242)	(0.258)	(0.250)	(0.253)
Peace years	−0.2203***	−0.2501***	−0.1745**	−0.1900**	−0.1932**
	(0.044)	(0.066)	(0.067)	(0.068)	(0.068)
Spline 1	−0.0019*	−0.0022	−0.0011	−0.0014	−0.0014
	(0.001)	(0.001)	(0.001)	(0.001)	(0.001)
Spline 2	0.0013	0.0017	0.0007	0.0009	0.0009
	(0.001)	(0.001)	(0.001)	(0.001)	(0.001)
Spline 3	−0.0005	−0.0006	−0.0002	−0.0003	−0.0003
	(0.000)	(0.000)	(0.000)	(0.000)	(0.000)
CONSTANT	−2.1844**	−1.7994*	−2.2533**	−2.0756	−6.1365***
	(0.765)	(0.908)	(0.852)	(1.151)	(1.150)
N	350203	284086	261992	254018	254018
Log-likelihood	−1777.35	−1212.30	−985.20	−966.73	−959.12
χ^2 (13, 14,15,16,17)	1685.29***	1566.57***	1548.84***	1573.89***	1476.20***

Significance: *$p < .05$; **$p < .01$; ***$p < .001$; p-values based on two-tailed tests.
[1]Dummy variable.
[2]Logged variable.

Capitalism, Commitment, and Peace

PATRICK J. McDONALD
The University of Texas at Austin

This paper builds on the growing capitalist peace research program by examining how large quantities of public property influence the likelihood of conflict between states. Drawing on the logic of the commitment problem, it develops two explanations linking the predominance of public property in an economy to the likelihood of being the target of military conflict, defined to include both militarized disputes and war. Empirical support for this hypothesis is generated with a brief illustrative case and a series of statistical tests with monadic and directed dyadic research designs. A final section discusses how these findings suggest that capitalism plays a larger role than democracy in limiting military conflict between states.

Recent contributions to the liberal peace debate have sought to shift the literature away from the Kantian tripod of international trade, democracy, and international organizations and toward a set of institutions or economic attributes often associated with capitalism as alternative and potentially competing causes of peace (Weede 1995; Mousseau 2000; Gartzke 2007; Gleditsch 2008; McDonald 2009). This paper draws on the bargaining literature (e.g., Fearon 1995; Powell 1999, 2006; Wagner 2007; Reiter 2009) to extend this work on the capitalist peace. It breaks from these broader literatures on the liberal peace and the bargaining model of war in two key ways to develop new tests of a mechanism by which capitalism promotes peace between states. First, rather than relying on concepts—like bilateral trade flows, interdependence, or capital mobility—that describe economic

---

Thank you to Terry Chapman, Paul Fritz, Ron Krebs, Dan Reiter, Bruce Russett, and Harrison Wagner for comments on previous versions of this manuscript.

relationships between states to understand how commerce promotes peace, it instead concentrates on the internal institutional attributes of states, namely the relative distribution of public and private property in an economy. Second, while most empirical and theoretical research on the bargaining model of war focuses on how informational problems impede peaceful compromise between states, I instead examine how large quantities of public property within economies can create a commitment problem between states that heightens the likelihood of military conflict.

This paper builds on the research linking capitalism to peace found in McDonald (2009) in three ways. First, it utilizes that theoretical framework to examine two mechanisms—one focused on internal political survival; the other on expected changes in the international distribution of military power—by which large quantities of public property within an economy increase the likelihood of war between states. Second, it offers new statistical evidence that extends the empirical support for a capitalist peace in three ways: a focus on how capitalism alters the likelihood of being the target of both militarized interstate disputes and war; by showing that the capitalist peace holds in both monadic and directed dyadic research designs; and by making reasonable interpolations of missing data to increase confidence that findings linking capitalism to peace do not depend on the exclusion of socialist countries for which economic data is lacking.[1] The statistical tests show robust support for the claim that the possession of high quantities of public property heightens the risk of being targeted in a military dispute. Third, given that the predominance of private property in an economy is a crucial institutional indicator of capitalism (e.g., Kornai 2000), these empirical extensions generate additional support for both of the central conclusions of McDonald (2009): capitalism promotes peace; and the pacific effects generated by capitalism are stronger than those of democracy.

These findings possess multiple theoretical and empirical implications for literatures in both political science and history. First, they extend the growing literature on the capitalist peace by highlighting an alternative mechanism by which governmental constraints on private property heighten the risks of war. Second, they build on the suggestion by Powell (2006) to devote more attention to commitment problems, rather than private information, to understand bargaining failures. With few exceptions, the liberal peace literature has focused on informational asymmetries to understand how democracy, international commerce, and international organizations might promote peace.[2] Third, these findings carry implications for the emerging debate over whether democracy or capitalism plays a larger role in promoting peace between states (Mousseau 2000, 2009; Gartzke 2007; Gleditsch 2008;

---

[1] McDonald (2009) does not extensively examine targeting, does not utilize a directed dyadic research design, and does not draw on the imputed data utilized here.
[2] These exceptions include Lipson (2003) and Eilstrup-Sangiovanni and Verdier (2005).

McDonald 2009). Democracy and capitalism shape the likelihood of being targeted in a military dispute in very different ways. While democracy heightens the risk of being targeted, capitalism reduces it. These differential effects help to account for the presence of a monadic capitalist peace, the absence of a monadic democratic peace, and show that the conditions of a capitalist peace are less restrictive than those of a democratic peace. While capitalism promotes peace irrespective of the economic institutional attributes of a dyadic partner, the capacity of democracy to promote peace is conditioned by the presence of democratic institutions in a dyadic partner.

The rest of this paper is divided into three sections. The first section reviews the growing literature on the capitalist peace, outlines two causal mechanisms linking the quantity of public property in an economy to the likelihood of that country being targeted in a military dispute, and presents some illustrative case evidence. The second section presents a series of statistical tests utilizing monadic and directed dyadic research designs. A third section concludes and discusses the implications of these findings for the democratic peace debate.

EXTENDING THE CAPITALIST PEACE

Often organized around the Kantian tripod, the debate on the sources and strength of a liberal peace has been among the most prominent in international relations over the past two decades (e.g., Russett and Oneal 2001). Many contributions to the growing literature on the capitalist peace criticize or extend the components of this larger debate examining the role of democracy and trade in promoting peace.[3] Focusing on libertarian states, Rummel (1983) links economic freedom to a reduction in military conflict. Weede (1995) argues that economic liberalization via free trade promotes peace by fostering democracy. Mousseau (2000, 2003) argues that dominance of contract-intensive transactions within societies conditions the democratic peace. The democratic peace only emerges among those states in which scarce resources are allocated via contractual relationships based on exchange. Gartzke (2007) argues that the presence of the statistical relationship between democracy and peace depends on the omission of variables he associates with capitalism. The inclusion of variables for common political interests, economic development, and capital account liberalization eliminates the statistical relationship between democracy and peace. McDonald (2009) argues that the domestic institutions associated with capitalism, namely the relative dominance of private ownership in a domestic economy

---

[3]For recent reviews see Schneider, Barbier, and Gleditch (2003), Mansfield and Pollins (2003), and Gleditsch (2008).

and competitive market structures, have played a larger role than democracy in promoting peace between states over the past two centuries.

This section blends components of this literature that focus on the internal institutional attributes of capitalism with insights from the bargaining framework to develop two theoretical mechanisms linking capitalism to peace. These mechanisms concentrate on how the fiscal independence generated by large quantities of public property impedes the ability of governments to commit to preserving the international status quo. By strengthening a government's hold on domestic power and enabling it to sustain arms races, large quantities of public property increase the risks of being targeted in a preventive attack.

Bargaining and the Outbreak of War

The bargaining framework draws on a common story to characterize the process by which political disputes between states can escalate to war (e.g., Fearon 1995; Powell 1999, 2006; Reiter 2003; Wagner 2000, 2007). Imagine two states disagree over how to distribute some resource, say territory, between them. Both states want to maximize the portion of the resource they control. They each possess two broad options by which to reach this goal. They could negotiate a compromise arrangement whereby each gains access to some portion of the resource. Alternatively, they could opt to settle the dispute with a military contest in which the victor captures the entire resource. The balance of military capabilities between the two states then shapes the war's outcome. States possessing more military capabilities are more likely to win. This war option carries the risk of losing the entire disputed resource. Moreover, the use of military force is inefficient as it imposes costs on all its participants. Consequently, a settlement provides a bonus by allowing states to avoid such costs. This bonus is large enough to compensate both governments so that they are at least as well off had they gone to war. Explanations for why wars occur therefore necessitate understanding the failure of states to reach a stable, negotiated compromise that avoids the costs of war.

Fearon (1995) focuses on two key impediments to peaceful bargains that avert war—private information and commitment problems.[4] Informational asymmetries about the balance of military capabilities or resolve can make states overly optimistic about their likelihood of prevailing in war. This optimism can encourage greater demands or a more intransigent bargaining stance that leads an adversary to choose to defend its interests with military force. The existence of private information coupled with incentives

---

[4] He identifies a third—issue indivisibilities. These occur when the disputed resource, say some strategically important piece of territory, is not easily broken apart and thus apportioned between the two parties. Powell (2006) argues that issue indivisibilities should instead be cast as a commitment problem.

to misrepresent information can thus impede states from identifying a potential settlement that that avoids the costs of war.

Powell (2006) criticizes the broad trend in the bargaining literature that has led to a concentration on informational problems as a cause of war and urges a new focus on commitment problems. The inability of states to commit to living with a bargain prevents them from agreeing to one in the first place. Accordingly, states go to war because they fear the political consequences of a peace in which their bargaining power is successively negotiated away. The problem here is not the identification of a peaceful bargain that leaves both parties better off than had they gone to war but the unwillingness of either to refrain in the future from demanding a renegotiation of the agreement once their bargaining leverage has improved.

Powell identifies five examples of bargaining failures caused by commitment problems. Four of these five—preventive war, preemptive war, bargaining over issues that change the balance of power, and a domestic version of preventive war—can be traced to a common mechanism: a large and rapid shift in the balance of military or political power between bargaining entities. War breaks out in these situations when the temporarily weaker side is unable to commit to refrain from exploiting the future improvement in its bargaining leverage caused by the shift of military power in its favor. His (2006:192–194) second key source of commitment problems integrates an aspect of the military balance often neglected in the bargaining literature: a government's ability to procure societal resources for national defense. Because governments do not own all the resources within their economy, they must also engage in negotiations with their own citizens to secure access to economic resources that can be utilized for national defense. Powell shows that states may opt to go to war to avoid paying the domestic costs, measured in terms of foregone consumption, of deterring an adversary by preserving the military balance. By eliminating a military rival, victory in war creates a peace dividend that allows a government to reduce the demands it places on societal resources.

Constraining Commitment: Public Property, Regime Stability, and the International Status Quo

Large quantities of public property within states aggravate commitment problems between states in two ways. Both follow from the tendency of large quantities of public property to strengthen a government politically at home.[5] First, this strength emboldens foreign policy by insulating it from internal opposition. Second, large quantities of public property enhance the

---

[5] For discussions of this relationship between public property and domestic political strength see Kiser (1986/87), Barnett (1990), McDonald (2007, 2009), and Morrison (2009).

capacity of governments to sustain arms races that alter the distribution of military power among states.

The relative distribution of public and private property in a domestic economy influences regime stability by shaping the scope to which governments rely on societal wealth to fund and implement public policy. If governments do not own all of the resources within the domestic economy, they must secure a transfer of these resources through fiscal policy. This transfer necessarily entails some type of bargain with the property holding class. Property holders do not willingly surrender their wealth without receiving some mix of services, like security from internal and external threats, and promises to impose limits on such transfers, such as government commitment to subject itself to legislative oversight for subsequent tax increases.[6] The nature of this bargain and, most importantly, the extent of the political concessions a government makes in these negotiations shapes its capacity to retain power at home, the quantity of societal wealth it can rely on to fund its war machine, the scope of its military power, and most importantly, its bargaining leverage relative to other governments in the international system. Alternatively, large quantities of nontax revenues render governments less dependent on large wealth transfers from society via taxation to implement policy, and most importantly, less politically constrained by the concessions necessary to extract such resources.[7]

McDonald (2007, 2009) integrates this logic into selectorate theory (Bueno de Mesquita, Smith, Siverson, and Morrow 2003) to link the possession of large quantities of public property with domestic political strength and a greater willingness to initiate military conflict. Selectorate theory traces variation in the size of a government's support coalition to its decisions for military conflict. While large support coalitions push governments to deploy fiscal resources to supply public goods, small coalitions alternatively encourage governments to cultivate loyalty via concentrated private goods payouts targeted only to members of their support coalition. Secure at home, leaders with small support coalitions are more likely to initiate military conflict because they are insulated from the political costs of policy failure. The maintenance of political support from small winning coalitions depends not on policy outcomes but on the continuation of private goods payouts. Consequently, such governments are free to pursue bold or aggressive foreign policies that increase a state's likelihood of initiating military conflict.

Similarly, large quantities of public property increase the likelihood that a government will be politically free to initiate military conflict by providing critical resources to maintain regime security in polities with either small or

---

[6]See for example North and Weingast (1989).
[7]Morrison (2009) generates a proof of the claim that higher levels of nontax revenue reduce taxation and presents statistical evidence showing that higher levels of nontax revenue lead to lower taxes on capital, profits, and income in democracies.

large winning coalitions. Because these resources are not garnered via taxation and do not necessitate its concomitant political concessions, these "free" resources can be deployed in one of three manners that all tighten a government's hold on power at home. First, they can be used to increase the loyalty of members of the existing support coalition by augmenting their private benefit payments. Second, they can be used to coopt some portion of an opposition movement by diverting private benefits to them and increasing the size of the support coalition. Third, these resources can weaken opposition from groups outside of the winning coalitions by increasing the supply of public goods more broadly in the polity.

While McDonald (2007, 2009) focuses on how these domestic dynamics influence the likelihood of military conflict by increasing a government's willingness to initiate it, these same dynamics can also heighten the risks of conflict by removing an important domestic mechanism that pushes governments to preserve their international commitments. Accordingly, states with high quantities of public property may be targeted in a preventive strike because an adversary recognizes that these resources create an internal political capacity to sustain the costs associated with using military force to alter the international political status quo. Multiple studies link regular leadership turnover within democracies to sustainable international commitments (e.g., Leeds 1999, Lipson 2003). The possibility of facing domestic political punishment for abrogating international agreements leads democratically elected leaders to uphold their commitments. This logic suggests any domestic attribute that impedes leadership turnover—like free resources stemming from public property, foreign aid, international borrowing, and natural resource wealth—could threaten international commitments and encourage an adversary to try and preserve them with military force. The British, French, and Israeli decision to launch a preventive strike against Egypt in 1956 illustrates this mechanism (McDonald 2009). British leaders, in particular worried that Nasser's nationalization of the Suez Canal and control of the revenues generated from it would enable him to consolidate his rule at home and embark on a much more expansionist foreign policy in the Middle East, altering the regional status quo.

Constraining Commitment: Public Property and Arms Races

This institutional separation between government authority and citizen ownership also bears on the connection among arms races, the distribution of power among states, commitment problems, and war. The domestic political capacity to sustain an arms race can shift the balance of military power between states, increase a government's bargaining leverage relative to its adversaries, and tempt adversaries to launch a preventive war that helps alleviate the long term domestic costs associated with sustaining a program of armaments expansion (Powell 2006).

Kydd (2000) and Wagner (2007) both compare an arms race to fighting a limited war. Just as a limited war is a form of bargaining while fighting that reveals information about which state is likely to win a total war in which one state completely disarms the other, an armaments competition is also a form of bargaining that precedes the outbreak of fighting. Greater defense spending increases the likelihood of victory in a military contest and enhances a state's capacity to extract more concessions during the bargaining process that precedes war. Like war, this struggle is costly in that resources deployed for military uses could instead expand the productive capacity of the domestic economy. Moreover, given the incentive of both sides to preserve bargaining power by matching an adversary's increase in military spending, the balance of military power could remain unchanged. Consequently, each side may "destroy" productive assets without improving their international bargaining position. Given this possibility, both parties have an interest in striking a bargain, namely an arms control agreement, that halts the joint diversion of economic resources to the military.

By increasing military expenditures, arms races can pose significant domestic challenges to governments by necessitating a revision of the fiscal contract between state and society that regulates the conditions under which the former gains access to the assets of the latter to secure the means of external defense. Despite characterizations of national defense as a public good, groups within society still disagree about the necessary quantity of the public good or an equitable distribution of its costs (e.g., Narizny 2007). Society can use such negotiations with the state to extract political concessions in the form of greater control over national security policy or future restrictions on military spending. Arms races can thus threaten any internal political equilibrium by forcing the state to violate past tax agreements while attempting to extract even more resources from society.

This possibility possesses important implications for thinking about how domestic institutional structures that regulate the economy may shape both a state's capacity to procure national resources for war and how this internal contract influences the terms of international settlements, including those created via war, governments make among themselves. First, significant domestic differences in the political process by which states mobilize societal wealth for defense can shape the military balance of power among states and expectations about the capacity of states to alter this balance in the future through an arms race. Second, this underlying domestic political capacity can threaten the sustainability of peaceful bargains among states via commitment problems. Domestic institutions that reduce the concessions made to society to mobilize national wealth for defense can make suspect any commitment by a government not to exploit such a political resource in an arms race.

A brief examination of the arms races on land and sea in the decade before 1914 illustrates this intimate connection between domestic and international bargaining. The British, French, and German governments adopted similar political strategies to sustain these arms races.[8] Prior to the turn of the century, they all relied primarily on regressive tax schemes that shifted most of the burdens of public finance on the political left via tariffs and consumption taxes. Because this constituency possessed a relatively smaller portion of the wealth in these societies, the arms race threatened this financial paradigm by exposing its limited capacity to generate sufficient revenue growth to match the exploding costs of manpower and capital-intensive equipment like battleships.[9] When faced with the need to mobilize more of society's wealth to augment military capabilities, all three governments revolutionized their systems of public finance by introducing property and incomes taxes whose burdens fell more on the political right. While the political left had long opposed armaments spending, governments bought their support via reform that promised to distribute the burdens of public finance more equitably. In France and Germany, these decisions upset traditional political coalitions and necessarily created great uncertainty as to whether the government could remain in power and/or sustain the arms race. Because the left had long opposed arms spending, its willingness to countenance future increases was highly unlikely. Moreover, these political tactics threatened to provoke a conservative revolt from the right that could leave both governments without any reliable coalition of support. In short, the arms race forced a revision of the domestic bargain by which governments secured societal resources for their war machines. This revision necessitated political concessions that circumscribed the ability of these governments to secure new financing in the future and created significant doubts about their capacity to sustain the arms race over the long term.

How did this arms race shape the decision for war in 1914? McDonald (2009) shows how French loans and the revenues generated from two key state-owned resources, namely railroads and vodka, gave Russia a distinct advantage in the armaments race on land beginning in 1912 that rapidly altered the balance of military power on the continent. Unconstrained by the need to renegotiate the basic tax contract with society, the Tsar dramatically increased Russian military expenditures. His capacity to surge ahead in the arms race simultaneously demonstrated to German leaders that they were politically incapable of making additional domestic political concessions necessary to maintain the pace of the arms race (Ferguson 1994). Peace may have been preserved with a Russian commitment to slow its program of military expansion. However, any promise to do so would have been incredible because the institutional separation between state control and private ownership necessary to force political leaders to bargain with

---

[8]This discussion draws largely on chapter 7 of McDonald (2009).

[9]Rowe (1999) examines the political consequences for defense procurement of rising labor and capital costs during this period.

society for the right to tax was simply absent in Russia. Germany launched a preventive war in 1914 in large part because it could no longer pay the domestic costs of preserving the balance of military power on the continent.

This example illustrates how the quantity of public property shapes the size of the resource transfer a state must secure from society to build and maintain its military power. Large quantities of public property free the state from having to mobilize more wealth from society, a process that often requires a series of political concessions, such as democratic oversight or fiscal reform. In this light, public property can serve as a revenue source for the state that is acquired independently of societal oversight. Alternatively, privatization necessarily reduces the amount of resources owned by the state. As public property decreases, the state must undertake a broader mobilization effort that either risks alienating societal support or results in voluntary limits on its own political autonomy as greater quantities of consumption are sacrificed to prepare for war.[10] By freeing a government from having to make domestic political concessions to obtain the resources necessary to construct a war machine, large quantities of public property enhance a government's capacity to sustain an arms race.

This political capacity to sustain an arms race shapes the likelihood of war by influencing expectations about the present and future balance of military power. While an arms race can reveal information about the balance of military capabilities between states, it can also reveal an organizational imbalance between two states in their respective political capacities to fund programs of armaments expansion. Powell's discussion about commitment problems suggests why the revelation of this organizational imbalance might lead to war. Because the state possessing the mobilizational advantage finds it difficult to commit to arms control that necessarily limits its ability to exploit this political resource, this disparity can lead its adversary to launch a preventive war to avoid either the costs of the arms race or detrimental shifts in the balance of military power.

In sum, large quantities of public property can make military conflict more likely by increasing the chances that its holders will be targeted in a preventive strike. This claim was built by examining two examples of how commitment problems can lead to bargaining failures and war. First, by strengthening a government at home, large quantities of public property eliminate domestic incentives to uphold international settlements. Second, large quantities of public property enable governments to sustain the domestic political costs associated with arms races and tempt adversaries to launch a preventive strike to avoid paying such costs. Alternatively, by forcing governments to renegotiate the basic tax contract with society, the

---

[10]Multiple scholars (e.g., Kiser 1986/87; Levi 1988; Barnett 1990) have noted how the state's bargaining position vis-à-vis society is strengthened when it does not rely on the wealth of private citizens within its polity to fund public policies such as war.

predominance of private property in an economy acts as a device by which governments can commit to some form of arms control.[11] The next section offers some statistical evidence supporting this relationship between public property and military conflict.

TARGETING PUBLIC PROPERTY REGIMES IN MILITARY CONFLICT

This section presents a series of statistical tests of the hypothesis that large quantities of public property heighten the risks of being targeted in a military conflict. These tests differ on three critical dimensions—the choice of monadic or directed dyadic research designs; operationalization of the dependent variable, namely being the target of a militarized interstate dispute or the target of a war; and the operationalization of the primary independent variable, the relative distribution of public and private property in a domestic economy.[12] Together, these regressions demonstrate robust support for this principal hypothesis and offer more empirical verification of the larger claim that capitalism promotes peace.

Research Design

The primary hypothesis in this paper examines how the economic attributes of one state alter its likelihood of participating in military conflict. This can be examined in two key ways. The first just focuses on how these economic attributes of one state alter its participation in military conflict, broadly defined to include military conflict with any other state in the international system. The second narrows the sample of states with which a government could be engaging to one. The former concentration utilizes a monadic research design in which the unit of analysis is a country year. The second utilizes a directed dyadic research design in which the unit of analysis is a

---

[11]This logic is similar to that found in Garfinkel (1994). In her model, partisan competition creates a downward bias in military spending that then enables democratic regimes to commit to arms control. She conceptualizes current arms expenditures as an investment in future consumption. Holding arms spending by all other nations equal, a state could use additional military resources to seize or defend a larger portion of the total pool of global resources. The possibility of getting voted out of office though reduces the likelihood that a democratic government will reap the benefits of this future capacity to seize more global resources. Consequently, this electoral uncertainty induces both parties in a democracy to adopt lower levels of military spending. In the same way, large quantities of private property force a government to renegotiate the basic tax contract with society to secure the revenues for greater military spending. By requiring political concessions that limit a government's ability to remain in office, this renegotiation with private wealth holders can similarly act as a commitment device by heightening a government's uncertainty about its ability to reap future advantages from any investment in military capabilities.

[12]These tests also differ from the statistical tests presented in McDonald (2009) by focusing on targeting, examining statistically the outbreak of war, utilizing a directed dyadic framework, and presenting robustness checks that make reasonable assumptions to impute missing economic data.

directed dyad year. In this latter setup, each state is paired with every other state in the international system. This pairing generates two observations for each year of the sample. The first observation identifies the factors that correlate with any decision by the first state (State A) to initiate a military dispute against the second state (State B) in a given year. The second observation identifies the factors that correlate with any decision by the second state (State B) to initiate a military dispute against the first state (State A) in a given year. For example, the U.S.-Canada pairing generates two observations in 1980. The United States is state A in the first observation; and is state B in the second observation.

There are advantages and disadvantages to each of these approaches. Because it only focuses on the economic and political attributes of one state rather than two, the monadic setup generally requires the deletion of a smaller percentage of cases due to missing data. By not restricting the states to which a government can engage in conflict with to a dyadic partner, the presence of military conflict in a monadic design is also a much less rare event among the sample of observations. Furthermore, these two hurdles can interact in the directed dyadic setup when listwise deletion due to missing data for critical independent variables alters the inclusion of an already very small number of observations of military conflict, heightening the sensitivity of the results to the composition of the sample created by data availability.[13] However, many of these disadvantages may be outweighed by the inclusion of well-known dyadic characteristics, like the distribution of military power and geographic distance, in a directed dyadic setup. Their inclusion ensures that any relationship between public property and military conflict does not depend on the exclusion of a standard group of control variables common in quantitative studies of military conflict. The tests employ both of these research designs to compensate for the relative weaknesses of each and ensure that any statistical conclusion does not depend on research design choice.

Data—Critical Independent and Dependent Variables

The primary independent variables (PUBLIC and $PUBLIC_{A,B}$) utilize data collected by McDonald (2007) from the IMF's *Government Finance Statistics*. McDonald (2007) argues that a government's nontax revenue—from such sources as its own property, dividends on financial assets, rents from leasing natural resources, and administrative fees—provides a proxy for the relative distribution of public and private property in an economy. Higher levels of nontax revenue signify greater quantities of public property a government can utilize to fund its activities. This indi-

---

[13]For a discussion of this issue and its relevance to the capitalist peace see Dafoe (2009).

cator is particularly apt here because of the theoretical focus on the political difficulties faced by governments seeking to renegotiate the basic tax contract with society. Higher levels of nontax revenue indicate a greater financial independence from society and a greater capacity to fund higher levels of military spending without renegotiating the basic tax contract with society. In both research designs, PUBLIC measures the percentage of annual government revenues derived from nontax sources respectively for a state.

I operationalize PUBLIC in two ways. The first relies solely on observed values reported by the International Monetary Fund. McDonald (2007, 2009) discusses the coverage that this data provides. With the exception of island states, most countries are included in the data set. However, because states joined the IMF at different points in this sample, data for some countries are missing for parts of the time series. In light of arguments made by Dafoe (2009) emphasizing the estimation risks associated with dropping socialist countries that were not members to the IMF, I employ a second means of operationalizing PUBLIC. This second measure implements a procedure similar to that recommended by Gleditsch (2002) to reduce the costs associated with deleting observations from regressions due to missing data. Because data for both socialist countries[14] and members of OPEC have a high rate of missingness, I construct sample averages of PUBLIC for socialist states (0.24) and members of OPEC (0.41) over the entire time period.[15] I then substitute these sample averages for the two respective types of economies whenever data on PUBLIC is missing for those states. These substitutions raise the potential number of country-years that could be included in the analysis from 3,110 to 3,660.[16]

In the directed dyadic setup, I include PUBLIC scores for both members of the directed dyad. $PUBLIC_B$ tests the primary hypothesis under investigation here. Higher values of $PUBLIC_B$ should be associated with a greater likelihood that state B will be targeted in a military dispute by state A in a given year (i.e., A will initiate a military dispute against B). $PUBLIC_A$ tests a key hypothesis of McDonald (2007) linking the possession of large quantities of public property to an increased willingness to initiate military disputes. To guard against endogeneity, I measure PUBLIC for each state in the year prior to which the observation for the dependent variable is made. Data for PUBLIC is available after 1970.[17]

---

[14]The list of socialist countries is drawn from Kornai (1992).
[15]This imputation raises the potential number of socialist state years that could be included in the analysis from 116 to 467. For OPEC, the number of potential case observations moves from 191 to 390.
[16]These sample averages for PUBLIC are 16.0 without the imputed data and 17.85 with it.
[17]The conflict data provides the temporal endpoint for the sample—1997 and 2001 for wars and MIDS, respectively.

I operationalize military conflict in two ways. The theory points directly to a focus on being the target of a preventive war. Consequently, one set of dependent variables (WARTARGET) takes on a value of one whenever the state in question is the target of a new war in a given year. To be coded as a target, the state in question must be an original party to the war when it first broke out. WARTARGET takes on the value of zero in all other years. These observations are collected from version 3.0 of the interstate war data set from the Correlates of War project (Sarkees 2000). However, because the number of interstate wars during the period under which data for PUBLIC is available is relatively small, I also use militarized interstate disputes to measure military conflict. This dependent variable (MIDTARGET) is also dichotomous. In the monadic setup, it takes on a value of one whenever the state in question is the target of a new militarized dispute. In the directed dyadic setup, it takes on a value of 1 when State A initiates a new military dispute against State B in a given year and State B is an original party to the dispute. This operationalization is equivalent to stating that the dependent variable takes on a value of 1 in a year when State B is targeted by State A in a military dispute. All other cases of either no conflict present in the directed dyad year or the continuation of a military dispute from a previous year are coded as 0. The coding of the dependent variable relies on version 3.0 of the Militarized Interstate Dispute data set (Ghosn, Palmer, and Bremer 2004).[18]

Control Variables

To ensure robustness of the results, I also include a set of control variables commonly utilized in quantitative research on international conflict. Both research designs include the standard spline technique to control for temporal autocorrelation (Beck, Katz, and Tucker 1998). In the monadic design, I include controls for regime type (DEMOCRACY), major power status (GREATPOWER), the number of states sharing a land border with the state in the observation (CONTIGUOUS COUNT), and trade levels as a portion of gross domestic product (OPEN). This model specification follows that in McDonald (2007). Descriptions of these variables can be found there.

In the directed dyad setup, I include controls for regime type, major power status, the dyadic balance of power, contiguity, the presence of an alliance agreement, geographic distance between the two states, bilateral trade dependence, and interest similarity. DEMOCRACY$_{A,B}$ indicate respectively the regime scores of states A and B as designated by the Polity IV

---

[18]The initiating state is identified as the one moving first in a military dispute, i.e., State A in the MID coding scheme.

project (Jaggers and Gurr 1995).[19] These variables range from −10 to 10, with higher levels associated with more democratic regimes. DEMAND$_{A,B}$ measures the relative importance of bilateral trade between states A and B as a function of the their respective aggregate economic sizes.[20] CONTIGUOUS is a dummy variable that indicates whether or not the two states in the dyad share a common border by land or are separated over water by less than 400 miles.[21] DISTANCE is the natural log of the distance in kilometers between the capital cities of states A and B. MAJORPOWER$_{A,B}$ are dummy variables that take on a value of 1 when the states in the directed dyad are designated a great power by the COW project. PREPONDERANCE measures the disparity in military capabilities between states A and B as indicated by their COW CINC scores. It is the natural log of the capability score of the more powerful state in the dyad divided by the capability score of the weaker state.[22] INTEREST SIMILARITY is the unweighted global S score (Signorino and Ritter 1999) for alliance portfolio similarity between the two states in the dyad. ALLIES is a dummy variable that takes on a value of 1 when states A and B are both members of the same alliance. With the exception of DEPEND, all of these control variables were generated with Version 3.201 of the Eugene data generating program (Bennett and Stam 2000).

Monadic Results

The monadic results are presented in Table 1. The first two columns utilize WARTARGET as the dependent variable. In the first column, PUBLIC does not contain any imputed observations. The positive and statistically significant coefficient on PUBLIC indicates that as a state's possession of public property increases it is more likely to be targeted in an interstate war. The second column utilizes averaged data for PUBLIC to fill in missing observations for socialist states and members of OPEC.[23] While the coefficient shrinks some in size, the basic conclusion remains: states are more likely to target economies with large quantities of public property in war. While the

---

[19] The observation for DEMOCRACY is made at $t-1$ to guard against endogeneity concerns. I utilize version two of the Polity 4 which converts regime scores previously classified as "interregnum" or "transition" to the 21-point scale. For a discussion of these coding rules see http://www.cidcm.umd.edu/inscr/polity/convert.htm
[20] Similarly, the observation for DEPEND is made at $t-1$ to guard against endogeneity concerns. Data for these variables are taken from Oneal and Russett (1999) and McDonald (2004).
[21] CONTIGUITY was coded with the updated COW contiguity data set (Stinnett, Tir, Schafer, Diehl, and Gochman 2002).
[22] I also ran robustness checks that measured the distribution of power with a variable that divided the capability score of one of the states in a dyad by the sum of the capability score of each of the two states. This alternative measurement did not change any of the primary relationships among the variables for democracy, capitalism, and military conflict.
[23] To maximize the number of observations, I also exclude the variable for trade openness, a second key source of data missingness for socialist states.

TABLE 1 Monadic Tests

	DV: WARTARGET	DV: WARTARGET (extended data)	DV: MIDTARGET	DV: MIDTARGET (extended data)
PUBLIC	0.049***	0.029***	0.012***	0.007**
	(0.014)	(0.011)	(0.004)	(0.003)
DEMOCRACY	0.034	0.028	0.0002	0.004
	(0.066)	(0.040)	(0.009)	(0.008)
OPEN	−0.009*		−0.004**	
	(0.005)		(0.002)	
TOTAL	0.121*	0.066	0.049**	0.057**
	(0.066)	(0.064)	(0.023)	(0.022)
GREATPOWER	1.123	0.332	1.160**	1.120**
	(1.184)	(1.269)	(0.494)	(0.447)
CONSTANT	−8.766***	−7.044***	−0.975***	−1.183***
	(2.065)	(1.869)	(0.272)	(0.216)
N	2,462	3,045	2,782	3,427
Loglikelihood	−45.73	−71.67	−1183.75	−1492.91

Note: Top number in each cell is estimated coefficient. Robust standard errors clustered on dyad listed below in parentheses. Two-tailed estimates are conducted for all estimates. ***$p \leq .01$; **$p \leq .05$; *$p \leq .10$. Splines (not shown) added to all models.

first regression shows that a finding linking public property to conflict does not need to rely on the use of imputed data, the second regression enhances confidence that the broader conclusion linking capitalism to peace does not depend on the systematic exclusion of certain classes of states for which economic data is often lacking.

The last two regressions in the table broaden the range of military conflict captured in the dependent variable by focusing on being the target of a militarized dispute rather than just the target of a war. This shift does not alter the key conclusion. Utilizing both means of operationalizing PUBLIC, high quantities of public property heighten the risks of being targeted in a military dispute.

The results for the control variables perform largely as expected when the dependent variable is a militarized dispute. Conforming to a wide range of evidence restricting the democratic peace to a dyadic result, regime type has no effect on the likelihood of being a target of military conflict in these monadic tests. Great power status and the number of contiguous states increase the likelihood of being targeted in a military dispute but not war. High trade levels as a portion of GDP reduce the likelihood of being a target of military conflict.

Directed Dyadic Results

The directed dyadic results can be found in Tables 2 and 3. These eight models can be divided into three categories. The first set of regressions, found in the first and third columns of each table, include only the unit level attributes of state B in the regression model. These specifications maximize the number of observations in the sample. The regressions found in the second and fourth columns of each table include the unit level attributes for both states in the directed dyad. The second category refers to the way in which military conflict is measured. In Table 2, WARTARGET is the dependent variable. The results in Table 3 instead use militarized interstate disputes to operationalize military conflict. The third category, found in the latter two columns of each table, utilize the extended data for PUBLIC.

The variable critical here to testing the argument linking the possession of large quantities of public property to being targeted in a military conflict

TABLE 2 Directed Dyad Tests

	DV: WARTARGET	DV: WARTARGET	DV: WARTARGET (extended data)	DV: WARTARGET (extended data)
$PUBLIC_A$		0.014		0.008
		(0.016)		(0.146)
$PUBLIC_B$	0.046***	0.028***	0.046***	0.043***
	(0.011)	(0.010)	(0.015)	(0.149)
$DEMOCRACY_A$		0.027		−0.032
		(0.067)		(0.058)
$DEMOCRACY_B$	0.117***	0.086*	0.097*	0.076
	(0.050)	(0.044)	(0.056)	(0.054)
$DEPEND_A$		−521.572***		
		(186.540)		
$DEPEND_B$	−373.49	−7.375		
	(329.82)	(53.406)		
CONTIGUOUS	0.614	3.950***	1.868***	1.588***
	(1.190)	(1.340)	(0.297)	(0.397)
DISTANCE	−1.123***	−0.746***	−0.735***	−0.730***
	(0.225)	(0.250)	(0.164)	(0.169)
$MAJORPOWER_A$		-----[a]		1.152
				(1.362)
$MAJORPOWER_B$	3.882**	7.106***	0.671	0.380
	(1.966)	(0.976)	(1.346)	(1.800)
PREPONDERANCE	−0.709	−0.624**	−0.334	−0.303
	(0.470)	(0.246)	(0.306)	(0.230)
INTEREST SIMILARITY	−7.057***	−8.308***	−3.910*	−4.078
	(1.552)	(2.275)	(2.347)	(2.727)
ALLIES	−0.781	0.033	−1.097	−1.158
	(1.400)	(1.821)	(0.974)	(1.138)
CONSTANT	−560.276**	−665.410	−10.107***	−9.931***
	(272.313)	(272.321)**	(2.468)	(2.662)
N	360,255	210,314	516,604	346,658
LOGLIKELIHOOD	−51.01	−36.68	−84.22	−75.07

Note: Top number in each cell is estimated coefficient. Robust standard errors clustered on dyad listed below in parentheses. Two-tailed estimates are conducted for all estimates. ***$p \leq .01$; **$p \leq .05$; *$p \leq .10$. Splines (not shown) added to all models.
[a]Because public property data is not available for China—the only great power that initiated a war during this time period—when it initiated the two wars against Vietnam, this variable drops from the analysis as it perfectly predicts the outcome variable.

TABLE 3 Directed Dyad Tests

	DV: MIDTARGET	DV: MIDTARGET	DV: MIDTARGET (extended data)	DV: MIDTARGET (extended data)
PUBLIC$_A$		0.013***		0.011***
		(0.003)		(0.002)
PUBLIC$_B$	0.009***	0.011***	0.007**	0.007**
	(0.003)	(0.004)	(0.003)	(0.003)
DEMOCRACY$_A$		−0.026***		−0.005
		(0.009)		(0.008)
DEMOCRACY$_B$	0.022**	0.015	0.020***	0.021**
	(0.009)	(0.011)	(0.007)	(0.009)
DEPEND$_A$		−4.860*		
		(2.521)		
DEPEND$_B$	−6.721*	−6.501*		
	(3.682)	(3.704)		
CONTIGUOUS	2.851***	2.482***	3.045***	2.588***
	(0.388)	(0.492)	(0.270)	(0.316)
DISTANCE	−0.180***	−0.191***	−0.144***	−0.173***
	(0.050)	(0.066)	(0.035)	(0.040)
MAJORPOWER$_A$		1.056***		0.835***
		(0.349)		(0.173)
MAJORPOWER$_B$	1.038***	1.438***	0.981***	0.638***
	(0.218)	(0.298)	(0.155)	(0.199)
PREPONDERANCE	−0.167***	−0.079	−0.200***	−0.116***
	(0.041)	(0.056)	(0.033)	(0.044)
INTEREST SIMILARITY	−1.272**	−0.374	−1.870***	−1.711***
	(0.500)	(0.707)	(0.483)	(0.581)
ALLIES	0.054	0.087	−0.093	−0.230
	(0.169)	(0.235)	(0.156)	(0.190)
CONSTANT	−2.767***	−3.518***	−2.563***	−2.497***
	(0.655)	(0.822)	(0.604)	(0.706)
N	398,878	238,146	573,712	377,620
LOGLIKELIHOOD	−2820.60	−1790.69	−4503.19	−3362.05

Note: Top number in each cell is estimated coefficient. Robust standard errors clustered on dyad listed below in parentheses. Two-tailed estimates are conducted for all estimates. ***$p \leq .01$; **$p \leq .05$; *$p \leq .10$. Splines (not shown) added to all models.

is associated with PUBLIC$_B$. Across all of these eight specifications, the coefficient on PUBLIC$_B$ is consistently positive and statistically significant. These results indicate that state A is more likely to initiate war or a militarized dispute against state B as the level of public property in state B increases. In short, state B is more likely to be the target of military conflict as it possesses more public property. Similarly, as state B possesses higher quantities of private property (lower PUBLIC scores) it is less likely to be targeted in a military dispute. Given that the predominance of private property is one of the defining institutional traits of capitalist economies, these results support the broader claim that capitalism promotes peace.

The performance of the control variables changes. Shown in Table 3, the coefficient on PUBLIC$_A$ is positive and statistically significant when the dependent variable includes all militarized disputes and not just war. This result supports the findings of McDonald (2007), which shows that higher quantities of public property encourage governments to initiate military disputes. High levels of bilateral dependence reduce the risks that a government will be the target of a MID. Great powers are more likely than smaller states to initiate and be targeted in militarized disputes, but not necessarily war. Traditional geographic constraints also shape the likelihood of military conflict between states. Contiguous states engage in more disputes than noncontiguous states. And as the distance between states increases, they are less likely to settle any political differences with military force.

Discussion: The Relative Role of Capitalism and Democracy

The coefficients attached to the variables for democracy in both the monadic and directed dyadic statistical models possess implications for a larger debate over the relative role of democracy and capitalism in promoting peace. As earlier sections of this paper noted, research on the capitalist peace emerged largely as a response to and as a critique of the democratic peace literature. Gartzke (2007) argues that the inclusion of variables for capitalism eliminate the negative and statistically significant relationship between democracy and peace in dyadic tests. McDonald (2009) offers a milder critique, arguing that the relative role of capitalism in promoting peace is larger than that of democracy and that the conditions limiting the presence of a democratic peace are more restrictive than much of the literature has acknowledged.

The results offered here suggest that the peace created by capitalism is stronger than that of democracy. This claim does not rely on a comparison of the size of the estimated coefficients on the variables used to operationalize capitalism or democracy but is instead nested in a relative comparison of the number of conditions that limit the capacity of democracy or capitalism *in any one state* to limit military conflict between states. It treats the dyadic restriction, namely that the capacity of institutional traits in one country to reduce conflict between states depends on the institutional traits of the country with which it is interacting, as one such restriction. Together with the results presented in McDonald (2007, 2009), the tests presented here show that the conditions that limit the capacity of capitalism to promote peace are fewer than those that limit the capacity of democracy to promote peace.

The monadic and directed dyadic tests demonstrate that high levels of public property in one state heighten the risks of military conflict between states. Large quantities of state-owned assets encourage governments to initiate military conflict and heighten the risks that they will be targeted in military conflict. Conversely, high levels of private property, one of the institutional hallmarks of capitalist economies, make military conflict less likely both in terms of initiating and targeting behavior.

The coefficient on the democracy variables in both the monadic and directed dyadic tests also suggests why the democratic peace is more restrictive, dependent on the presence of democracy in a dyadic partner. This coefficient was either insignificant, or positive when significant. These regressions modestly support a claim that democracy, unlike capitalism, encourages the initiation of military conflict by adversaries. Even if democracy inhibits the initiation of military conflict, it might simultaneously aggravate the risks of being targeted in a dispute. Thus, the absence of a monadic democratic peace may emerge from the counteraction of any tendency by competitive elections to dampen the incentive by democracies to initiate military conflict by the concurrent tendency to aggravate the risks associated with being the target of military conflict. More importantly, these results show that such targeting effects are the opposite of those associated with capitalism. At least in directed dyadic tests utilizing militarized disputes, low levels of public property in state A dampened its likelihood to initiate military conflict and low levels of public property in state B reduced the likelihood that it would be the target of military conflict.

While showing that the capacity of capitalism to promote peace is less restrictive than that of democracy, it should be pointed out that these results do not challenge the presence of a dyadic democratic peace. Drawing on Oneal (2006), I also conducted a series of auxiliary regressions in the directed dyadic setup that confirmed the presence of a dyadic democratic peace in the sample examined here.[24] However, these tests also demonstrated that democracies are often targeted by mixed regimes. The peace created by democracy depends on the presence of democratic restraints in multiple states. The monadic and directed dyadic tests presented here show that peace fostered by capitalism is not subject to a similar restriction. Capitalism in one state promotes peace between states irrespective of the institutional attributes of any dyadic partner.

CONCLUSION

This paper combined emerging literatures on the capitalist peace and bargaining models of war to examine how high levels of public property

---

[24] I thank Bruce Russett for suggesting the following tests to me. The results are omitted here for reasons of space but are available from me via email. These tests utilized a three-fold regime typology that distinguished among democracies (Polity score greater than 6), mixed regimes (Polity score greater than −7 and less than 7), and autocracies (Polity score greater less than −6). I created nine dummy regime variables that matched the regime typologies for states A and B in the directed dyad: democracy$_a$democracy$_b$, democracy$_a$mixed$_b$, democracy$_a$autocracy$_b$, mixed$_a$democracy$_b$, mixed$_a$mixed$_b$, mixed$_a$autocracy$_b$, autocracy$_a$democracy$_b$, autocracy$_a$mixed$_b$, autocracy$_a$autocracy$_b$. I then ran regressions that dropped the dummy variable indicating whether both states were democratic to utilize that dyad type as the baseline category. The coefficients on the variables for mixed$_a$democracy$_b$, mixed$_a$mixed$_b$, mixed$_a$autocracy$_b$, and autocracy$_a$democracy$_b$ were all positive and significant.

generate commitment problems that increase the likelihood of military conflict between states. Large quantities of public property create domestic political freedom that insulates governments from internal political opposition and enables them to undertake military buildups without having to renegotiate the basic tax contract with society. This financial strength undermines the credibility of promises to preserve the international status quo by increasing a government's ability to retain power at home and enhancing its domestic capacity to shift regional or global balances of military power in its favor. The predominance of private property in an economy promotes peace by forcing governments to renegotiate the basic tax contract with society when shifting substantial resources from the civilian economy to national defense. Because this renegotiation process generally requires a government to make political concessions to society, it renders promises by capitalist states to restrain military spending and abide by the international status quo more credible.

These claims linking large quantities of public property to preventive war were primarily examined with quantitative evidence that extended the research of McDonald (2009). Three sets of regression results utilizing different research designs, different operationalizations of the dependent variable, and different data sources for public property all showed that high levels of public property heighten the risks that a state will be the target of military conflict. Given that low levels of public property are a critical indicator of capitalism, these results support the broader claim that capitalism promotes peace. Finally, these statistical tests also offered some evidence that the capitalist peace is stronger than the democratic peace. While democracy seems to heighten the risks of being targeted in military conflict, capitalism dampens those risks.

REFERENCES

Barnett, Michael. (1990) High Politics is Low Politics: The Domestic and Systemic Sources of Israeli Security Policy, 1967–1977. *World Politics* 42(4):529–562.
Beck, Nathaniel, Jonathan Katz, and Richard Tucker. (1998) Taking Time Seriously: Time-series-cross-section Analysis with a Binary Dependent Variable. *American Journal of Political Science* 42(4):1260–1288.
Bennett, D. Scott, and Allan Stam. (2000) EUGene: A Conceptual Manual. *International Interactions* 26(2):179–204.
Bueno de Mesquita, Bruce, Alistair Smith, Randolph M. Siverson, and James D. Morrow. (2003) *The Logic of Political Survival*. Cambridge, MA: MIT Press.
Dafoe, Allan. (2009) Democracy Still Matters: The Risks of Sample-censoring, and Cross-sectional and Temporal Controls. Typescript. University of California at Berkeley.
Eilstrup-Sangiovanni, Mette, and Daniel Verdier. (2005) European Integration as a Solution to War. *European Journal of International Relations* 11(1):99–135.

Fearon, James D. (1995) Rationalist Explanations for War. *International Organization* 49(3):379–414.
Ferguson, Niall. (1994) Public Finance and National Security: The Domestic Origins of the First World War Revisited. *Past and Present* 142(1):141–168.
Garfinkel, Michelle R. (1994) Domestic Politics and International Conflict. *American Economic Review* 84(5):1294–1309.
Gartzke, Erik. (2007) The Capitalist Peace. *American Journal of Political Science* 51(1):166–191.
Ghosn, Faten, Glenn Palmer, and Stuart A. Bremer. (2004) The MID3 Data Set, 1993–2001: Procedures, Coding Rules, and Description. *Conflict Management and Peace Science* 21(2):133–154.
Gleditsch, Kristian Skrede. (2002) Expanded Trade and GDP Data. *Journal of Conflict Resolution* 46(5):712–724.
Gleditsch, Nils Petter. (2008) The Liberal Moment Fifteen Years On. *International Studies Quarterly* 52(4):691–712.
Jaggers, Keith, and Ted Robert Gurr. (1995) Tracking Democracy's Third Wave with the Polity III data. *Journal of Peace Research* 32(4):469–482.
Kiser, Edgar. (1986/87) The Formation of State Policy in Western European Absolutisms: A Comparison of England and France. *Politics and Society* 15(3):259–296.
Kornai, Janos. (1992) *The Socialist System: The Political Economy of Communism*. Princeton: Princeton University Press.
Kornai, Janos. (2000) What the Change of System from Socialism to Capitalism Does and Does Not Mean. *Journal of Economic Literature* 14(1):27–42.
Kydd, Andrew. (2000) Arms Races and Arms Control: Modeling the Hawk Perspective. *American Journal of Political Science* 44(2):228–244.
Leeds, Brett Ashley. (1999) Domestic Political Institutions, Credible Commitments, and International Cooperation. *American Journal of Political Science* 43(4):979–1002.
Levi, Margaret. (1988) *Of Rule and Revenue*. Berkeley: University of California Press.
Lipson, Charles. (2003) *Reliable Partners: How Democracies Have Made a Separate Peace*. Princeton: Princeton University Press.
Mansfield, Edward D. and Brian M. Pollins, eds. (2003) *Economic Interdependence and International Conflict: New Perspectives on an Enduring Debate*. Ann Arbor: University of Michigan Press.
McDonald, Patrick J. (2004) Peace Through Trade or Free Trade? *Journal of Conflict Resolution* 48(4):547–572.
McDonald, Patrick J. (2007) The Purse Strings of Peace. *American Journal of Political Science* 51(3):569–582.
McDonald, Patrick J. (2009) *The Invisible Hand of Peace: Capitalism, the War Machine, and International Relations Theory*. New York: Cambridge University Press.
Morrison, Kevin M. (2009) Oil, Nontax revenue, and the Redistributional Foundations of Regime Stability. *International Organization* 63(1):107–138.
Mousseau, Michael. (2000) Market Prosperity, Democratic Consolidation, and Democratic Peace. *Journal of Conflict Resolution* 44(4):472–507.

Mousseau, Michael. (2003) The Nexus of Market Society, Liberal Preferences, and Democratic Peace: Interdisciplinary Theory and Evidence. *International Studies Quarterly* 47(4):483–510.

Mousseau, Michael. (2009) The Social Market Roots of Democratic Peace. *International Security* 33(4):52–86.

Narizny, Kevin. (2007) *The Political Economy of Grand Strategy*. Ithaca: Cornell University Press.

North, Douglas C. and Barry R Weingast. (1989) Constitutions and Commitment: The Evolution of Institutions Governing Public Choice in 17th Century England. *The Journal of Economic History* 49(4):803–832.

Oneal, John R. (2006) Confirming the Liberal Peace with Analyses of Directed Dyads, 1885–2001. In *Approaches, Levels, and Methods of International Politics*, edited by Harvey Starr. New York: Palgrave-Macmillan, pp. 73–94.

Oneal, John R., and Bruce M. Russett. (1999) The Kantian Peace: The Pacific Benefits of Democracy, Interdependence, and International organizations, 1885–1992. *World Politics* 52(1):1–37.

Powell, Robert. (1999) *In the Shadow of Power: States and Strategies in International Politics*. Princeton: Princeton University Press.

Powell, Robert. (2006) War as a Commitment Problem. *International Organization* 60(1):169–203.

Reiter, Dan. (2003) Exploring the Bargaining Model of War. *Perspectives on Politics* 1(1):27–43.

Reiter, Dan. (2009) *How Wars End*. Princeton: Princeton University Press.

Rowe, David M. (1999) World Economic Expansion and National Security in Pre-World War I Europe. *International Organization* 53(2):195–231.

Rummel, Rudolph J. (1983) Libertarianism and Interstate Violence. *Journal of Conflict Resolution* 27(1):27–71.

Russett, Bruce, and John R. Oneal. (2001) *Triangulating Peace: Democracy, Interdependence, and International Organizations*. New York: Norton.

Sarkees, Meredith Reid. (2000) The Correlates of War Data on War: An Update to 1997. *Conflict Management and Peace Science* 18(1): 123–144.

Schneider, Gerald, Katherine Barbieri, and Nils Petter Gleditch, eds. (2003) *Globalization and Armed Conflict*. Lanham, MD: Rowman and Littlefield.

Signorino, Curtis S., and Jeffery Ritter. (1999) Tau-b or not Tau-b: Measuring the Similarity of Foreign Policy Positions. *International Studies Quarterly* 43(1):115–144.

Stinnett, Douglas M., Jaroslav Tir, Philip Schafer, Paul F. Diehl, and Charles Gochman. (2002) The Correlates of War Project Direct Contiguity Data, Version 3. *Conflict Management and Peace Science* 19(2):58–66.

Wagner, R. Harrison. (2000) Bargaining and War. *American Journal of Political Science* 44(3):469–484.

Wagner, R. Harrison. (2007) *War and the State: The Theory of International Politics*. Ann Arbor: University of Michigan Press.

Weede, Erich. (1995) Economic Policy and International Security: Rent-seeking, Free Trade, and Democratic Peace. *European Journal of International Relations* 1(4):519–537.

Capitalism, Peace, and the Historical Movement of Ideas

JOHN MUELLER
Ohio State University

A logical and causal exploration of the growing acceptance of capitalism and peace, or war aversion, is part of what Robert Dahl has called "the historical movement of ideas." Although war aversion and the acceptance of free-market capitalism have undergone parallel and substantially overlapping historical trajectories, support for capitalism does not on its own logically or necessarily imply war aversion or support for peace. Not only must capitalism be embraced as an economic system, but at least three other ideas must be accepted as well: prosperity and economic growth must be taken as a dominant goal; peace must be seen as a better motor than war for development, progress, and innovation; and trade, rather than conquest, must be held to be the best way to achieve the dominant goal. Moreover, the causal direction may well be misspecified: it is not that free-market capitalism and the economic development it spawns cause peace, but rather that peace causes—or facilitates—capitalism and its attendant economic development. This also may explain why peace is more closely associated with capitalism than with democracy.

Robert Dahl has observed that "because of their concern with rigor and their dissatisfaction with the 'softness' of historical description, generalization, and explanation," most social scientists have turned away from what he calls, "the historical movement of ideas". The result, he suggests, is that their theories, "however 'rigorous' they may be, leave out an important explanatory variable and often lead to naive reductionism." Since beliefs and ideas are often, as Dahl notes, "a major independent variable," to ignore changes in ideas, ideologies, and attitudes is to leave something important out of consideration (1971:182–183, 188).

Over the last few centuries there have been remarkable changes in many major ideas about the way societies and the world should be arranged. For example, there have been notable declines in formal slavery, capital and corporal punishment, torture, vendetta, blood feuds, monarchy, and smoking, and there has been the rising acceptance of humane prisons, pornography, abortion, racial and class political equality, women's rights, labor unions, environmentalism, gay rights, and the determined application of the scientific method.

Important in this process, it appears, are the exertions of idea entrepreneurs. Beginning in the late nineteenth century, for example, groups began assiduously to market the idea that war—or at least war among developed countries—is a bad idea, and, despite many setbacks, their efforts seem to have been at least partly responsible for the historically-unprecedented absence of major war for most of a century now (Mueller 1989, 1995: chapter 9, 2004, 2009). And over the course of the last couple of centuries other idea entrepreneurs sought to market the ideas that democracy is the most desirable form of government and that free-market capitalism is the best way to organize the economy, in each case with what looks today to have been a fair amount of success (Mueller 1999: chapters 5 and 8).

A focus on idea entrepreneurs recommends itself because it is often difficult to come up with material reasons to explain the historical movement of ideas. For example, slavery declined over the nineteenth century when, as Seymour Drescher points out, the Atlantic slave trade "was entering what was probably the most dynamic and profitable period in its existence" (1987:4). Stanley Engerman notes that, in "the history of slave emancipation in the Americas, it is difficult to find any cases of slavery declining economically prior to the imposition of emancipation." Rather, very much in line with Dahl, he stresses the importance of "political, cultural, and ideological factors" to explain the phenomenon (1986:322–333, 339; see also Eltis 1987). Similarly, one might be inclined to argue that the remarkable decline in war among developed states is due to the increasing costs of such wars (for example, Kaysen 1990). But medieval wars were often absolutely devastating (Kaeuper 1988:77–117), while within a few years after a terrible modern war, World War I, most of the combating nations had substantially recovered economically (Overy 1982:16). The "most meaningful question," observes Alan Milward, "is whether the cost of war has absorbed an increasing proportion of the increasing Gross National Product of the combatants. As an economic choice war, measured this way, has not shown any discernable long-term trend towards greater costliness" (1977:3). Democracy began to take root in substantial countries by the end of the eighteenth century even though it had been known as a form of government for millennia and even though there seem to have been no technological or economic advances at the time that impelled its acceptance (Mueller 1999:197–200).[1]

None of this is to suggest that the efforts of idea entrepreneurs invariably succeed. Many, probably most, promoted ideas meet with far more failure than success, and some, like Communism and fascism, have enjoyed a period of considerable success only eventually to die out. Indeed, if extensive purposeful promotion could guarantee acceptance, we'd all be driving Edsels. Or, put another way, anyone who can accurately and persistently predict or manipulate tastes and desires would not be writing about it, but would move to Wall Street to become in very short order the richest person on the planet.

Many of the ideas that have grown in acceptance over the last few centuries relate to one another, and sometimes they have been promoted by the same idea entrepreneurs. However, although the ideas have taken parallel—and often overlapping or correlated—trajectories, it is not clear they are consequentially or logically or necessarily dependent on each other. It is quite possible, for example, to oppose slavery or capital punishment, but not war; to promote the political freedoms necessary for democracy without accepting the economic liberties necessary for free-market capitalism; to embrace class or ethnic equality, but not gender equality. And people who strongly oppose abortion on moral grounds may still accept capital punishment and may be appalled by those who have the opposite predispositions.

In assessing the relationship, if any, between capitalism and peace (or war aversion) in this article, I will first explore the logical connection between the two ideas and then their possible causal connection.

CONNECTING CAPITALISM AND PEACE: LOGIC

Although the idea strands of war aversion and the acceptance of free-market capitalism have undergone parallel and substantially overlapping historical trajectories, support for capitalism does not on its own necessarily imply war aversion or support for peace. In fact, for people to embrace the slogan "Make money, not war!" as proposed by Nils Petter Gleditsch (2008:707), they must not only embrace capitalism as an economic system, but must logically accept at least three other, or underlying, ideas. They must take economic prosperity and development as a dominant goal; they must see

---

[1] For a critique of the notion that economic development is a prerequisite for democracy, see Mueller 1999.

peace as a better motor than war for development, progress, and innovation; and they must come to believe that trade, rather than conquest, is the best way to achieve their chief goal.

The Growth of Economic Well-being Should be a Dominant Goal

For capitalism—or indeed economic considerations in general—to have an effect on war aversion, it would be necessary, first, to convince people that getting rich is an important goal—for the world to come to value economic well-being above passions that are often economically absurd (see also Hirschman 1977; McCloskey 2006: part 3). That is, for capitalism, or economic development, to have much bearing on decisions about war, it is necessary for the single-minded pursuit of wealth to be unashamedly accepted as behavior that is desirable, beneficial, and even honorable.

The general acceptance of capitalism—the notion that the economy should be arranged to allow for the free exchange of goods and services with minimal government intervention—will be of little consequence, or even interest, to those who do not think achieving wealth is a particularly important goal. And, traditionally the notion that one should give favor to people who are acquisitive—to people who are centrally, indeed entirely, occupied with advancing their own long-term wealth—has been repulsive to those who aspire to values and goals they consider far superior such as honor, heroism, empathy, altruism, sacrifice, selflessness, generosity, piety, patriotism, racism, self-respect, spirituality, nationalism, and compassion. In contrast, economic motives have been routinely condemned as crass, materialistic, cowardly, vulgar, debased, hedonistic, uncaring, selfish, immoral, decadent, and self-indulgent. Thus, as Simon Kuznets has pointed out, the quest for otherworldly eternity and the quest to maintain inborn differences as expressed in class structure have often been taken to be far superior to economic advancement (1966:12–14).

An important area in which noneconomic values have commonly dominated is war. For centuries, thinkers have held peace to be immoral, decadent, corrupt, materialistic, and base. According to Friedrich Nietzsche, "It is mere illusion and pretty sentiment to expect much (even anything at all) from mankind if it forgets how to make war," and Prussian General Von Moltke declared "perpetual peace" to be "a dream and not even a beautiful one . . . Without war, the world would wallow in materialism." Similarly, J.A. Cramb, a British professor of history, characterized universal peace as "a world sunk in bovine content." In the United States, the president of the Naval War College found peace to be "more degrading" than war's "simple savagery." Aristotle held that "a time of war automatically enforces temperance and justice: a time of the enjoyment of prosperity, and license accompanied by peace, is more apt to make men overbearing." And five years before writing his treatise, *Perpetual Peace*, Immanuel Kant maintained that "a prolonged peace" tended "to degrade the character of the nation" by favoring "the predominance of a mere commercial spirit, and with it a debasing self-interest, cowardice, and effeminacy" (Kant 1952:113; for other sources see Mueller 1989: chapter 2; see also Mueller 2004; Lebow 2008).

In result, capitalism—or economic development in general—has regularly been irrelevant to war's prosecution. Whether war does or does not advance economic well-being has often been of no interest whatever because the people prosecuting the war do not value economic development. When economic motivations have been put forward, they have often seemed like a rationale for impulses that are actually more nearly moral, aesthetic, emotional, or psychological. As Quincy Wright observed after a lifetime of study of the matter:

> Studies of both the direct and the indirect influence of economic factors on the causation of war indicate that they have been much less important than political ambitions, ideological convictions, technological change, legal claims, irrational psychological complexes, ignorance, and unwillingness to maintain conditions of peace in a changing world (1968:463).[2]

An important reason economic development issues have traditionally played such a limited role in war initiation is that full recognition of the notions that economic growth is possible and that wealth can be "created" are fairly new. Over the course of most of history, wealth has routinely been held to be a zero-sum game: if one person becomes rich, some other person must be becoming poorer.

This lack of appreciation of the notion of economic growth is understandable because, throughout most of history, economies have, in fact, *not* grown. Perhaps the most important single fact about economics, economic history, and economic development—and, indeed, about human material well-being—is tidily conveyed in Figure 1. In 1750, as can best be determined, all areas of the world were fairly equal economically—actually, equally poor by contemporary standards since the vast majority of people everywhere, and at all times up until then, lived in severe misery, even wretchedness.[3] Economic historian Paul Bairoch, whose data are displayed in the figure, estimates that the ratio in per capita wealth between the richest

---

[2] For an extensive discussion of the varying role of economics as a motivation, or excuse, for war, see Luard 1986.

[3] As Rosenberg and Birdzell put it: "If we take the long view of human history and judge the economic lives of our ancestors by modern standards, it is a story of almost unrelieved wretchedness. The typical human society has given only a small number of people a humane existence, while the great majority have lived in abysmal squalor. We are led to forget the dominating misery of other times in part by the grace of literature, poetry, romance, and legend, which celebrate those who lived well and forget those who lived in the silence of poverty. The eras of misery have been mythologized and may even be remembered as golden ages of pastoral simplicity. They were not" (1986:3; see also Marshall 1890:2–4).

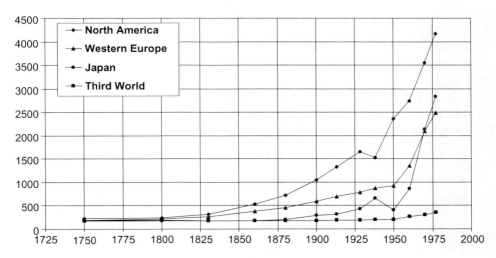

FIGURE 1 Real GNP per capita, 1750–1982 (1960 U.S. dollars and prices). Source: Bairoch 1993:95.

and poorest countries was then no more than 1.6 to 1. However, beginning in the nineteenth century, and accelerating thereafter, an enormous gap opened when North America, Europe, and, eventually, Japan began to grow significantly. And in more recent years, growth from historic (and low) levels has begun to take place worldwide (Bairoch 1981:3, 80).

This remarkable, even astounding, historic change has been dubbed "the European miracle" by Eric Jones (1987). But whatever the reasons for this remarkable development, until pretty much the end of the nineteenth century, the idea that economies could actually grow could scarcely have been appreciated by most people because, in fact, during just about the whole of the previous course of human development, none, essentially, had.

Economic development did lead Europeans to an increased appreciation for capitalism. However, capitalist development alone did not cause most people to fully embrace economic growth as a dominant goal even in rapidly-developing Europe.

Michael Howard notes that at one time the developed world was organized into "warrior societies" in which warfare was seen to be "the noblest destiny of mankind." This was changed, he suggests, by industrialization which "ultimately produces very unwarlike societies dedicated to material welfare rather than heroic achievement" (1991:176). The main problem for this generalization is that industrialization spoke with a forked tongue. The developed world may have experienced the industrial revolution, enormous economic growth, the rise of a middle class, a vast improvement in transportation and communication, surging literacy rates, and massive increases in international trade.[4] But if this experience encouraged some people to abandon the war spirit, it apparently propelled others to fall, if anything, more fully in love with the institution. Howard himself traces the persistence, even the rise, of a militaristic spirit that became wedded to a fierce and expansionist nationalist impetus as industrialization came to Europe in the nineteenth century. And, of course, in the next century industrialized nations fought two of the greatest wars in history. Thus, industrialization can inspire bellicism as much as pacifism. Howard never really provides much of an explanation for how or why industrialization must inevitably lead to an antimilitary spirit, and he simply attributes the horrors and holocausts that accompanied industrialization to "the growing pains of industrial societies" (1991:1).

The remarkable capitalistic development of the nineteenth century was accompanied by a rising antiwar movement, particularly in its last decade. However, this set of idea entrepreneurs remained a small, gadfly enterprise, and it took the experience of the cataclysm of World War I, perhaps embellished by that of its even more violent successor twenty years later, to fully undercut the appeal of the martial virtues (Mueller 1989:24–30, 1995:9). Capitalist economic development alone, no matter how impressive, was clearly insufficient to do that.

Peace Is Better than War for Promoting Innovation, Progress, and Growth

Even if one accepts free-market capitalism and holds economic development and the growth of material well-being to be dominant goals, it does not necessary follow that peace is the best engine for development and progressive innovation. Many who have accepted the importance of innovation and development have also argued that war is a more progressive engine than peace—that war, and the preparations for it, act as a stimulus to economic and technological innovation and to economic growth.

In 1908, for example, H. G. Wells, who was by no means a warmonger, found commercial advances to be "feeble and irregular" compared to the "steady and rapid development of method and appliances in naval and military affairs." He noted that the household appliances of his era were "little better than they were fifty years ago" but that the "rifle or battleship of fifty years ago was beyond all comparison inferior to those we now possess" (1908:215–216). And Wells was hardly alone: the argument that war was an important stimulus to technological development was common in his era (Milward 1977:2).

---

[4] For sources of data on these trends, see Mueller 1995:143n.

Taking the consideration further, many have found war to be a key element in promoting civilizational and evolutionary progress more generally. The Prussian historian, Heinrich von Treitschke, proclaimed that "the great strides which civilization makes against barbarism and unreason are only made actual by the sword" and that "brave people alone have an existence, an evolution or a future; the weak and cowardly perish, and perish justly" (1916: Vol. 1, 21, 29, 65). General Friedrich von Bernhardi maintained that war was a "powerful instrument of civilization" and "a political necessity . . . fought in the interest of biological, social and moral progress." For him it had "a necessary place in historical development" because it was "a regulative element in the life of mankind which cannot be dispensed with," and he warned that "without war inferior or decaying races would easily choke the growth of healthy budding elements, and a universal decadence would follow" (1914:18, 20, 111).

In this Treitschke and Bernhardi were reflecting the views of some Social Darwinists like the British statistician Karl Pearson, who felt he had discovered a correlation in 1900: "The path of progress is strewn with the wreck of nations . . . who found not the narrow way to great perfection. These dead people are, in very truth, the stepping stones on which mankind has arisen to the higher intellectual and deeper emotional life of today." In 1871 a French intellectual, Ernest Renan, called war "one of the conditions of progress, the cut of the whip which prevents a country from going to sleep, forcing satisfied mediocrity itself to leave its apathy"; and in 1899 British intellectual H.W. Wyatt argued, "The only means, revealed to us by past experience, whereby the vigorous people has supplanted the weaker, has been war without which change and movement must have ceased." In 1891, Émile Zola declared that "it is only warlike nations which have prospered: a nation dies as soon as it disarms." In America, Henry Adams concluded that war "called out the qualities best fitted to survive in the struggle for existence"; and Admiral Stephen Luce declared that "war is one of the great agencies by which human progress is effected." In like manner, Russian composer Igor Stravinsky once declared war to be "necessary for human progress."[5]

Wealth Is Best Achieved Through Exchange, Not Through Conquest

In 1795, reflecting a view of Montesquieu and others, Immanuel Kant argued that the "spirit of commerce" is "incompatible with war" and that, as commerce inevitably gains the "upper hand," states would seek "to promote honorable peace and by mediation to prevent war" (1957:24; see also Hirschman 1977:79–80, 134–135). However, this notion is incomplete

---

[5]For sources for these quotes, see Mueller 1989:44–45. See also Stromberg 1982. Even some war opponents have bought the notion that war could be progressive; they tried to argue, however, that while war may once have been productive and necessary, it was no longer so: Emerson 1904:151, 152, 155, 156, 159, 161; Spencer 1909:664–665).

because, as nineteenth-century British historian, Henry Thomas Buckle pointed out, "the commercial spirit" has often been "warlike" (1862:157).

Buckle did, however, see this changing, and he hailed Adam Smith's *Wealth of Nations* as "probably the most important book that has ever been written" because it convincingly demonstrated that gold and silver are not wealth, but are merely its representatives and because it shows that true wealth comes not from diminishing the wealth of others, but rather that "the benefits of trade are of necessity reciprocal" (1862:154, 157). These conclusions are elemental and profound, and, as Buckle suggests, they had once been counterintuitive—that is, Smith and others had to discover them and point them out. Buckle went on to conclude that Smith's key economic discovery was the "leading way" in which the "warlike spirit" had "been weakened" (1862:146, 151–158).

The problem is, however, that, even if one embraces material well-being as a dominant goal, even if one rejects the notion that war is better than peace as an engine of progress, and even if one accepts the notion that wealth comes from exchange, it does not necessarily follow that war—and particularly conquest—is a bad idea.

Indeed, an important reason why "the commercial spirit" has so frequently been "warlike" is that it is entirely possible that military conquest can be economically beneficial. As free traders would stress, the United States owes much of its prosperity to the fact that it is the world's largest free trade zone. But its enormous size was quite notably established by various forms of *Lebensraum*-like conquest—victory in a war with Mexico and with a series of them against Indians, who happened to occupy turf Americans were systematically determined to occupy.

Particularly in the early years, West European populations conquered by the Nazis during World War II, while deeply resenting the occupiers, kept out of trouble by cooperating in the sense of carrying out their normal occupations and functions, and this, as Norman Rich as observed, "kept the routine business of government and the economy going and thereby enabled the Nazis to rule, and to exploit, the occupied countries with a minimum investment of German personnel" (1974:423). Indeed, the Germans often found that occupation could be quite profitable. The people of the occupied territories continued to turn out products necessary for Germany's war, and the occupiers levied taxes, charged "occupation costs," and engaged in other financial devices to obtain revenue. The sums so received were far higher than the actual costs of maintaining the occupying army; the occupation of France was particularly profitable (Milward 1977:137–141; Rosecrance 1986:35–36; Liberman 1996).

Logically, in fact, an ardent free trader should favor conquest—at least when damage is minimal and when long-term resentments are not stirred up—since this would expand the free trade zone to the general benefit. For example, free traders would presumably hold that all North Americans would be better off economically if Canada were able consensually, and at low cost benevolently, to conquer the United States because the Canadians in their wisdom would doubtless eliminate all trade barriers that currently exist between the two countries.

Thus, commerce becomes, in Kant's phrase, "incompatible with war" *only* when it is accepted that wealth is best achieved through exchange rather than through conquest. It was with that goal in mind that antiwar idea entrepreneurs like the English journalist and economic writer, Norman Angell, sought to undercut the appeal of empire by convincing people that trade, not conquest, is the best way to accumulate wealth.[6]

In 1908 he declared it "a logical fallacy to regard a nation as increasing its wealth when it increases its territory." Adopting a free trade perspective, he pointed out that Britain "owned" Canada and Australia in some sense, yet did not get the products of those countries for nothing—it had to pay for them just as though they came "from the lesser tribes in Argentina or the USA." The British, in fact, could not get those products any cheaper than the Germans. Thus, he asked, "If Germany conquered Canada, could the Germans get the wheat for nothing? Would the Germans have to pay for it just as they do now? Would conquest make economically any difference?" The popular notion that there were limited supplies in the world and that countries had to fight to get their share was nonsense, Angell argued. Indeed, he contended, "the great danger of the modern world is not absolute shortage, but dislocation of the process of exchanges, by which alone the fruits of the earth can be made available for human consumption" (1914:31; 1933:108, 17).

Critics, such as the prominent American naval historian Admiral A.T. Mahan, countered this economic argument by noting that some wars, particularly short and cheap ones, could be economically beneficial. Not only could conquest provide a place to send excess population and establish a country in a predominant position, but it could break down invidious tariff barriers by superimposing wider governments over pettier factions; after all, large businesses are often more profitable than small ones (1912:131). Angell countered that a nation's "wealth, prosperity, and well-being . . . depend in no way upon its military power," noting that the citizens of such war-avoiding countries as Switzerland, Belgium, or Holland were as well off as the Germans, and much better off than the Austrians or Russians. Moreover, he continued to insist that, on balance, the inescapable economic chaos of war "makes economic benefit from victory impossible" (1914:36; 1933:89–92, 230; 1951:165)—something likely to hold for the vast majorities of wars.

Idea entrepreneur Angell helped to crystallize a line of reasoning that has been gaining in acceptability ever since, and this has helped lead to one of the most remarkable changes in world history: the virtual eradication of the ancient and once-vital notion of empire. Thus, as Richard Rosecrance

---

[6]On this issue, see also Nadelmann 1990; Rosenberg and Birdzell 1986:17; Crawford 2002.

observes in *The Rise of the Trading State*, more and more countries have come to the conclusion that the path to wealth is through trade rather than through conquest, and he cites the striking and important examples of two recent converts: "Today West Germany and Japan use international trade to acquire the very raw materials and oil that they aimed to conquer by military force in the 1930s. They have prospered in peaceful consequence." Among trading states, Rosecrance observes, "the incentive to wage war is absent" (1986:16, 24; see also Gleditsch 2008:707). Put another way, free trade furnishes the economic advantages of conquest without the unpleasantness of invasion and the sticky responsibility of imperial control.

CONNECTING CAPITALISM AND PEACE: CAUSATION

Logic suggests, then, that international war is unlikely if people come to accept three additional ideas: they must take prosperity and economic growth as a dominant goal; they must see peace as a better motor than war for development, progress, and innovation; *and* they must come to believe that trade, rather than conquest, is the best way to achieve their dominant goal. All three propositions have now gained wide currency, and, although international war has hardly evaporated from the planet, it is worth noting that the nations of the developed world have avoided war with each other for the longest period of time in millenia and that, despite the great increase in the number of independent countries, international war has become quite rare (Mueller 2009; see also Gleditsch 2008). This remarkable development may at least partly be due to the increasing joint acceptance of the capitalist/peace propositions. Over time, most countries in most areas of the world have opted for peace and, not unrelatedly, for the banal pleasures of capitalist economic development.[7]

---

[7]Kant was probably right to suggest that the "commercial spirit" wallows in "self-interest, cowardice, and effeminacy," something that might be called the Kantian triangle (compare Russett and Oneal 2001). However, under that "commercial spirit," people can service their long-term economic *self-interest* only if they are able to provide a good or a service other people freely find of value, and they will generally profit best if they adopt business practices that are honest, fair, civil, and compassionate (Mueller 1999: chapter 2). In addition, although it may be an act of *cowardice* by the standards of those who exalt the martial virtues to turn one's back when insulted, it is possible, by other standards, to suggest that lethal battles fought over the cut of one's coat or over the color of one's sneakers or over "spheres of influence" are not only economically foolish, but quite childish. And if it is a sign of *effeminacy* to avoid unnecessary conflict, to temper anger, and to be guided by the not entirely unreasonable notion that other people do, in fact, sometimes have feelings, that gentle, accommodating behavior is, in general, economically beneficial and facilitates trade and prosperity, and might be quite desirable even if it does sometimes come laden with a degree of treacly sentimentality. Thus, despite Kant's stern and intemperate disapproval, a society—indeed, a world—dominated by self-interest, cowardice, and effeminacy might turn out to be entirely bearable. As both peace and the "commercial spirit" have been embraced and as they interact productively, many areas of the world have increasingly moved in that direction. See also McCloskey 2006.

But there is another consideration. One of the curiosities about the historical movement of ideas is that over the last few centuries ideas that have successfully filtered throughout the world have tended to do so in one direction—from West to East. Indeed, the process has often been called "Westernization." Thus, Taiwan has become more like Canada than Canada has become like Taiwan, Gabon more like Belgium than Belgium like Gabon (on this issue, see also Nadelmann 1990:84). This means there is something of a standard geographic correlation or clustering: countries that early embraced war aversion were also generally early to take up democracy, capitalism, science, pornography, gay rights, and abortion, and early as well to abandon slavery, monarchy, blood feuding, capital punishment, and the church.

As suggested earlier, it may in general be best to see each idea movement as an independent phenomenon rather than contingent on something else or on another idea stream, rather in the way that skirt lengths are determined far more by fashion whims than by the availability of cloth and thread. There will be a correlation between the acceptance of the ideas, but it may be essentially spurious: countries that come to embrace international peace in about the same order as they embrace democracy and capitalism, but that should not be taken to imply that democracy or capitalism necessarily "lead to" peace or that there is a "democratic peace" or a "capitalist peace."

In fact, it may well be that any causal relationship between capitalism, democracy, and peace needs reexamination, and that the literature on the subject has it backwards. Insofar as there is a causal relationship between the ideas, it may be best to see peace as an independent variable not, as in the common approach, as a dependent one.

Thus, it may not be that the cluster of ideas about capitalism leads to peace, but the other way around. Although there may be a correlation between the rise of free-market capitalism and of war aversion, any causal relationship between them is rather different—indeed, just the opposite—of what has just been implied. It is not so much that free-market capitalism and the economic development it spawns cause peace, but rather that peace causes—or perhaps better, facilitates—capitalism and its attendant economic development. It is peace, not capitalism, that is the determining factor in the relationship.

Something like this may also hold for the correlation between the rise of war aversion and the rise of democracy. Peace may furnish countries with security and space in which to explore and develop democracy (see also Pietrzyk 2002, Payne 2006). That is, democracy (or democratic idea entrepreneurs) are more likely to flourish when the trials, distortions, and disruptions of war are absent. Countries often restrict or even abandon democracy when domestic instability or external military threat seems to loom. By the same token, when they are comfortably at peace, people may come to realize that they no longer require a strongman to provide order and can afford to embrace the benefits of democracy even if those might come with somewhat heightened uncertainty and possibly with the potential for less reliable leadership.

However, the relationship by which peace facilitates market capitalism and economic growth is likely to be considerably stronger than the one by which it facilitates democracy. This presumably holds especially with respect to international trade. International tensions and the prospect of international war have a strong dampening effect on trade because each threatened nation has an incentive to cut itself off from the rest of the world economically in order to ensure that it can survive if international exchange is severed by military conflict. Thus, it has frequently been observed that militarized disputes between countries reduce trade between them (Pollins 1989a, 1989b; Li and Sacko 2002). By contrast, if a couple of countries that have previously enjoyed a conflictual relationship lapse into a comfortable peace and become extremely unlikely to get into war, businesses in both places are likely to explore the possibilities for mutually beneficial exchange. The Cold War could be seen in part as a huge trade barrier and, with the demise of that politically-derived and economically-foolish construct, trade has been liberated. And the long and historically-unprecedented absence of war among the nations of Western Europe has not been caused by their increasing economic harmony. Rather, their economic harmony has been caused, or at least substantially facilitated, by the long and historically unprecedented peace they have enjoyed.[8]

This line of thought also relates to studies concluding that any democratic peace is conditioned by economic development (Mousseau 2009:56). As noted, peace does probably facilitate democratic development, but it likely facilitates economic development far more—hence there is a closer relationship between peace and capitalism than between peace and democracy. But the causal relationship is not that democracy and/or capitalism cause peace. Rather, if other issues are in proper alignment, it is peace that causes—facilitates, makes more possible—democracy and capitalism.

---

[8]The same may hold for the rise of international institutions and norms. They often stress peace but, like expanded trade flows, they are not so much the cause of peace as its result. Many of the institutions that have been fabricated in Europe—particularly ones like the coal and steel community that were so carefully forged between France and Germany in the years following World War II—have been specifically designed to reduce the danger of war between erstwhile enemies. However, since it appears that no German or Frenchman in any walk of life at any time since 1945 has ever advocated a war between the two countries, it is difficult to see why the institutions should get the credit for the peace that has flourished between those two countries for the last half century and more (as in Russett and Oneal 2001:158; Ikenberry 2001: chapter 6). They are among the consequences of the peace that has enveloped Western Europe since 1945, not its cause. As Richard Betts puts it for institutions of collective security, "peace is the premise of the system, not the product" (1992:23–24, emphasis removed; see also Schweller 2001:183).

REFERENCES

Angell, Norman. (1914) *The Great Illusion: A Study of the Relation of Military Power to National Advantage.* London: Heinemann.
Angell, Norman. (1933) *The Great Illusion 1933.* New York: Putnam's.
Angell, Norman. (1951) *After All: An Autobiography.* New York: Farrar, Straus and Young.
Bairoch, Paul. (1981) The Main Trends in National Economic Disparities since the Industrial Revolution. In *Disparities in Economic Development since the Industrial Revolution,* edited by P. Bairoch and M. Levy-Leboyer. London: Macmillan, pp. 3–17.
Bairoch, Paul. (1993) *Economics and World History: Myths and Paradoxes.* Chicago, IL: University of Chicago Press.
Bernhardi, Friedrich von. (1914) *Germany and the Next War.* New York: Longmans, Green.
Betts, Richard K. (1992) Systems for Peace or Causes of War? Collective Security, Arms Control, and the New Europe. *International Security* 17(1):5–43.
Buckle, Henry Thomas. (1862) *History of Civilization in England,* Vol. I. New York: Appleton.
Crawford, Neta C. (2002) *Argument and Change in World Politics: Ethics, Decolonization, and Humanitarian Intervention.* Cambridge, UK: Cambridge University Press.
Dahl, Robert A. (1971) *Polyarchy.* New Haven, CT: Yale University Press.
Drescher, Seymour. (1987) *Capitalism and Antislavery: British Mobilization in Comparative Perspective.* New York: Oxford University Press.
Eltis, David. (1987) *Economic Growth and the Ending of the Transatlantic Slave Trade.* New York: Oxford University Press.
Emerson, Ralph Waldo. (1904) War. In *The Complete Works of Ralph Waldo Emerson: Vol. 11, Miscellanies.* Boston and New York: Houghton Mifflin, pp. 148–176.
Engerman, Stanley L. (1986) Slavery and Emancipation in Comparative Perspective. *Journal of Economic History* 46(2):317–339.
Gleditsch, Nils Petter. (2008) The Liberal Moment Fifteen Years On. *International Studies Quarterly* 52(4):691–712.
Hirschman, Albert O. (1977) *The Passions and the Interests: Political Arguments for Capitalism Before Its Triumph.* Princeton, NJ: Princeton University Press.
Howard, Michael. (1991) *The Lessons of History.* New Haven, CT: Yale University Press.
Ikenberry, G. John. (2001) *After Victory: Institutions, Strategic Restraint, and the Rebuilding of Order After Major Wars.* Princeton, NJ: Princeton University Press.
Jones, E. L. (1987) *The European Miracle: Environments, economies, and geopolitics in the history of Europe and Asia*m, 2nd ed. Cambridge, UK: Cambridge University Press.
Kaeuper, Richard W. (1988) *War, Justice, and Public Order: England and France in the Later Middle Ages.* New York: Oxford University Press.
Kant, Immanuel. (1952) *The Critique of Judgement.* Trans. James Creed Meredith. London: Oxford University Press.

Kant, Immanuel. (1957) *Perpetual Peace*. Trans. Louis White Beck. Indianapolis, IN: Bobbs-Merrill.

Kaysen, Carl. (1990) Is War Obsolete? *International Security* 14(4):42–64.

Kuznets, Simon. (1966) *Modern Economic Growth: Rate, Structure, and Spread*. New Haven, CT: Yale University Press.

Lebow, Richard Ned. (2008) *A Cultural Theory of International Relations*. Cambridge, UK: Cambridge University Press.

Li, Quan, and David Sacko. (2002) The (Ir)Relevance of Militarized Interstate Disputes for International Trade. *International Studies Quarterly* 46(1): 11–34.

Liberman, Peter. (1996) *Does Conquest Pay? The Exploitation of Occupied Industrial Countries*. Princeton, NJ: Princeton University Press.

Luard, Evan. (1986) *War in International Society*. New Haven, CT: Yale University Press.

Mahan, Alfred Thayer. (1912) *Armaments and Arbitration: The Place of Force in the International Relations of States*. New York: Harper.

Marshall, Alfred. (1890) *Principles of Economics*. London: Macmillan.

McCloskey, Deirdre N. (2006) *The Bourgeois Virtues: Ethics for an Age of Commerce*. Chicago, IL: University of Chicago Press.

Milward, Alan S. (1977) *War, Economy and Society, 1939–1945*. Berkeley, CA: University of California Press.

Mousseau, Michael. (2009) The Social Market Roots of Democratic Peace. *International Security* 33(1):52–86.

Mueller, John. (1989) *Retreat from Doomsday: The Obsolescence of Major War*. New York: Basic Books.

Mueller, John. (1995) *Quiet Cataclysm: Reflections on the Recent Transformation of World Politics*. New York: HarperCollins.

Mueller, John. (1999) *Capitalism, Democracy, and Ralph's Pretty Good Grocery*. Princeton, NJ: Princeton University Press.

Mueller, John. (2004) *The Remnants of War*. Ithaca, NY: Cornell University Press.

Mueller, John. (2009) War Has Almost Ceased to Exist: An Assessment. *Political Science Quarterly* 124(2):297–321.

Nadelmann, Ethan A. (1990) Global Prohibition Regimes: The Evolution of Norms in International Society. *International Organization* 44(4):479–526.

Overy, Richard. (1982) *The Nazi Economic Recovery 1932–1938*. London: Macmillan.

Payne, James L. (2006) Election Fraud: Democracy is an effect, not a cause, of nonviolence. *American Conservative* 5(5):11–12.

Pietrzyk, Mark E. (2002) *International Order and Individual Liberty: Effects of War and Peace on the Development of Governments*. Lanham, MD: University Press of America.

Pollins, Brian. (1989a) Conflict, Cooperation, and Commerce: The Effect of International Political Interactions on Bilateral Trade Flows. *American Journal of Political Science* 33(3):737–761.

Pollins, Brian. (1989b) Does Trade Still Follow the Flag? *American Political Science Review* 83(2):465–480.

Rich, Norman. (1974) *Hitler's War Aims: The Establishment of the New Order*. New York: Norton.

Rosecrance, Richard. (1986) *The Rise of the Trading State: Conquest and Commerce in the Modern World*. New York: Basic Books.

Rosenberg, Nathan, and L.E. Birdzell. (1986) *How the West Grew Rich: The Economic Transformation of the Industrial World*. New York: Basic Books.

Russett, Bruce M., and John R. Oneal. (2001) *Triangulating Peace: Democracy, Interdependence, and International Organizations*. New York: Norton.

Schweller, Randall L. (2001) The Problem of International Order Revisited: A Review Essay. *International Security* 26(1):161–186.

Spencer, Herbert. (1909) *The Principles of Sociology*, Vol. II. New York: Appleton.

Stromberg, Roland N. (1982) *Redemption by War: The Intellectuals and 1914*. Lawrence, KS: Regents Press of Kansas.

Treitschke, Heinrich von. (1916) *Politics*. New York: Macmillan.

Wells, H. G. (1908) *First and Last Things: A Confession of Faith and a Rule of Life*. New York: Putnam's Sons.

Wright, Quincy. (1968) War: The Study of War. In *International Encyclopedia of the Social Sciences*, Vol. 16, edited by D. L. Sills. New York: Macmillan-Free Press, pp. 453–468.

Capitalism and Peace: It's Keynes, not Hayek

MICHAEL MOUSSEAU
OMER F. ORSUN
JAMESON LEE UNGERER
DEMET YALCIN MOUSSEAU
Koç University, Turkey

Can capitalism promote peace among nations? For many this might seem like an odd proposition, given the strong traditional view in the field of international relations that capitalism produces "merchants of death" (Engelbrecht and Hanighen 1934). Lenin blamed World War I on the capitalist quest for investment outlets (1970 [1917]). While Karl Deutsch et al. (1957) observed the existence of a "security community" among the highly capitalist states of Europe, neo-Marxist world-systems theory blamed five centuries of war, imperialism, and slavery all on the shoulders of capitalism (Wallerstein 1974).

But what exactly do we mean by "capitalism"? For Wallerstein (1974:399–400) and others in the world-systems school, "capitalism" can include any form of economic exchange, including the outright robbery of colonial imperialism, slavery, and even Soviet-style communism, as long as an economy is linked with global markets. By this definition every major economic system that has existed in the modern era is capitalist; according to this definition, capitalism must be associated with both peace and war, lacking all analytical value. Obviously, any coherent discussion of capitalism must give the concept analytical teeth, and in the newly burgeoning capitalist peace literature two distinctive definitions have emerged. Other chapters in this volume by Gartzke and Hewitt, and McDonald outline what we call "free-market" theories of capitalist peace, which equate "capitalism" with free markets or smaller government at home and abroad. Since these views also assume that free markets and less government ownership of property promote economic growth spontaneously, while government plays, at most, a minimal role in market creation and only a regulatory role in its maintenance, this view is perhaps best represented by the works of Friedrich Hayek (1994 [1944], 1960).

However, neo-classical liberals do not have a monopoly on the definition of capitalism, and a second definition defines it simply as a way of life: the extent to which citizens in a society regularly contract with strangers located in a market to obtain goods, services, and incomes (Mousseau 2000). In this "social-market" definition there is no assumption that markets emerge spontaneously, or that state policies of interference and redistribution impede them. In fact, in all social-market (henceforth "market") capitalist economies of the modern era the state has historically been highly involved in promoting capitalist development, often by subsidizing various enterprises and, most consistently, by spending lavishly to maintain steady rates of market growth (Gurr et al. 1990). Market capitalism is thus historically linked much more with the economic philosophy of John Maynard Keynes (1935), who advocated government spending to promote consumption, rather than with a small unobtrusive government that lets it rise (and fall) on its own.

It is this second, more-Keynesian, definition of capitalism and its role effecting foreign policy that is the subject of this chapter. As identified by economic norms theory (Mousseau 2000, 2009), social market capitalism causes peace by way of micro-level dependency on a market, which causes citizenry dependence on a third party—government—for the enforcement of contracts. This micro-level dependency on contracting with strangers produces two nontrivial results. First, it creates a direct interest in the democratic rule of law as the best means for ensuring that government enforces contracts reliably and impartially. Second, it creates a direct interest in the health and welfare of everyone else in the market, since there is more opportunity to be had when others in the market are healthy and wealthy rather than dead or poor. Since others in the market can be both inside and outside a nation, dependency on a market makes war, both within and among capitalist nations, virtually unthinkable. Moreover, since nations have interests in each other's welfare, economic norms theory explicitly predicts a positive peace, rather than just a cold absence of militarized conflicts—an achievement unmatched by competing democratic peace and capitalist peace theories in the literature, all of which predict only a dearth of militarized conflict rather than actual friendship based on mutual interests. The ability to explain a shared positive peace offers a scientifically more progressive explanation of the observed phenomenon (Ungerer 2012), providing added explanatory power beyond free-market capitalist and democratic peace theories, at the same time posing the far greater paradigmatic challenge to the strong anarchic assumptions of mainstream realism and liberalism.

Because economic norms theory explicates how market capitalism can cause both democracy and peace among nations, it offers a full explanation for the famous democratic peace—the observation that democratic nations rarely fight each other—as well as the extant peace among the advanced nations. Prior research has corroborated this view: Mousseau (2009) showed that in the modern era not a single fatal conflict has occurred among nations with impersonal economies, which was gauged using a binary measure of contract flows within nations. Furthermore, the analysis found that democracy has no significant impact on peace. However, some defenders of the democratic peace have challenged these results: Russett (2010:201) thinks democracy might be revived if control is added for regime differences; Dafoe (2011) asserts that Mousseau's results are not a "compelling" explanation for the democratic peace, owing to the moderate correlation of capitalism and democracy only 26% of democratic dyads are excluded from the democratic peace. Moreover, he also calculates that if the democracy measure is made binary and far more restrictive, then democracies too have not had fatal disputes.

This chapter extends our understanding of the impacts of democracy and capitalism on peace in several significant ways. First, we report results using Mousseau's (2009) newer continuous measure of contract flows, providing a solution to the perfect prediction problem that besets analyses of conflict using the binary measure. Second, we switch from analyses of militarized interstate disputes (MIDs) to analyses of interstate crises using the Interstate Crisis Behavior (ICB) dataset (Hewitt 2003). Whereas MIDs are events that may not reflect actual state intentions, crises are defined by perceptions of threats, including value threats, by policymakers, so we can be more confident in analyzes of crises that the antagonists genuinely perceive themselves as in conflict and thus engaging in actions that would be inconsistent with, and uncharacteristic of, nations engaged in a positive peace. Third, to address Russett's concern about control for regime differences, this factor is considered in the analyses. Finally, we examine all the capitalist peace theories together in head-to-head tests.

The analyses of most dyads from 1961 to 2001 yield clear and compelling results: neither measures of democracy nor free markets have any significant impact on peace once social-market capitalism is considered, and the latter emerges as the most robust correlate among the crucial explanatory variables of interstate crises. The implications of these findings are far from trivial: economic norms theory provides an empirically corroborated explanation for why the advanced capitalist economies have been long adherents to the principles of democracy, while at the same time providing a theoretically powerful explanation of capitalism that consistently renders the existence of a negative and positive peace among nations. The real-world applicability is direct and clear: to promote peace among nations the successful strategy is not the support of democracy in other countries, but rather the promotion of their national economies.

This chapter is organized as follows. After reviewing economic norms theory, we offer a theoretical account of capitalism that we believe more accurately accounts for the nature of the advance of developed capitalist nations. We then delineate the causal process that leads to the market capitalist peace, further arguing that it is a "market capitalist" rather than a "democratic" peace that has been prolifically observed throughout the literature. We then detail the procedures of our analysis, before discussing our results. We conclude by emphasizing that the market capitalist explanation continues to receive empirical corroboration, while providing greater explanatory power for a peace among nations, consistent with expectations across all specifications. As other chapters in this volume have addressed the free-market capitalist peace, we begin by explicating the substantial differences between free market and social market theories of capitalist peace.

A TALE OF TWO CAPITALISMS

The free-market theories of capitalist peace that have preceded us in this volume all define capitalism as less government interference in the private sector. For Gartzke and Hewitt, "capitalism" means fewer governmental restrictions on foreign trade and investment; for McDonald, "capitalism" means less government ownership of property. Weede (2011:20) is most explicit in this regard: "for me … capitalism and economic freedom are synonyms."

The embrace of free and private markets is widely associated with the classical (or neo-classical) liberal tradition of Adam Smith's hidden hand and, in the modern era, the works of Hayek. While accepting a role for the state as an impartial regulator of the economy, and even allowing for social security and assistance for the poor, Hayek believed that the market was a natural phenomenon which emerged from the spontaneous interactions of those acting in it, and that state interference in the market by way of government ownership, spending, and redistribution impeded its efficiency (Hayek 1960). Moreover, he believed that state interference led inexorably to totalitarianism, arguing that it fostered rent seeking and other conflicts over the nature of state interference, and that these conflicts can ultimately be resolved only with totalitarian solutions (Hayek 1994 [1944]). Hayek was thus adamantly opposed to state interference in the market with spending and redistribution policies on moral as well as utilitarian grounds, and as such he is widely identified today as a major influence on the leading advocates of freer markets, including Margaret Thatcher and Milton Friedman, as well as the pro-free-market Tea Party movement in the USA.

All the free-market theories of capitalist peace seem to adopt the classical/Hayekian assumption that freer markets or smaller governments do a better job at promoting growth in markets compared to less free markets or larger governments. Weede (2011:2) simply assumes that freer markets promote "prosperity." The two other free-market models seem less explicit about their free market assumptions, but they nevertheless assume freer (rather than less free) private markets promote wealth when they claim that their measures of free markets or private property can explain "the absence of war among states in the developed world" (Gartzke 2007:166) and the linkage of peace with "modernization and economic development" (McDonald 2007:569).

In direct opposition to Hayek is Keynes (1935), who advocated government spending and redistribution to promote consumption and thus market growth. Since government interference is necessary to ensure the efficiency of markets, for Keynes there is no assumption that freer markets are better than less free ones in promoting market growth. Rather, the Keynesian tradition is based on the premise that markets are not natural or spontaneous but rather constructed and maintained, particularly with government policies of increased taxation, spending, and redistribution—policies adamantly opposed by Hayek.[1] Today Keynesianism is most closely associated with the left social democratic parties of Europe, which explicitly embrace policies of spending and redistribution. Nevertheless, all the advanced capitalist states have regimes of heavy spending aimed at promoting market growth. While parties of the right often deny their Keynesian proclivities, in fact when in power they usually spend heavily on military and other matters to keep unemployment rates low; for evidence, just recall the socialization and management of the banks in 2008 by the supposedly pro-free-market W. Bush administration.

As we will see in the following section, economic norms theory is quite distinctive from the other capitalist peace theories in that it makes no claim that freer markets do better than less free ones in promoting wealth or peace. Moreover, in making no fixed human nature assumption, economic norms theory explicitly rejects the market-as-natural or spontaneous assumptions of the classical liberals and Hayek. Finally, because it accepts that markets can be created and maintained with governmental policies of spending and redistribution, it fits snugly into the social democratic Keynesian view on the role of government in the advancement of market capitalism.

ECONOMIC NORMS THEORY

The market capitalist peace is deduced from economic norms theory (Mousseau 2000, 2009), which starts with the observation, widely documented by economic historians (Polanyi 1957 [1944]), of two kinds of economies in history: impersonal markets and personalist clientelism. As is suggested by their names, each form of economic exchange is differentiated by the manner in which the potential for prosperity is acquired. In impersonal economies, citizens normally obtain goods and services by contracting with

---

[1]Polanyi (1944[1957]) also argued that markets are created, but with a thesis that opposed markets as alien to human nature.

strangers in the marketplace, ably trusting the contractual commitments, given a credible third-party enforcer. Contrastingly, personalist economies rely primarily on personal relationships as the primary determinant factor for economic exchange, as individuals give or withhold favors, or trust in contractual commitments, based on in-group orientation or in light of prior interactions with individuals they know personally.

Personalist-clientelist economies have encompassed the majority of human history, still characterizing the economies of many nations today (Hicken 2011). A well-known historical example is European feudalism, where client serfs pledged loyalty, including military service, to patron vassals in exchange for economic and physical security, with vassals in turn pledging their loyalty to patron lords, and so on. While contracting has long coexisted with clientelism, in feudal Europe and today, the key difference in personalist economies is that third-party enforcement is unnecessary for most contracting that does occur. Many contracts take the form of spot trades, such as retail contracts, and thus do not require trust in the credibility of commitments. Other contracts, such as wholesale contracts, may require credibility of commitments, but, more often than not, the credibility emanating from these forms of contractual commitments rests on a personalized form of trust, including the fear of future sanctions in the event of violations of this trust (Kohn 2003).

The kind of transaction that affects interests and outlooks is the impersonal contract, which is distinguished by the fact that the credibility of commitments depends entirely on third-party enforcement. To gauge the extent at which impersonal contracting is the modal form of transaction in an economy, we directly observe contract flows in life insurance, a sector that is unique in that all its transactions are necessarily impersonal. First, life insurance exchanges cannot take the form of spot trades because the commitments of insurers must occur after the commitments of policyholders. Second, these transactions cannot rest on personal trust among contractees, and the threat of the loss of future contracts in the event the insurer fails to fulfill its commitments, because the delivery of service is expected only after the relationship ends with the death of the policyholder.

The history of personalist economies indicates a transition in the form of redistribution. Wealth in feudal Europe was based primarily on land, in contrast in many developing countries today, where the market remains comparatively peripheral to everyday life, clientelist relationships are more likely to be centered on access to state rents (Hicken 2011:303). Rather than manors and fiefs, clientelist-oriented networks take a variety of forms, including, but not limited to, tribes, clans, neighborhood associations, gangs, mafias, labor unions, religious sects, political parties and other forms of in-group orientation. Patrons may be local government officials, landowners, respected business people, or other local notables (ibid.:291). It is common that families or extended families maintain all major forms of economic exchange within the family, sharing loyalty and obligation only among other members of the group. For instance, in an extended family an uncle may have access to discounted goods, a cousin may do all the electrical work, and an aunt active in a political party may find local government jobs for various family members—all of whom are obligated in turn to take care of fellow family members, and all family members are obligated to serve her political party as asked, including showing up at rallies. Crucial for the reciprocity of a clientelist political economy to work, representatives of patrons continuously monitor the behavioral loyalty of their clients (ibid.:292–93).

Economic norms theory begins with the assumption that everybody in all societies seeks goods and services, highlighting that the aforementioned differentiated manner in the form of economic exchange differs according to the socioeconomy: in impersonal economies the dominant strategy is to contract with strangers located in the marketplace; in clientelist economies the dominant strategy is to nourish personal relationships and participate in group struggles over state rents (Mousseau 2000, 2009). However, owing to human cognitive limitations, it is not likely that individuals rationally decide which form of exchange maximizes their interest each time they have an economic need. Rather, as was identified by Simon (1955), human beings deal with repetitive decision-making environments by forming habitual responses to them. As such, habitual responses are dependent on the economy in which they are embedded. Thereby, acting according to market norms is not rational in a clientelist order, and acting according to clientelist norms is not rational in a market order, most economies tend to lean one way or the other and socioeconomic transitions are rare. Denzau and North (1994) suggest that individuals with common experiences share similar mental models (ideologies, models, or institutions to interpret the world). In short, the well-documented distinction of the two economic orders, tied with the insights of Nobel laureates Herbert Simon and Douglass North, lead inexorably to the deduction that individuals across the two types of economies must have different outlooks, producing the divergent cultures of contracting and clientelism.

While contracting and clientelism coexist in all economies, the crucial distinction of the two orders is the manner in which the majority of individuals obtains and holds their primary economic assets. Where securities are habitually held in contract, there is widespread dependency on third-party—government—enforcement of contracts. This is another reason why we observe life insurance contracts, which are crucial securities. Because the purpose of a life insurance contract is to promote the economic security of one's closest family members, life insurance contract flows are a direct gauge of the theorized causality of the extent at which individuals depend on the impersonal market and the credibility of the impersonal state in enforcing it. Where securities are primarily distributed by patrons, in contrast, there is little dependency on third-party enforcement, but widespread dependency on the health and good fortune of one's own patrons. As a consequence, individuals in the two orders have divergent interests, in several identifiable ways; furthermore these divergent interests have political ramifications.

First, only a contract-intensive economy, not a clientelist one, requires *a strong state that uniformly enforces the rule of law*. Individuals cannot automatically trust the commitments of strangers, so high levels of impersonal exchange cannot occur unless the commitments in contracts are widely credible. Third-party enforcement mechanisms can be private or public. However, the private enforcement of contracts, such as the use of notaries, is costly, so individuals economically dependent on strangers have an interest in an authority that offers the enforcement of contracts as a public good. For an authority's enforcement of a contract to be credible, however, it must possess a monopoly on violence over a fixed and declared geographic space. It must also maintain bureaucracies and court systems that are capable of reaching and protecting the contract rights of every actor in the marketplace. Therefore, when exogenous factors render the benefits of contracting in the market greater than the benefits of clientelist ties, members of a society develop an interest in a state that has the capability and will to effectively and efficiently enforce contracts. To the extent that those dependent on the market, such as merchants or a large middle class, have political influence, they will affect state decisions to construct effective bureaucracies and impartial court systems (Mousseau 2009).

Owing to the way in which profits are primarily sought in personal-clientelist ties, in contrast, there is little benefit from a bureaucratic rational state. The dominant strategy for most is to stay loyal to patrons, since patrons distribute wealth with partiality according to loyalty, rank, and service to the group. Because they have the loyalty of clients, patrons have the capacity to wage violence: order in these societies is maintained via gift exchanges among patrons and between patrons and clients that reinforce paths of hierarchy and loyalty among them. The state is an oppressive force to be evaded for those in groups that are not in control of, or connected to it; for those privileged in groups with ties to the state, utility is maximized with loyalty to specific personalities in the state, not the state itself. In this way clientelist economies can be democratic, with political action for the group central to one's economic well-being, yet the state still partial in its enforcement of law—or illiberal—favoring those in power over those not in power (Mousseau 2009).

A second change in preferences resulting from an exogenous rise in contracting in a society is for *legal equality*. For a contract to be credible all parties to it must be equally obligated to its terms. Therefore, states that wish to promote impersonal exchange must have not only the capacity to protect the contract rights of every actor in the market, but they must also do so with renowned credibility. States wishing to promote markets must therefore construct bureaucracies and court systems that are not only effective and efficient, but also widely recognized as impartial. In clientelist political economies, in contrast, such credibility is largely irrelevant, since utility is normally maximized through personalist relationships and rankings in group hierarchies. For those in groups tied to the state, an impartial and transparent bureaucracy and court system is an economic threat that must be undermined in order to maintain control of the distribution of state rents. In these ways, the modern bureaucratic rational state may be an epiphenomenon of market capitalism: for the commitments of contracts to be widely credible an effective state must first exist, and then it must be widely respected as both capable and impartial.

Once micro-level dependency on impersonal contracting is correctly understood as a variable rather than a constant, it is easy to see the third way micro-level preferences change with a rise in contracting: *a rise in markets promotes an interest in freedom*. For anyone dependent on impersonal exchanges in a market, a larger market offers more opportunities than a smaller one. Individuals seeking wealth in the market thus have interests not only in their own freedom to contract, but also in the freedom of everyone else to contract. There is no apparent reason to limit this interest to one's own ethnic group, religious sect, or nation. In fact, the delimitation of freedom creates more opportunity for economic prosperity as there is a larger pie from which portions are served. For individuals seeking wealth through personal ties in politics, in contrast, there is no apparent interest in the freedom of strangers, because there is little to be gained from strangers located in a market, as the same state rents will be distributed amongst a greater number of people, thus freedom and wealth are part of the same zero-sum-like equation. Nor is there much interest in one's own freedom, due to tactical reasons, whereby the incentive is to at least appear to conform with alacrity to the norms and values of patrons.

In these ways, a rise in contracting dependent on third-party enforcement in a society can cause a change in prevailing mental models, and the emerging culture of capitalism can legitimate liberal democratic institutions. Individuals routinely dependent on trusting strangers in contract will develop the habits of trusting strangers and preferring universal freedom and rights; and strong and impartial states for protecting these rights. This is so even though most, acting on bounded norms rather than on instrumental rationality, do not know why they have these universalistic liberal values. Individuals in personalist economies, in contrast, habitually trust only those they know personally or those that they can identify as part of their in-groups; and routinely abide by the commands of patrons, distrusting those from out-groups, including their states. Acting on bounded norms rather than on instrumental rationality, most do not know why they fear outsiders, or why they place such great value in loyalty to their groups and group leaders. In these ways, capitalist development gives rise to stable and liberal democracy. Can the culture of capitalism also cause peace among nations?

THE MARKET CAPITALIST PEACE

A complete theory of peace is also a theory of war: it should explain why states fight as well as why they do not. Free-market theories of capitalist peace fail to explain why states fight, limiting their explanatory value to why some do not. This is because they are all firmly nestled in the mainstream realist-liberal tradition that assumes away the important question of why states fight by simply assuming a highly anarchic and competitive world. Due to the costliness of war, it is commonly thought that war does not pay, and thus war is deduced to occur by mishap, resulting from weak information or from an inability of nations to credibly commit to peace (Keohane and Martin 1995; Fearon 1995). From these starting assumptions, freer markets abroad are suggested to yield better information regarding states' resolve in crises, thus averting war (Gartzke et al. 2001); and less government ownership of property at home is thought to constrain the autonomy of governments and make their foreign policy commitments more credible (McDonald 2007, 2009). For Weede (2011:2–3), freer markets at home and abroad constrain states from fighting due to private ownership of the media, and because it gives politicians jobs if they lose office; free markets also indirectly constrain states from fighting because they are presumed to cause democracy and, possibly, membership in international governmental organizations (ibid.:7).

The market capitalist peace of economic norms theory, in contrast, offers an account for both sides of the war puzzle: why states fight and why they do not. Starting with why personalist states fight, recall that clientelist political economy is zero-sum like: a gain in state rents for one group must always equal a loss for another. It follows that ruling groups within these nations—whether democratically elected or not—have little incentive to produce public goods, preferring the distribution of private goods to supporters. In this way, foreign war can serve two purposes. First, it can be in the economic interests of the ruling coalition of in-groups, with its costs imposed on repressed out-groups. Second, war can be a means for ruling group coalitions to stay in power. Because individuals are bound to their groups, rather than their states, personalist states tend to lack widespread legitimacy and are thus less stable than impersonal ones. In addition, the zero-sum nature of their political economies means that ruling groups must continuously seek wealth for supporters and, as a consequence, repress out-groups who can be allotted few, if any, state rents. Yet repression is costly. To reduce this cost many state leaders have learned to play on clientelist bounded norms by propagandizing the state as an in-group patron providing economic and physical security to all; that is, ruling groups have learned to foster nationalism. Nationalist identities, however, require an out-group. The most convenient and successful way to foster a nationalist identity is to maintain a quarrel with another state. While the diversionary theory of war literature has long emphasized such motives in war making (Levy 1988), economic norms theory informs us that contract-poor nations are far more susceptible to this malady than contract-rich ones, particularly when facing internal crises.

Market capitalist economy, in contrast, is positive-sum like: any improvement in the welfare of anyone else in the market increases the odds that one's own welfare will improve. Everyone in the market thus has a principal interest in the public good of an ever expanding growth in the market. While some individuals might rank some other preference or preferences higher than market growth, more individuals rank market growth at or near the top of their preference ordering than they do any other preference, and, as a result, the voter preference for market growth is Pareto optimal: in an impersonal political economy there is no other preference that a citizenry, as a group, will rank higher. Since impersonal states are largely democratic, successful political parties have learned that performance in fostering market growth, rather than the promotion of fears of others, is the winning strategy for staying in power.

The consequence is that market capitalist states do not fight each other, for three primary reasons. Of great salience is the two ways they lack the personalist state's motives for war. First, they lack the incentive and capability to promote nationalist xenophobia with aggressive foreign policies, since they have stable and widely legitimate governments, and because voters are not as susceptible to supporting the state in response to nationalist/aggressive rhetoric in the foreign policy discourse. Second, because impersonal states are more constrained than personalist ones to produce public goods, there is less incentive to promote the rent-seeking interests of any private interest group with foreign conquest.[2]

The second reason market capitalist states do not fight each other is because they share common foreign policy interests. Successful political parties of these states have learned to promote exports to enhance market growth, and in this way impersonal states share a common interest in the

---

[2]Bueno de Mesquita et al.'s (1999) selectorate theory also links public goods provision with fewer foreign policy demands for private goods, but predicts the government incentive to produce public goods from democratic rather than economic institutions. Economic norms theory is a much larger theory than selectorate theory, as it also predicts common interests and a dearth of relative gains seeking among capitalist nations, as discussed below. Moreover, Bueno de Mesquita et al. (1999) ignore the cost of repression of all disfranchised citizens with no say in the choice of leadership and its relation to diversionary use of foreign enmities, which is endogenized in economic norms theory to the prevailing economy type and works as one of the causal mechanisms that links economy type to interstate conflict behavior.

vitality of the global marketplace. Personalist states, because they are most interested in the distribution of private goods to supporters, are comparatively less interested in promoting the public good of market growth and, as a consequence, have comparatively less interest in the global market.[3] The wellbeing of any marketplace depends on the credibility of contractual commitments and thus the credibility of third-party enforcement; thus all markets require the uniform application of law and order. There is no reason this dictum does not apply to the global level, and since market capitalist nations have common interests in the vitality of the global marketplace, they too have common interests in the vitality of global law and order. Thus market capitalist nations not only lack any motive to fight each other, they are in a fundamental natural alliance against any threats to global law and order.

The third reason market capitalist states do not fight each other is because they have direct interests in each other's welfare. As was previously observed, market capitalism is positive-sum like: any improvement in the welfare of anyone else in the market increases the odds that one's own welfare will improve. This means that the leaders of market capitalist nations have direct interests in the economic health of any nation that joins the global market. It follows that there can be no concern with relative economic gains among market capitalist nations, since comparatively rapid growth in one nation has the result of promoting market growth in the others. For leaders interested in their political party's electoral fortunes, market growth in another nation in the global market cannot be perceived as a threat because it is *preferred*. Obviously, no leader wishing foremost to promote exports in the global marketplace can have any interest in threatening disorder or harming another capitalist state's economy; even the perception of such threats harms the global marketplace and must be steadfastly avoided. The result is a perfect peace in formal anarchy, making war virtually unspeakable.

DEMOCRATIC OR CAPITALIST PEACE?

The democratic peace—the observation that democratic nations rarely fight each other—is easily the most cited empirical regularity in the field of international relations.[4] Although a number of democratic causal mechanisms have been proffered, there is no consensus as to which, if any, can serve as the active key explanatory variable of the observed democratic peace. If a

---

[3] The primary exceptions are cases where rent-seeking supporters of a personalist state rely on exports, usually primary exports such as oil. Even in these cases, however, the personalist state is usually concerned narrowly on the specific market for the particular export, not the general vitality of the global marketplace.
[4] For the most recent comprehensive review of this literature, see Ungerer (2012).

third variable were to be postulated as the root cause of the observed peace, it must satisfactorily account for both the *explanans* (democracy) and the *explanandum* (militarized interstate conflict) (Blalock 1979:468–474; Thompson and Tucker 1997: 434–35; Ray 2003a:14). Among the free-market capitalist peace theories, none offer both an explanation for democracy and corroborating evidence in support of the posited causality. Gartzke (2007) offers no theory of how free markets are supposed to cause democracy, but offers corroborative evidence for this chain of causation anyway, reporting that consideration of free markets in foreign investment renders the democratic peace spurious. But others report that this result is due to errors in sampling and specification (Choi 2011; Dafoe 2011; see also Russett 2010). Weede (2011:2) offers a way free markets might cause democracy, but in an elaborate chain of causation that remains uncorroborated: free markets are assumed to cause prosperity and prosperity is assumed to cause democracy, rendering the "democratic peace a mere component of the capitalist peace." But to our knowledge there is no corroborative evidence that free markets cause prosperity (cf. Gurr et al. 1990), no corroborated theory in the literature (prior to economic norms theory) of how prosperity can cause democracy, and no corroborated evidence that democracy is rendered insignificant after consideration of free markets.

Economic norms theory, in contrast, offers a specific explanation for the coincidence of market capitalism and democracy, directly pinpointing how a rise in contract-intensive economy can cause both democratic transitions and peace, as discussed above. Moreover, this path of causation has substantial corroborated evidence. As Gleditsch (1992:371) has pointed out, the absence of war among democracies is such a perfect relationship that a confounding factor would "need to have a near-perfect relationship with both the other variables." CONTRACT-INTENSIVE ECONOMY (CIE), the operationalized measurement of market capitalism (see below) possesses this near-perfect relationship with both democracy and peace. Regarding democracy, almost all nations with contract-intensive economies (as indicated with above-median values of CIE, see below) are democratic by normal standards of measurement (polity >6, see below)—Singapore is the *only* long-term exception. Yet roughly half of all democratic nation-years do not have contract-intensive economies, and these democracies do not appear to be in any sort of peace (Mousseau 2009, 2012a, 2012b).

Regarding conflict, market capitalism has a near-perfect relationship with peace: not only have no wars occurred among nations with impersonal economies, but in all recorded history these nations have not had a single battlefield-connected fatality among them (Mousseau 2009, 2012a). The perfect absence of fatalities among market capitalist nations means that the market capitalist peace is far more substantial than the democratic one, which boasts only an absence of wars, not fatalities, among democratic nations. Ironically, however, the near-perfect dearth of militarized interstate disputes (MIDs) among market capitalist nations means that there is no point in studying the impact of market capitalism on escalation once a pairing of nations is already in militarized conflict: there are simply too few militarized events among market capitalist nations to draw any generalizations on their behavior once in mutual militarized conflict.

However, there is an alternative dataset on interstate conflict, one that focuses on crises among nations: the ICB dataset (Hewitt 2003). A crisis occurs when key foreign policy decision makers in a state "perceive a threat to one or more basic values, along with an awareness of finite time for response to the value threat and a heightened probability of involvement in military hostilities" (Brecher and Wilkenfeld 2000:3), whereas MIDs involve only explicit threats, displays or actual uses of military force (Gochman and Maoz 1984). There are three major differences between MIDs and crises that have implications for our analysis.[5] First, perceptions are the defining feature of a crisis, whereas they play no role in defining MIDs, since explicit threats, displays or actual uses of force do not necessarily involve any perceived infringement of closely held values or value threats. Second, crises are triggered by the actions of key foreign policy decision makers, representing the realm of political actions such as overt gripes, insinuations and arraignments uncharacteristic of cooperative behavior and a positive peace shared between nations, while MIDs solely capture military threats and actions that would be uncharacteristic of a negative peace. In this sense, although not truly a measurement of a shared positive peace, the ability to explain crises would represent a positive endowment for any theory attempting to explain state behavior beyond a mere lack of conflict events in interstate relations. Third, a significant portion of international crises do not necessarily involve a threat, display or use of force. A crisis can involve a vast array of actions including verbal acts such as accusations, political acts in the form of alliance formation with adversaries, economic acts of withholding economic aid, nationalization of property, and so forth.

In this way, analyses of the onset of crises offers a new test of the market capitalist peace, since it is possible that while market capitalist nations avoid each other in wars and all types of MIDs, they may yet confront each other without explicit threat, display or use of force such as in the form of alliance formation with adversaries or diplomatic sanctions—outcomes that would be clear and direct anomalies for economic norms theory. Moreover, while the democratic peace is found to be spurious in analyses of MIDs (Mousseau 2009, 2012a), analyses of the ICB dataset can examine whether the democratic peace is also spurious in tests of interstate crises. Finally, while among the free-market capitalist peace variables only trade interdependence remains robust after consideration of market capitalism in analyses of MIDs (Mousseau

---

[5]For a detailed overview, see Hewitt (2003).

2012a), these may yet be potent factors in analyses of crises. The remainder of this chapter examines democratic and capitalist behavior in interstate crises.

ANALYTIC PROCEDURES

The analyses herein are constructed in accordance with the standard procedures used in interstate conflict studies. The unit of analysis is the nondirectional dyad year. The dependent variable CRISIS will indicate whether a particular dyad experiences an international crisis in year $t + 1$. A dyad experiences a crisis if at least one member perceives crisis conditions with the other member of a dyad (Hewitt 2003). Most of the independent variables are conventional to the conflict studies literature, so to save space their justification can be reviewed elsewhere (e.g. Oneal and Russett 2005). Data sources and measures are listed at the bottom of Tables 1 and 2. The exception is the measure for impersonal economy, which is discussed at length below. All data are available for replication purposes at http://home.ku.edu.tr/~mmousseau/.

As discussed above, we gauge the intensity of impersonal contracting in nations directly using data on life insurance contracts in force, which have been compiled under the auspices of the World Bank (Beck and Webb 2003). These data are available for 64 of the 157 nations identified as sovereign by the Correlates of War Project from 1960 to 2000 (Small and Singer 1982) and for which data on democracy and wealth are also available.[6] Unfortunately, theory and evidence indicate that missing values are probably not random, as theory informs us that missing values may indicate contract-poor economies, for two reasons. First, for enforcement purposes contracts are normally recorded, leaving a history based on written records. Reciprocating transactions, in contrast, cannot be recorded because they are framed as favors. Missing life insurance data can thus result from there being few life insurance contracts to record. Second, as discussed above, governments of market capitalist nations are constrained by voters to ardently pursue continued growth in their markets. They have thus learned to collect, analyse, and make widely available all kinds of economic data. Governments of clientelist nations, in contrast, have the opposite incentive of hiding data, given that they must redistribute government funds to their supporters, often illegally. The systematic difference of the missing data from the known data is confirmed with validity tests, which show that most nations with low levels of private consumption and investment (Heston, et

---

[6]That is, in the Polity IV democracy data (Marshall and Jaggers 2003), and the Penn World Tables data (Heston et al. 2002) with populations greater than 500,000.

al. 2002)—roughly reflecting impersonal economy—are not recorded in the life insurance data.

To assuage concern that the test results below may be due to a bias caused by missing data, we follow the recommendation of King et al. (2001; see also Gleditsch 2002) and report results with missing values estimated using secondary data. Missing values are not a blank slate: we know a great deal about political economies from a variety of sources, and personal and impersonal economies are very different from one another in a number of dimensions. Tests confirm that the following variables yield an imputed measure that correlates at 0.97 with life insurance contracts in force: per capita private consumption (KC) and investment (KI); ratios of KC and KI to foreign trade; energy consumption per capita; communist economy; post-communist economy; oil-export dependency; population; and various controls for regions and sample size variations that occur over time. The extremely high correlation of the predicted measure with the original data indicates that the imputed values yield a highly reliable estimate of the missing values. We refer to the variable as CONTRACT-INTENSIVE ECONOMY (CIE), measured as the natural log of USA dollars per capita.[7]

RESULTS

Model 1 in Table 1 replicates the null model of democratic peace in analyses of militarized interstate crises as reported in multiple studies. As expected, the coefficient for DEMOCRACY (LOW) (–0.10) is negative and highly significant. Since this variable indicates the lower value of democracy of the two regimes in a dyad, high values indicate that both states are highly democratic; the value of this coefficient serves as corroborating evidence for the democratic peace. The coefficient for REGIME DIFFERENCE (0.05), gauged in standard form as the higher regime score in the dyad minus the lower regime score, is positive and significant, confirming that the likelihood of conflict increases as the regime difference increases in a dyad.[8] All remaining variables perform as expected, as in prior studies, and need not be reviewed here.

Model 2 provides novel insight by testing for the hypothesis that impersonal economy is a confounding variable in the democracy promotes peace equation. To capture the dyadic expectation of peace among social-market

---

[7]Details in the construction of the imputed data can be reviewed and replicated at http://home.ku.edu.tr/~mmousseau/.

[8]See Choi (2011: 783–784) for superiority of the REGIME DIFFERENCE measure over DEMOCRACY (HIGH), the higher democracy score in a dyad, which nullifies the purpose of the weak link assumption and leads to a biased estimation of DEMOCRACY (LOW).

capitalist nations, the variable CIE (LOW) indicates insurance contracts in force per capita of the state with the lower level of CIE in the dyad; a high value of this measure indicates both states have contract-intensive economies. As can be seen, the coefficient for CIE (LOW) (–0.39) is negative and highly significant ($p<0.001$). This confirms that an impersonal economy is a highly robust force for peace. The coefficient for DEMOCRACY (LOW) (–0.05) is negative, but now much closer to zero and no longer significant when the control for impersonal economy is included. There are no other differences between Models 1 and 2, whose samples are identical, and, apart from Mousseau (2009), no one has directly examined any role for contract flows in the democratic peace. Therefore, Model 2 yields the nontrivial result that all prior reports of democracy as a force for peace are probably spurious; a result predicted and fully accounted for by economic norms theory.

CIE (LOW) and DEMOCRACY (LOW) correlate only in the moderate range of 0.46 (Pearson's r), so the insignificance of democracy is not likely to be a statistical artifact resulting from multicollinearity. This is confirmed by the variance inflation factor for DEMOCRACY (LOW) in Model 2 of 1.83, which is well below the usual rule-of-thumb indicator for multicollinearity of 10 or more. Nor should readers assume most democratic dyads also include both states with impersonal economies: while almost all nations with contract-intensive economies (as indicated with below-median values of CIE) are democratic (Polity2>6) (Singapore is the only long-term exception), more than half—55%—of all democratic nation-years have personalist economies. At the dyadic level in this sample, this translates to 82% of democratic dyad years (all dyads where DEMOCRACY$_{binary6}$ = 1) that are not both social-market capitalist. In other words, not only does Model 2 show no significant evidence of causation from democracy to peace (as reported in Mousseau 2009), but it also illustrates that this absence of democratic peace includes the vast majority—82%—of democratic dyad years over the sample period.

Model 3 estimates the standard binary measure of democracy (Polity2>6). As can be observed, the coefficient for CIE (LOW) (–0.46) remains negative and highly significant, while DEMOCRACY$_{binary6}$ (–0.42) is again insignificant. Model 4 uses another binary measure for democracy (DEMOCRACY (LOW) = 10), as advocated by Dafoe (2011) in response to Mousseau (2009). As can be seen, DEMOCRACY$_{binary10}$ predicts peace perfectly and is dropped from the model along with 11,339 unused observations due to quasi-complete separation, a problem which leads to an infinite coefficient and standard error estimates for the offending variable. Since this problem leaves the remaining variables relatively unscathed, we can tell from Model 4 that CIE (LOW) (–0.44) remains negative and highly significant even with the removal of all highly joint-democratic dyads from the sample.

As far as we are aware, the application of the Polity2=10 measure had not been used in the literature prior to Dafoe (2011) advocating it. We caution that by changing the operationalization of democracy as a variable to a score of +10, all the previous research on the democratic peace is automatically rendered inconsequential as affected by measurement error. This change also implies that much of the research on democratic norms, structures, or institutions may have little bearing on the phenomena of the democratic peace, as the question shifts to what aspects of +10 democracies would enable such causal mechanisms to work that inevitably fail at lower levels of democracy.

Furthermore, from a perspective of scientific progress, such a theoretical emendation represents stagnation, at best, in the research of the democratic peace, according to Lakatosian standards that have often been applied in International Relations (e.g. Vasquez 1997; James 2002; Ray 2003b). The post-hoc emendation of the Polity +10 measure is adapted to the data on the basis of its ability to better conform to the previously observed phenomena of the democratic peace. However, two critical observations need to be made concerning this adjustment. First, the explanatory power of the democracy leads to peace causal path is vastly diminished as it only applies to a significant minority of democratic dyad years and the causal mechanism that differentiates +10 democracies from others remains unspecified. Second, the focus on sustaining the statistical significance of democracy through a post-hoc adjustment to its measurement obscures the necessity to maintain substantive significance – the engine that has driven the democratic peace, thus far – in that it both loses its theoretical connection and turns it into a finding that is merely trivial and uninteresting as it cannot usefully show that a theory has been corroborated nor prove that an important empirical fact has been established (Lakatos 1978 [1970]:87–88).

Moreover, following Bayer and Bernhard (2010)—and as suggested by Russett (2010) —we use Aike Information Criterion (AIC) to test how good the fit is across the different operationalizations of democracy.[9] Accordingly, if different measures of democracy yield different results in terms of significance and magnitude, we expect the results generated by the better measure to provide a better fit with the data. The results clearly indicate that the continuous measure DEMOCRACY (LOW) outperforms the other operationalizations with the lower AIC value of 4,554.1, whereas $DEMOCRACY_{binary6}$ has an AIC value of 4583.1 and $DEMOCRACY_{binary10}$ has a value of 4,582.6. The correlation of DEMOCRACY (LOW) with crisis onset is –0.0108, much stronger than the correlations of $DEMOCRACY_{binary6}$ (–0.0068) and $DEMOCRACY_{binary10}$ (–0.0054). Therefore, diverting from the usage of

---

[9] AIC is calculated as $-2 \times \log(L) + 2 \times K$, where L is log-likelihood, K is the number of parameters in the model. Schwarz's information criterion (BIC) results were almost identical so we report the AIC values only. Following Bayer and Bernhard, AIC values are acquired from baseline models of democratic peace, which exclude CIE (Low) and where DEMOCRACY (LOW), $DEMOCRACY_{binary6}$ and $DEMOCRACY_{binary10}$ are reported as highly significant. The results of these analyses can be easily replicated from the do file and dataset.

the richer standard continuous measure, DEMOCRACY (LOW), is neither theoretically nor empirically justifiable based on Lakatosian standards and information criteria tests.

The problem of quasi-complete separation also occurs in analyses of fatal MIDs (Mousseau 2009)—thus we employed the continuous CIE measure in all analyses herein—and Dafoe (2011) has cautioned against attributing Mousseau's (2009) finding of a perfect absence of fatal MIDs among CIE countries only to impersonal economy because countries with the highest democracy score (DEMOCRACY (LOW) = 10) also never experienced a fatal conflict over the 1961 to 2001 period of observation. Therefore to test if $DEMOCRACY_{binary10}$ may have a significant impact in crises, we transformed the DEMOCRACY (LOW) measure to model the binary impact of $DEMOCRACY_{binary10}$ by squaring it (after adding 10), which implies that the likelihood of conflict decreases more quickly toward the high values of DEMOCRACY (LOW). This new measure provides an even better fit than DEMOCRACY (LOW) with an AIC value of 4,546.4. As can be seen in Model 5, however, CIE (LOW) (−0.37) is highly significant, whereas DEMOCRACY (LOW)^2 (−0.003) is insignificant. Without the control of CIE (LOW), however, DEMOCRACY (LOW)^2 (−0.005) is negative and highly significant ($p = 0.001$) (see Appendix Table A1), indicating again that the impact of very high levels of democracy on peace is best explained by social-market capitalism.

In all our tests democracy is insignificant, but only after consideration of social-market capitalism. Since this outcome was predicted a priori with theory that links impersonal economy with both democracy and the democratic peace, we seem to have a prima facie case for the democratic peace being spurious. However, it is also apparent in the democracy measures that while they are insignificant in every model, they remain consistently in the negative direction. This suggests that even after consideration of impersonal economy there may be a small pacifying impact of democracy. However, further calculations of the coefficients in Model 2 indicate that this impact seems to be largely inconsequential. Since the coefficients reflect the impact of each after excluding the impacts of the others, the coefficients for CIE (LOW) and DEMOCRACY (LOW) inform us that even the autocratic social-market nations are in a peace that is about 20% stronger than the peace among the democratic dyads where at least one state has a personalist-clientelist economy. Most of the autocratic social-market nations in the data were simply in transition to democracy (as mentioned above, the only exception appears to be Singapore), and we have strong theory that fully accounts for this direction of causation. The state of the evidence thus follows that it is social-market capitalism, not democracy, that is the driving force for the noted zone of peace in global politics.

Given the insignificance of democracy in Models 1–5, Model 6 reports the winning specification of international crises. The democracy variables as well as REGIME DIFFERENCE are dropped due to endogeneity, given that all may be partially explained by impersonal economy. Further calculations indicate that impersonal economy is the most robust correlate among the nontrivial explanatory variables of interstate crises, tying or being surpassed only by the relatively trivial MAJOR POWER and CONTIGUITY variables.

Table 2 provides an examination of whether wealth and the free-market capitalist factors can account for the effect of impersonal economy. The first column reports the correlation of each factor with CIE (LOW), showing that all of the correlations with CIE are well below the rule-of-thumb danger zone of 0.70 or higher.[10] Nor does any variable in Table 2 yield a variance inflation factor above 2, which is well below the rule-of-thumb threshold of 10. As can be seen in Model 1, the coefficient for CIE (LOW) (–0.66) remains negative and highly significant even while controlling for WEALTH (LOW) (0.62), which is positive and significant. Most relatively wealthy states with personalist economies are communist regimes or oil-exporting states, both of which are often highly clientelist, as authorities distribute rents with partiality; examples include Iraq, Russia, Saudi Arabia, and the Soviet Union.

As can be seen in Model 2, the coefficient for CIE (LOW) (–0.58), while slightly smaller than it is in Model 1, is still highly robust, with a control added for TRADE (LOW) (–0.44), which is insignificant. Even though Hewitt (2003) presents similar results for trade interdependence using an alternative measure, in a separate analysis (see Appendix Table A2), it was significant before CIE (LOW) is introduced into the Model 2 ($\beta = –1.14$, SE = 0.33, $p = 0.001$). Therefore, corroborating Mousseau (2009)'s analysis of MIDs, this study provides further evidence that an impersonal economy is a cause of both trade interdependence and peace among nations. This result makes sense from the perspective of economic norms theory, which predicts peace to emerge from a state preference for trade, rather than trade dependency and its effect on the opportunity costs of war and signaling at the dyadic level, and dyads where both states prefer to trade will be, ceteris paribus, more likely than others to be trade interdependent.

Model 3 examines if capital openness (Gartkze et al. 2001) can account for the impact of impersonal economy.[11] In order to construct the test conditions, we first consider the missing data in the CAPITAL OPENNESS

---

[10]Wealth is gauged using energy consumption per capita. Energy consumption is preferred over gross domestic product (GDP) as a measure of wealth because GDP and CIE are axiomatically related as GDP is partly constructed from data on contract flows reported to government agencies. Also, because GDP is partly constructed from data on contract flows it is comparatively biased towards impersonal economy. As expected, CIE (LOW) correlates with GDP comparatively higher at 0.71, which is also above the rule-of-thumb threshold for multicollinearity.

[11]We thank Erik Gartzke and Patrick McDonald for kindly providing their data for inclusion in the models.

(LOW) variable, which suffered from ad hoc methods of (i) list-wise deletion (Gartkze 2007), which requires the missing data to be MCAR (missing completely at random) assumption and (ii) imputation of missing values with a zero (Gartzke and Hewitt 2010), which requires the contradictory MNAR (missing not at random) assumption. Usage of these two contradictory methods for the same measure is neither coherent nor correct and efficient. What is more, the missing data encompasses more than half of the crisis years (146 out of 285 crises) over the period of 1966–1992, which may cause false positives in coefficient and standard error estimates if these values are assumed as zero by Gartzke and Hewitt (2010) or left as missing as done by Gartkze (2007).

In order to lessen the biases inherent in these methods, we first interpolate between the known values of CAPITAL OPENNESS (LOW) and fill all the missing observations that are allowed by this method, then, following Gartzke and Hewitt (2010), we replace all the remaining missing values with a zero. This procedure shows that at least 2,432 missing observations are incorrectly coded as zero for this variable by Gartzke and Hewitt (2010), corresponding to around 10% of the crisis years (30 out of 285). Therefore, caution is necessary for analyses with this variable. As can be seen, the coefficient for CIE (LOW) (−0.56) holds firm, while the coefficient for CAPITAL OPENNESS (LOW) (−0.08) is insignificant. Additional tests of this same model and sample without CIE (LOW), reported in Appendix Table A2, show CAPITAL OPENNESS (LOW) to be significant (ß = −0.18, SE = 0.05, p = <0.001). It thus appears that impersonal economy can account for prior reports of capital openness causing peace (Gartzke 2007). Just as economic norms theory predicts increased trade among social-market capitalist states, it also predicts capital openness.

Model 4 investigates if the size of the public sector (McDonald 2009) can account for the impact of impersonal economy. McDonald hypothesizes that nations with large public sectors are more prone to militarized conflict than those with smaller ones, an expectation that can be modeled among pairs of nations by observing the size of the public sector of the state with the higher level of public sector, a variable we call PUBLIC (HIGH). As can be seen, the coefficient for CIE (LOW) (−0.34) holds firm and significant, while the coefficient for PUBLIC (HIGH) (0.00) is insignificant. Additional tests of this same model and sample with CIE (LOW) excluded (see Appendix Table A2) show PUBLIC (HIGH) to be still insignificant (ß = 0.008, SE = 0.007, p = 0.263). The results of Model 4 thus indicate that the size of the public sector does not account for the pacific impact of impersonal economy, while at the same time providing no evidence that it can account for peaceful relations among states in analyses of international crisis onset.

IMPLICATIONS AND CONCLUSION

This chapter sought to review the economic norms explanation for the capitalist peace and democratic peace. We showed that not only does social-market capitalism successfully account for the empirical peace among nations, but it also provides a definition of capitalism that offers more explanatory power and theoretical force than the alternative definitions. In addition to the rise of social-market capitalism serving as a precursor to the modern rise of democracy, it also accounts for the effect of peace that was previously attributed to democracy. Moreover, the levels of empirical corroboration achieved, as well as the generation of novel hypotheses that prove to be substantiated predictions, are unmatched by the competing explanations of peace among states examined in this chapter.[12] Application of the continuous variable (CIE (LOW)) to capture the level of impersonal economy removes any bias that was previously present with the use of the binary measure (Mousseau 2009), clarifying the path of causation from social-market capitalism to peace.

Furthermore, the use of the ICB data set provides a progressive step beyond the perfect prediction of peace for contract-intensive economies in analyses of fatal militarized interstate disputes (Mousseau 2009). One advantage of using the ICB data is that crises are defined by the perception of a value threat by key decision makers in a regime. Nations that share in common the priorities of the unbiased enforcement of law, at home and abroad, do not have opposing foreign policy values and thus cannot end up on opposite sides of international crisis situations. Although not a true measure of a positive peace between nations, the role of perception in value threats does examine a set of crises that would be inconsistent with nations that were fully engaged in such a peace. Therefore, the level of success in predicting that the more a state transitions to social-market capitalism, the less likely it is to engage in crises based on the perception of value threats with other social-market capitalist states represents progressive corroborating evidence for the existence of a "security community" amongst the advanced capitalist nations.

In contrast, the free-market theories of capitalist peace—addressed in this volume by Gartzke and Hewitt, and McDonald—do not attempt to account for this peace, instead focusing on a negative peace that constrains states only from engaging in militarized conflict in an assumed anarchic and competitive world. We think such explanations for the peace among the

---

[12] To date, empirical corroboration of novel facts includes: the economic conditionality to the democratic peace (Mousseau 2000); cooperation (Mousseau 2002) and common preferences (Mousseau 2003) among nations; variance in social trust within nations (Mousseau 2009:61), state respect for human rights (Mousseau and Mousseau 2008), public support for terrorism (Mousseau 2011), and the onset of civil wars (Mousseau 2012c).

advanced capitalist nations are incomplete, as it must be clear to even the most casual observer of global affairs that the capitalist security community is a phenomenon much larger than anything that can result from simple cost–benefit calculations of leaders (Weede 1996, 2011), signals of resolve (Gartzke et al. 2001), or domestic constraints and credibility of commitments (McDonald 2007, 2009).

By returning to the Hayek (free market) and Keynes (social market) capitalism debate, it becomes clear that only one form of capitalism leads to a shared positive peace among nations. Regardless of their respective ability to produce economic growth and development, there is no clear direct linkage of free markets or private property on peace; only the socioeconomic condition of impersonal economy does so. Based on the analyses presented herein and the general state of evidence (Gurr et al. 1990), states that wish to engage in a shared peace should seek to construct or maintain impersonal economy with Keynesian-like policies of spending and redistribution, not Hayekian-like spending cuts and smaller government with the hope that these will promote market growth. Moreover, the adoption of the Keynesian economic policy can serve to bolster any internal democratization attempts by promoting more equal access to the marketplace.

Furthermore, not only do the analyses indicate that the free-market theories are not empirically corroborated, but it is also apparent that the advanced capitalist nations do more than just avoid fighting each other: they are in a permanent state of positive peace, based not on self-help, but shared-help, where each demonstrates concern in the health and welfare of the other in a deeply embedded natural alliance. The evidence suggests that the assumption of anarchy is null and void among social-market capitalist nations, where peace and cooperation is highly institutionalized with a thick web of norms rooted not in mutually constituted perceptions, as most constructivists would contend, but rather individual-level micro-economic conditions that, through processes of pursuing happiness in the market, give rise to a state of permanent positive peace. Among nations where most citizens have a stake in the market, the world may be less anarchic and competitive than previously supposed.

REFERENCES

Bayer, Resat and Michael Bernhard. (2010) The Operationalization of Democracy and the Strength of the Democratic Peace: A Test of the Relative Utility of Scalar and Dichotomous Measures. *Conflict Management and Peace Science* 27(1):85–101.

Beck, Thorsten and Ian Webb. (2003) Economic, Demographic, and Institutional Determinants of Life Insurance Consumption across Countries. The World Bank Economic Review, 17(1):51–88.

Blalock, Hubert M. Jr. (1979) *Social Statistics,* 2nd edition. New York: McGraw-Hill.

Brecher, Michael and Jonathan Wilkenfeld (2000) *A Study of Crisis*. Ann Arbor, MI: University of Michigan Press (paperback and CD version).

Bueno de Mesquita, Bruce, James D. Morrow, Randolph M. Siverson, and Alastair Smith (1999) An Institutional Explanation of the Democratic Peace. *American Political Science Review* 93(4):791–807.

Choi, Seung-Whan (2011) Re-evaluating Capitalist and Democratic Peace Models. *International Studies Quarterly* 55(3):1–11.

Dafoe, Allan (2011) Statistical Critiques of the Democratic Peace: Caveat Emptor. *American Journal of Political Science* 55(2): 247–62.

Denzau, Arthur T. and Douglass C. North (1994) Shared Mental Models: Ideologies and Institutions, KYKLOS 47:3–31.

Deutsch, Karl W., et al. (1957) *Political Community and the North Atlantic Area*. Princeton, NJ: Princeton University Press.

Engelbrecht, Helmuth C. and Frank C. Hanighen (1934) *Merchants of Death: A Study of the International Armament Industry*. London: Routledge. Available at http://greatwar.nl/frames/default-merchants.html

Fearon, James D. (1995) Rationalist Explanations for War. *International Organization* 49(3):379–414.

Gartzke, Erik (2007) The Capitalist Peace. *American Journal of Political Science* 51(1):166–191.

Gartzke, Erik, Quan Li and Charles Boehmer (2001) Investing in the Peace: Economic Interdependence and International Conflict. *International Organization* 55(2):391–438.

Gartzke, Erik and J. Joseph Hewitt (2010) International Crises and the Capitalist Peace. *International Interactions* 36(2):115–145.

Gleditsch, Nils Petter (1992) Democracy and Peace. *Journal of Peace Research* 29(4):369–376.

Gleditsch, Kristian S. 2002) Expanded Trade and GDP data. *Journal of Conflict Resolution* 46(5):712–724.

Gochman, Charles S. and Zeev Maoz (1984) Militarized Interstate Disputes, 1816–1976: Procedures, Patterns, and Insights. *Journal of Conflict Resolution* 28(4):585–616.

Gurr, Ted Robert, Keith Jaggers and Will H. Moore (1990) The Transformation of the Western State: The Growth of Democracy, Autocracy, and State Power Since 1800. *Studies in Comparative International Development* 25(1):73–108.

Hayek, Friedrich A. von (1994 [1944]) *The Road to Serfdom*. Chicago, Il.: University of Chicago Press, 1994.

Hayek, Friedrich A. von (1960) *The Constitution of Liberty*. Chicago, Il.: University of Chicago Press.

Heston, Alan, Robert Summers and Bettina Aten (2002) *Penn World Table Version 6.1*. Center for International Comparisons at the University of Pennsylvania (CICUP), October.

Hewitt, J. Joseph (2003) Dyadic Processes and International Crises. *Journal of Conflict Resolution* 47(5):669–692.

Hicken, Allen (2011) Clientelism. *Annual Review of Political Science* 14(1):289–310.

James, Patrick (2002) *International Relations and Scientific Progress*. Columbus, OH: Ohio State University Press.

Keohane, Robert O. and Lisa L. Martin (1995) The Promise of Institutionalist Theory. *International Security* 20(1):39–51.

Keynes, John Maynard (1935) *The General Theory of Employment, Interest, and Money / 1883–1946*. New York : Harcourt, Brace and Company.

King, Gary, James Honaker, Anne Josephy and Kenneth Scheve (2001) Analyzing Incomplete Political Science Data: An Alternative Algorithm for Multiple Imputation. *American Political Science Review* 95(1):49–69.

Kohn Meir (2003) Organized Markets in Pre-Industrial Europe. Working Paper. Dartmouth College.

Lakatos, Imre (1978 [1970]) Falsification and the Methodology of Scientific Research Programs. In *Mathematics, Science and Epistemology: Philosophical Papers, Volume 1*, ed. John Worrall and Gregory Currie. Cambridge, UK: Cambridge University Press.

Lenin, Vladimir (1970 [1917]) *Imperialism: The Highest Stage of Capitalism*. Reprint. Peking: Foreign Language Press. Available at http://www.marxists.org/archive/lenin/works/1916/imp-hsc/

Levy, Jack S. (1988) Domestic Politics and War. *Journal of Interdisciplinary History* 18(4):653–673.

Marshall, Monty G., and Keith Jaggers (2003) *POLITY IV PROJECT: Political Regime Characteristics and Transitions, 1800–2002, Dataset Users' Manual*. Center for International Development and Conflict Management, University of Maryland College Park and Colorado State University.

McDonald, Patrick J. (2007) The Purse Strings of Peace. *American Journal of Political Science*. 51(3):569–582.

McDonald, Patrick J. (2009) *The Invisible Hand of Peace: Capitalism, the War Machine, and International Relations Theory*. New York: Cambridge University Press.

Mousseau, Michael (2000) Market Prosperity, Democratic Consolidation, and Democratic Peace. *Journal of Conflict Resolution* 44(4):472–507.

Mousseau, Michael (2002) An Economic Limitation to the Zone of Democratic Peace and Cooperation. *International Interactions* 28(2):137–164.

Mousseau, Michael (2003) The Nexus of Market Society, Liberal Preferences, and Democratic Peace: Interdisciplinary Theory and Evidence. *International Studies Quarterly* 47(4):483–510.

Mousseau, Michael (2009) The Social Market Roots of Democratic Peace. *International Security* 33(4):52–86.

Mousseau, Michael (2011) Urban Poverty and Support for Islamist Terror: Survey Results from Muslims in Fourteen Countries. *Journal of Peace Research* 48(1):35–47.

Mousseau, Michael (2012a) Does the Capitalist Peace Trump the Democratic Peace? *International Studies Quarterly* (forthcoming).

Mousseau, Michael (2012b) Market-Capitalist or Democratic Peace. In *What Do We Know About War?* 2nd. edition, ed. John Vasquez. Langham, MD: Rowan-Littlefield.

Mousseau, Michael (2012c) Capitalist Development and Civil War. *International Studies Quarterly* 56(3): 470–483.

Mousseau, Michael and Demet Yalcin Mousseau (2008) The Contracting Roots of Human Rights. *Journal of Peace Research* 45(3):327–44.

Oneal, John R. and Bruce Russett (2005) Rule of Three, Let It Be? When More Really Is Better. *Conflict Management and Peace Science* 22(4):293–310.

Polanyi, Karl (1957 [1944]) *The Great Transformation: The Political and Economic Origins of Our Time*. Boston: Beacon Press. Available at http://uncharted.org/frownland/books/Polanyi/POLANYI%20KARL%20-%20The%20Great%20Transformation%20-%20v.1.0.html

Ray, James Lee (2003a) Explaining Interstate Conflict and War: What Should Be Controlled For? *Conflict Management and Peace Science* 20(2):1–31.

Ray, James Lee (2003b) A Lakatosian View of the Democratic Peace Research Program. In *Progress in International Relations Theory: Appraising the Field*, ed. Colin Elman and Miriam Fendius Elman. Cambridge, MA: MIT Press.

Russett, Bruce (2010) Capitalism or Democracy? Not So Fast. *International Interactions* 36(2):185–205.

Russett, Bruce and Oneal, John R. (2001) *Triangulating Peace: Democracy, Interdependence, and International Organizations*. New York: W. W. Norton & Company.

Simon, Herbert (1955) A Behavioral Model of Rational Choice. *The Quarterly Journal of Economics* 69(1):99–118.

Small, Melvin, and J. David Singer (1982) *Resort to Arms: International and Civil Wars, 1816–1980.* 2nd edition. Beverly Hills, CA: Sage.

Thompson, William R. and Richard Tucker (1997) A Tale of Two Democratic Peace Critiques. *Journal of Conflict Resolution* 41(3):428–454.

Ungerer, Jameson (2012) Assessing the Progress of the Democratic Peace Research Program. *International Studies Review* 14(1): 1–31.

Vasquez, John A. (1997) The Realist Paradigm and Degenerative versus Progressive Research Programs: An Appraisal of Neotraditional Research on Waltz's Balancing Proposition. *American Political Science Review* 91(4):899–912.

Wallerstein, Immanuel (1974) The Rise and Future Demise of the World Capitalist System: Concepts for Comparative Analysis. *Comparative Studies in Society and History* 16(4):387–415.

Weede, Erich (1996) *Economic Development, Social Order, and World Politics.* Boulder, CO: Lynne Rienner.

Weede, Erich (2011) Does the Capitalist Peace Exist? Yes, it Did! But Will it Apply to China and the West? *Conflict Management, Peace Economics and Development* 18:1–29.

TABLE 1 Capitalist Peace Versus Democratic Peace in Analyses of International Crisis, Behavior Onset 1961 to 2001[±]

Variables	Model 1	Model 2	Model 3	Model 4	Model 5	Model 6
Democracy (Low)	−0.10***	−0.05	—	—	—	—
	0.03	0.04				
Democracy$_{binary6}$	—	—	−0.42	—	—	—
			0.69			
Democracy$_{binary10}$	—	—	—	[†]	—	—
				[†]		
Democracy (Low)^2	—	—	—	—	−0.00	—
					0.00	
CIE (Low)	—	−0.39***	−0.46***	−0.44***	−0.37***	−0.52***
		0.11	0.11	0.09	0.12	0.08
Regime Difference[a]	0.05***	0.05***	0.06***	0.06***	0.05***	—
	0.01	0.01	0.01	0.01	0.01	
Capability Ratio[b]	−0.27***	−0.30***	−0.30***	−0.30***	−0.30***	−0.32***
	0.09	0.09	0.09	0.09	0.09	0.09
Major Power[c]	2.36***	2.52***	2.51***	2.50***	2.53***	2.63***
	0.30	0.29	0.28	0.28	0.29	0.31
Contiguity[d]	2.12***	2.07***	2.11***	2.11***	2.06***	1.89***
	0.28	0.29	0.28	0.27	0.29	0.26
Distance[e]	−0.61***	−0.66***	−0.66***	−0.66***	−0.66***	−0.68***
	0.09	0.09	0.09	0.09	0.09	0.09
Number of States[f]	−0.00	−0.01*	−0.01*	−0.01*	−0.01*	−0.01***
	0.00	0.00	0.00	0.00	0.00	0.00
Intercept	−0.92	0.04	0.50	0.48	0.51	1.43
Pseudo log-likelihood	−1,768	−1,753	−1,757	−1,754	−1,752	−1,800
Pseudo R^2	0.25	0.25	0.25	0.25	0.25	0.24
Observations	321,811	321,811	321,811	310,502	321,811	328,424

[±] Standard errors corrected for clustering by dyad. *** $p < 0.01$, ** $p < 0.05$, * $p < 0.10$. Peace years and cubic spline variables, calculated for crises back to the start of the Cold War in 1947, not shown for reasons of space.
[a] Polity2 higher minus polity2 lower, Polity IV data (Marshall and Jaggers 2003).
[b] COW Index of National Capability, higher/lower (logged + 1) (Singer et al. 1972).
[c] At least one state is a major power (Small and Singer 1982).
[d] States are contiguous by land.
[e] Inter-capital distance (logged).
[f] Number of states in system.
[†] Variable predicts peace perfectly and 11,309 observations, containing 279 clusters, are not used.

TABLE 2 Tests for Spuriousness in the market Capitalist Peace Crisis Onset 1961 to 2001[±]

Variables	Correlation with CIE (Low)	Model 1 ß	Model 1 SE	Model 2 ß	Model 2 SE	Model 3 ß	Model 3 SE	Model 4 ß	Model 4 SE
CIE (Low)	1.00	−0.66	0.08***	−0.58	0.10***	−0.56	0.10***	−0.34	0.15**
Wealth (Low)[a]	0.56	0.62	0.16***	0.66	0.16***	0.63	0.16***	−0.39	0.47
Trade (Low)[b]	0.30			−0.44	0.27				
Capital Openness (Low)[c]	0.29			−0.08					
Public (High)[d]	−0.15					0.05		0.00	0.01
Capability Ratio	0.00	−0.29	0.09***	−0.30	0.09***	−0.29	0.09***	−0.00	0.11
Major Power	0.13	2.37	0.27***	2.38	0.27***	2.03	0.29***	1.54	0.54***
Contiguity	0.03	1.91	0.25***	1.99	0.25***	1.91	0.29***	3.66	0.51***
Distance	−0.03	−0.63	0.09***	−0.63	0.09***	−0.61	0.10***	−0.44	0.16***
Number of States	0.08	−0.01	0.00***	−0.01	0.00***	−0.01	0.01*	−0.02	0.01*
Intercept	—	1.49	0.88*	1.45	0.89	1.81	1.37	0.83	2.27
Pseudo log-likelihood		−1,787		−1,767		−1,217		−348	
Pseudo R^2		0.25		0.25		0.26		0.33	
Observations		328,424		323,318		206,943		123,661	

[±]All independent variables lagged one year. Standard errors (SE)corrected for clustering by dyad. Peace years and cubic spline variables not shown for reasons of space. *** p<0.01, ** p<0.05, * p<0.10.
[a] Energy consumption per capita logged, COW Index of National Capability (Singer et al. 1972).
[b] (Exports$_{ij}$ + imports$_{ji}$)/GDP$_i$, lower (Gleditsch 2002).
[c] Index of government restrictions on foreign exchange, current and capital accounts, lower (Gartzke 2007:174).
[d] Proportion of state revenue from nontax sources, higher of both states in the dyad (McDonald 2009:79).

Appendix

TABLE A1 Capitalist Peace Versus Democratic Peace, Results in Table 1 without CIE (Low)±

Variables	Model 1	Model 2
Democracy$_{binary6}$	−1.52**	−
	0.63	−
Democracy (Low)^2	−	−0.01***
	−	0.00
Regime Difference	0.06***	0.04***
	0.01	0.01
Capability Ratio	−0.27***	−0.28***
	0.09	0.09
Major Power	2.28***	2.40***
	0.29	0.30
Contiguity	2.17***	2.08***
	0.28	0.28
Distance	−0.61***	−0.63***
	0.09	0.09
Number of States	−0.01**	−0.00*
	0.00	0.00
Intercept	−0.15	0.09
Pseudo log-likelihood	−1,778	−1,765
Pseudo R^2	0.25	0.25
Observations	321,811	321,811

± All independent variables lagged one year. Standard errors corrected for clustering by dyad. Peace years and cubic spline variables not shown for reasons of space. Same sample used as in Table 1. *** p<0.01, ** p<0.05, * p<0.10.

TABLE A2 Market Capitalist Peace, Results in Table 2 without CIE (Low)±

Variables	Correlation with CIE (Low)	Model 1 ß	Model 1 SE	Model 2 ß	Model 2 SE	Model 3 ß	Model 3 SE	Model 4 ß	Model 4 SE
Wealth (Low)[a]	0.56	−0.05	0.18	0.32	0.19*	0.08	0.19	−0.99	0.38***
Trade (Low)[b]	0.30			−1.14	0.33***				
Capital Openness (Low)[c]	0.29					0.05***			
Public (High)[d]	−0.15				−0.18				
Capability Ratio	0.00	−0.25	0.08***	−0.31	0.09***	−0.27	0.09***	0.01	0.01
Major Power	0.13	2.09	0.27***	2.31	0.28***	1.89	0.29***	−0.01	0.11
Contiguity	0.03	2.02	0.26***	2.23	0.24***	1.98	0.29***	1.38	0.56**
Distance	−0.03	−0.56	0.10***	−0.61	0.09***	−0.57	0.10***	3.63	0.53***
Number of States	0.08	−0.01	0.00***	−0.01	0.00***	−0.01	0.01	−0.45	0.16***
Intercept	—	0.43	0.86	0.92	0.82	0.77	1.29	−0.02	0.01*
								0.83	2.25
Pseudo log-likelihood		−1,847		−1,800		−1,242		−351	
Pseudo R^2		0.22		0.23		0.25		0.33	
Observations		328,424		323,318		206,943		123,661	

±All independent variables lagged one year. Standard errors (SE) corrected for clustering by dyad. Peace years and cubic spline variables not shown for reasons of space. *** p<0.01, ** p<0.05, * p<0.10.

Does Capitalism Account for the Democratic Peace? The Evidence Still Says No[1]

ALLAN DAFOE
Yale University, USA, and Uppsala University, Sweden

BRUCE RUSSETT
Yale University, USA

The democratic peace—the empirical association between democracy and peace—is an extremely robust finding. More generally, many liberal factors are associated with peace and many explanations have been offered for these associations, including the effects of: liberal norms, democratic signaling, credible commitments, the free press, economic interdependence, declining benefits of conquest, signaling via capital markets, constraints on the state, constraints on leaders, and others. Scholars are still mapping the contours of the liberal peace, and we remain a long way from fully understanding the respective influence of these different candidate causal mechanisms.

All this being said, the robustness of the democratic peace, as one interrelated empirical aspect of the liberal peace, is impressive. The democratic peace has been interrogated for over two decades and no one has been able to identify an alternative factor that accounts for it in cross-national statistical analyses. Democracy in any two countries (joint democracy) has been shown to be robustly negatively associated with militarized interstate disputes (MIDs), fatal MIDs, crises, escalation, and wars. The democratic peace is for good reason widely cited and regarded as one of the most productive research programs.[2]

We also agree with the editors and contributors to this volume that additional study of the capitalist peace is likely to generate substantial insight. Our mandate in this chapter, however, is to respond to the specific claims made by Mousseau, Orsun, Ungerer, and Mousseau (2013, henceforth denoted MOUM) that social-market capitalism "accounts for the effect of peace that was previously attributed to democracy" (2013:101), extending

---

[1] Replication code and data can be found at http://hdl.handle.net/1902.1/17726
[2] 45% of the respondents to the 2007 TRIP Survey of International Relations judged democratic peace to be one of the three most productive controversies or research programs, getting 9% more respondents than the closest runner-up (Maliniak et al. 2007:29).

the alleged finding that "the democratic peace is found to be spurious in analyses of MIDs (Mousseau 2009, 2012)" (MOUM 2013:93). We show that these claims are unsubstantiated, and that their results contra the democratic peace are fragile and unpersuasive. Before turning to the details of the analysis of MOUM, we reflect on the nature of causal inference using the kinds of cross-national analyses typical to this research.

CAUSAL INFERENCE IS HARD

Strong causal inference requires finding evidence that is unlikely under one theory, but is relatively likely under another theory.[3] Do MOUM present evidence that is unlikely if democracy is a true cause of peace, but likely under their alternative? The answer is no. A handful of correlations based on cross-national data such as those presented by MOUM could arise for many reasons even if democracy is a potent force for peace.

MOUM present estimated coefficients from three statistical models as sufficient evidence that social-market capitalism "accounts for the effect of peace that was previously attributed to democracy" (p.101). For this evidence to support the inference they claim, the evidence would have to be highly unlikely to arise if democracy was truly a force for peace. However, there are many reasons why a few regression results on observational data may fail to generate appropriately signed significant results for a variable that actually plays an important causal role. The analysis may: (i) induce post-treatment bias from conditioning on a post-treatment variable; (ii) mismeasure a variable; (iii) misspecify the functional form on some variable; (iv) omit an important confound; (v) have insufficient power to reject a false null hypothesis; (vi) suffer from multiple comparisons bias due to systematic (usually unconscious) biases in the reporting of results; (vii) fail on any of the other many assumptions required for regression results to have clear causal interpretations. For further discussion of the many assumptions required for and limits of model-based causal inference, see the works of Berk (2004), Morgan and Winship (2007), Sekhon (2009), Freedman (2010), Dunning (2010), Angrist and Pischke (2010), Imai, Keele, Tingley, and Yamamoto (2011), and others.

What should a scholar believe after reading MOUM (2013), Mousseau (2009), or other statistical critiques of the democratic peace? First, one should be very cautious about accepting interpretations that overturn large bodies of evidence and theory. The idea that democracy causes peace has been elaborated, formally and informally, in many theoretical works, with detailed discussion of many possible causal mechanisms. Many qualitative analyses support it (most recently Hayes 2012). So do hundreds of statistical studies,

---

[3]This can be expressed formally using Bayesian inference; see Appendix B.

many of which look at the occurrence of (fatal) militarized interstate disputes and wars (Dafoe 2011; Oneal 2006; Oneal and Russett 1997, 1999a, 1999b, 2001; Russett 1993; Russett and Oneal 2001) or at other behavior related to interstate escalation or civil conflict (Hegre et al. 2001; Huth and Allee 2002), and many of which test other predictions on entirely new empirical domains, such as using content analysis of documents (Schafer and Walker 2006) and laboratory and survey experiments (Geva, DeRouen, and Mintz 1993; Mintz and Geva 1993; Tomz 2007; Tomz and Weeks 2012).[4] Relevant work is not just by political scientists, but by anthropologists, economists, historians, and psychologists. While there is no consensus about how democracy causes peace, the weight of evidence in favor of a pacifying effect of democracy is certainly much stronger than the evidence in favor of the hypothesis of no (or a very small) effect. Until the contrary evidence at least partially approaches the supportive evidence, a reader should be wary about rejecting the various causal conjectures of the democratic peace research program.

Second, one should look in detail at the contrary results to see exactly what is driving these results. Contrary results may be driven by an error, by an otherwise arbitrary aspect of the specification, or by some noteworthy aspect of the data or analysis procedure that has been heretofore insufficiently appreciated by scholars. Whatever the cause, contrary results suggest that something may be learned from unpacking it.

In the case of MOUM (2013) we identify several problematic features. Those we discuss here are: (i) failing to appreciate that an inability to reject a null of no effect is not the same as the rejection of a null of a negative effect; (ii) using an unconventional operationalization of the key variable DEMOCRACY (LOW) that involves a fundamental reinterpretation of the estimand; (iii) ignoring an alternative specification used and justified by Mousseau (2009) involving an interaction between CIE (LOW) and DEMOCRACY (LOW), again for which DEMOCRACY (LOW) has a significant association with peace for much of the sample; (iv) failing to address the existence of an alternative dyadic specification for CIE that has better fit with the data and for which DEMOCRACY (LOW) is significantly associated with peace. (v) We also respond to MOUM's criticism of alternative cut points for operationalizing joint democracy. Each of these points is discussed in the following sections.

In summary, MOUM's evidence is in fact consistent with the democratic peace, and when any of the above reasonable alternative specifications are employed, the estimated coefficient on DEMOCRACY (LOW) is again significantly less than zero.[5] Even if MOUM presented robust results based on unproblematic analyses, one would want to be very cautious before assigning those results a clear causal interpretation. In this case, however, we need not

---

[4]A valuable annotated bibliography is Reiter (2013).
[5]Dafoe and Russett (2013) discuss these and other problems further.

contemplate too much the subtleties of causal inference since the empirical evidence presented against the democratic peace is thin and fragile.

A NEGATIVE ESTIMATE IS NOT EVIDENCE AGAINST A NEGATIVE EFFECT

The coefficient estimates in MOUM's Models 2, 3, and 5 are presented as evidence against the democratic peace. Each of these estimates, however, is still negative: the direction predicted by the democratic peace literature. Assuming for now that the model specification is appropriate, these results say that we cannot reject the null that there is no significant association between democracy and peace. However, it does not imply that we can reject the hypothesis that democracy is associated with peace. Suppose the null hypothesis is that the coefficient on DEMOCRACY (LOW) is −0.10, as estimated in Model 1; a test against this null using Model 2 would yield an insignificant result ($p = 0.2$). Similarly, the estimated coefficients in Models 3, 4 and 5 are each negative. They are closer to zero than before CIE (LOW) was included in the regression, but not so much that we can reject the hypothesis of an association the size of that estimated in Model 1, let alone reject a hypothesis that there is a weak peaceful association. This error is related to the error of interpretation that Gelman and Stern (2006:328) label as when "the difference between 'significant' and 'not significant' is not itself statistically significant." If we continued to collect data that provided similar results as MOUM (2013) present, DEMOCRACY (LOW) would eventually again be significantly less than zero.

FUNDAMENTAL CHANGE IN THE CONCEPTUALIZATION OF DYADIC DEMOCRACY

Oneal and Russett (1997) introduced a means of operationalizing dyadic democracy involving two variables, one measuring the lowest democracy level of the pair of countries in the dyad (DEMOCRACY (LOW)), and one for the highest democracy level of the pair of countries in the dyad (DEMOCRACY (HIGH)). The relevant portion of the statistical model is:

$$\beta_{OR,DL} \text{ DEMOCRACY (LOW)} + \beta_{OR,DH} \text{ DEMOCRACY (HIGH)} \qquad (1)$$

The OR subscripts denote that this is the Oneal and Russett operationalization. We refer to this operationalization as the *lowest-counterfactual* because the coefficient on DEMOCRACY (LOW) implicitly estimates the effect of changing the democracy level of the country with the lowest level of democracy (holding the level of democracy of the other country constant).

MOUM 2013 (citing Choi 2011) employ an alternative operationalization involving DEMOCRACY (LOW) and a measure of REGIME DIFFERENCE = DEMOCRACY (HIGH) − DEMOCRACY (LOW). The relevant portion of the statistical model would then be $b_{M,DL}$ DEMOCRACY (LOW) + $b_{M,RD}$ REGIME DIFFERENCE. By basic algebra we see that MOUM's statistical model involves estimating:

$$\beta_{M,DL} \text{ DEMOCRACY (LOW)} +$$
$$\beta_{M,RD} (\text{DEMOCRACY (HIGH)} - \text{DEMOCRACY (LOW)})$$

$$\Rightarrow (\beta_{M,DL} - \beta_{M,RD}) \text{ DEMOCRACY (LOW)} + \beta_{M,RD} \text{ DEMOCRACY (HIGH)} \quad (2)$$

This implies that:

$$\beta_{M,DL} - \beta_{M,RD} = \beta_{OR,DL}$$

and

$$\beta_{M,RD} = \beta_{OR,DH}$$

Since $\beta_{OR,DH}$ is almost always estimated to have a positive association, this implies that

$$\hat{\beta}_{M,DL} > \hat{\beta}_{OR,DL}$$

That is, this new operationalization involves estimating exactly the same statistical model—compare Models (1) and (2)—and merely redefines the interpretation of the DEMOCRACY (LOW) coefficient in a manner that will make the estimated coefficient closer to zero or positive. Nothing new has been revealed about the empirical association DEMOCRACY (LOW) between democracy and peace. We refer to MOUM's operationalization as the *both-counterfactual,* because the coefficient on DEMOCRACY (LOW) implicitly estimates the effect of changing the level of democracy of both countries simultaneously.

If the goal of a study is to demonstrate that some factor better accounts for peace than democracy, that study should be able to demonstrate this result without reconceptualizing dyadic democracy through a novel operationalization. MOUM write that "most of the independent variables are conventional to the conflict studies literature," but this operationalization of the central independent variable has little precedent. As reported in Dafoe and Russett (2013), a survey of the operationalization of democracy in a sample of articles ranked highest in a Google Scholar search of "democratic peace" found that 78% (32/41) implemented a specification that we interpret as consistent with the *lowest-counterfactual* conceptualization;[6] 15% (6/41) implemented the precise *lowest-counterfactual* (DEMOCRACY (LOW) and DEMOCRACY (HIGH)) that we recommend; zero articles[7] in our sample implemented the *both-counterfactual* employed by MOUM.[8] At the least we can say that the *both-counterfactual* operationalization is unconventional, and ought not to be included if the purpose is to demonstrate the effect of including a new variable on the standard models used in the literature.

How should we decide between these two (econometrically equivalent) specifications? It depends on what is the counterfactual of interest. A heuristic for clarifying thinking about the counterfactual of interest is to ask oneself: what is the experiment that researchers would run if they could? (Dorn 1953:680; Sekhon 2009:496). The counterfactual implicit to most democratic peace research, we argue, is that of increasing (or decreasing) the level of democracy of the least democratic country in a dyad. This is the same as the *lowest-counterfactual* implicit to the operationalization suggested by Oneal and Russett. By contrast, the *both-counterfactual* implicit to Choi and MOUM's coding involves increasing (or decreasing) the level of democracy of *both* countries in a dyad *simultaneously* and by *exactly* the same amount. It is hard to imagine a policy manipulation or historical process that would generate this counterfactual, and hence why we should be interested in it. In fact, by consequence of the dyadic data structure, even if we experimentally created the *both-counterfactual* by manipulating the democracy level of two countries, this experiment would induce as a byproduct many *lowest-counterfactuals*; specifically, all other dyads where the country with the lowest democracy level was also a member of this treatment dyad would experience the *lowest-counterfactual* manipulation.

Scholars who want to direct attention towards the conflict inducing aspects of increases in democracy, perhaps because they are considering the counterfactual of an increase in the democracy level of the most democratic country in Africa, should consider the estimated coefficient for DEMOCRACY (HIGH). Thus, irrespective of whether a scholar's counterfactual of interest involves changes in the democracy level of the less democratic or more

---

[6] Technically, we count all papers with some version of DEMOCRACY (LOW) or JOINT DEMOCRACY (an indicator variable for DEMOCRACY(LOW)), so long as the specification doesn't also have a control variable for REGIME DIFFERENCE or some close variant thereof.

[7] The analyses that we know of that employ the *both-counterfactual* operationalization are Choi (2011) and Henderson (2002); neither of these were among the literatures' top 100. Other operationalizations found in the literature include a monadic coding (DemA, DemB), an interaction monadic coding (DemA, DemB, DemA* × DemB), and (variants of) Maoz and Russett's "Joinreg" variable (Maoz and Russett 1993).

[8] This survey was performed by M.A. research assistants Olga Vera Hänni, Lars Osterberg, and Riho Palis, under supervision by Allan Dafoe. Our coding rubric and data is included in the replication files for (Dafoe and Russett 2013). Dafoe checked a random subset 20% (8/41) of the codings and found no errors in the coding, whether an article involved the *lowest-counterfactual or both-counterfactual*.

democratic country in a dyad, $\beta_{OR,DL}$ DEMOCRACY (LOW) + $\beta_{OR,DH}$ DEMOCRACY (HIGH) is the correct specification.

We include in Table A1 of Appendix a (trivial) replication of MOUM's (2013) Table 1, this time using the *lowest-counterfactual* specification. This confirms that, as expected, this modification makes the coefficient on DEMOCRACY (LOW) more negative and that this single modification returns a significant result on DEMOCRACY (LOW) to all of MOUM's models.

INTERACTION BETWEEN CIE_L AND DEMOCRACY (LOW)

Mousseau (2009) claims to provide evidence that contract-intensive development "appears to account for" the democratic peace. MOUM (2013:93) make the stronger claim that "the democratic peace is found to be spurious in analyses of MIDs (Mousseau 2009, 2012)." This interpretation, however, involves a misreading of interaction terms. Properly interpreted, leaving aside other questions about the statistical models, Mousseau's (2009) analyses show that DEMOCRACY (LOW) has an insignificant association with peace for the 26% of the dyad years with low values of CIE (LOW),[9] but a negative and significant association for the 74% of the dyad years with higher values of CIE (LOW), as pointed out in (Dafoe 2011, 249). This is an important qualification of the empirical finding of the democratic peace, but can hardly be read as evidence that contract-intensive development "appears to account for" the democratic peace, or that "the democratic peace [has been] found to be spurious in analyses of MIDs" (MOUM 2013:7).

MOUM (2013) do not include an interaction between CIE (LOW) and DEMOCRACY (LOW). Why, given that Mousseau's (2009) theory presumably suggested that an interaction should be included? Given its use and significance in Mousseau's prior work, we investigated what happens when CIE (LOW) is interacted with DEMOCRACY (LOW) in MOUM's (2013) analysis. Figure 1 summarizes the results for the *both-counterfactual* operationalization of DEMOCRACY (LOW) and Figure 2 for the preferred *lowest-counterfactual* operationalization. Otherwise the statistical model is identical to MOUM's Model 2.[10] Figures 1 and 2 plot the estimated change in the probability of crisis from changing DEMOCRACY (LOW) from the

---

[9]Technically, Mousseau (2009) employs a dichotomous measure of the lower level of CIECIE in a dyad. This is thus conceptually close to CIECIEl, (LOW) but differs only with respect to the functional form. For convenience of notation, we refer to Mousseau's (2009) variable of ONE STATE CIECIE by the variable name of its 2012 transformation: CIE (LOW)CIEl.

[10]To estimate first differences, CLARIFY (King, Tomz, and Wittenberg 2000) was used. MAJOR POWER was set to 0, CONTIGUITY to 1, *Distance* to its minimum, PEACE YEARS and temporal splines to 0, and CAPABILITY RATIO and NUMBER OF STATES to their median. The treatment variables, DEMOCRACY (LOW) in Figures 1 and 2, and CIE_L in Figure A1, were altered in their respective analysis from the value at their median to the value at their 90th percentile

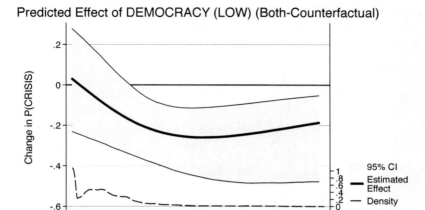

FIGURE 1 The estimated change in the probability of crisis from changing DEMOCRACY (LOW) from the median value (−7) to the 90th percentile value (7), for different values of CIE (LOW) = ln(LIFE INSURANCE PREMIUMS/CAPITA), holding all other variables constant. Estimates based on MOUM's (2013) Model 2, with a DEMOCRACY (LOW) CIE (LOW) interaction added. The bottom line graphs the density, scale on the right. 95% CI = 95% Confidence Interval.

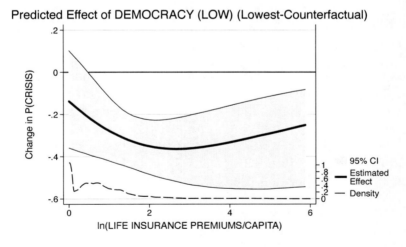

FIGURE 2 The estimated change in the probability of crisis from changing DEMOCRACY (LOW) from the median value (−7) to the 90th percentile value (7), for different values of CIE (LOW) = ln(LIFE INSURANCE PREMIUMS/CAPITA), holding all other variables constant. Estimates based on MOUM's (2013) Model 2, with a DEMOCRACY (LOW) CIE (LOW) interaction added and REGIME DIFFERENCE replaced with DEMOCRACY (HIGH). The bottom line graphs the density, scale on the right. 95% CI = 95% Confidence Interval.

median value (–7) to the 90th percentile value (7), for different values of CIE (LOW), holding all other variables constant.

Figures 1 and 2 illustrate the (statistically significant) interaction between CIE (LOW) and DEMOCRACY (LOW), and specifically that the estimated coefficient on DEMOCRACY (LOW) is significantly less than zero for sufficiently high values of CIE (LOW). That is, by just adding an interaction term to MOUM's Model 2 (using the *both-counterfactual*) we see that DEMOCRACY (LOW) is significant for CIE (LOW) values greater than 1.3 (which accounts for 32% of the sample). Using the preferred *lowest-counterfactual* operationalization in Figure 2, we see that for 66% of dyads (dyads with a CIE (LOW)>0.5) the estimated effect of DEMOCRACY (LOW) is significantly less than 0 and for all dyads the estimated effect is negative. That is very similar to what Mousseau (2009) reported, and once again provides an important empirical qualification of the democratic peace association, but by no means strong evidence against it. In Figure A1 in the Appendix we also graph the estimated effect of CIE (LOW) for MOUM's Model 2 with an interaction; this figure reveals very similar associations on CIE (LOW); the estimated coefficient on CIE (LOW) is not significant for low values of DEMOCRACY (LOW) (which includes 32% of the sample), but is negative and significant for higher values.

ANOTHER SOURCE OF NONROBUSTNESS: SPECIFICATION OF CONTRACT-INTENSIVENESS

Another modification that we investigated was whether a different specification of how CIE is dyadically operationalized would affect results. Inspired by the above discussion, we control for a measure of the higher level of CIE for a dyad (CIE (HIGH)), so as to have a specification that more closely represents the *lowest-counterfactual* for CIE. We control for CIE (HIGH): the higher level of ln(LIFE INSURANCE PREMIUMS/CAPITA) within a dyad. As evidence by its absence from MOUM (2013) and Mousseau's (2013) model specifications, Mousseau's theory seemingly doesn't anticipate associations related to CIE (HIGH), but CIE (HIGH) is in fact positive and very significant for all six of MOUM's models (see Table 1). This one modification makes DEMOCRACY (LOW) significant ($p<0.05$) in Model 2 and DEMOCRACY (LOW)^2 significant in Model 5.

To summarize, even ignoring the massive problems of drawing strong causal claims from a handful of regression results, MOUM's results themselves (i) are not in fact evidence against the democratic peace; and are not robust to a variety of reasonable modifications of the specification, such as (ii) using the standard and more appropriate *lowest-counterfactual* operationalization, (iii) interacting CIE (LOW) and DEMOCRACY (LOW) as Mousseau (2009) theorized and implemented, and (iv) modifying how CIE is dyadically operationalized.

TABLE 1

	(1) Crisis $t+1$	(2) Crisis $t+1$	(3) Crisis $t+1$	(4) Crisis $t+1$	(5) Crisis $t+1$	(6) Crisis $t+1$
CIE (Low)		−0.49*** (0.11)	−0.56*** (0.11)	−0.56*** (0.10)	−0.47*** (0.12)	−0.70*** (0.08)
CIE (High)		0.23*** (0.05)	0.20*** (0.05)	0.18*** (0.05)	0.24*** (0.05)	0.26*** (0.05)
Democracy (Low)	−0.10*** (0.03)	−0.08* (0.04)				
Democracy$_{binary6}$			−0.80 (0.68)			
Democracy$_{binary10}$				−∞		
Democracy (Low)^2					−0.00* (0.00)	
Regime Difference	0.05*** (0.01)	0.02 (0.01)	0.03** (0.01)	0.04*** (0.01)	0.01 (0.01)	
Capability Ratio	−0.27** (0.09)	−0.29*** (0.09)	−0.30*** (0.09)	−0.29*** (0.09)	−0.29*** (0.09)	−0.30*** (0.09)
Major Power	2.36*** (0.30)	2.21*** (0.26)	2.23*** (0.26)	2.23*** (0.26)	2.21*** (0.26)	2.19*** (0.26)
Contiguity	2.12*** (0.28)	2.36*** (0.30)	2.38*** (0.30)	2.39*** (0.30)	2.36*** (0.31)	2.39*** (0.29)
log(Distance)	−0.61*** (0.09)	−0.60*** (0.10)	−0.61*** (0.10)	−0.61*** (0.10)	−0.61*** (0.10)	−0.61*** (0.09)
Number of States	−0.00 (0.00)	−0.01** (0.00)	−0.01** (0.00)	−0.01** (0.00)	−0.01** (0.00)	−0.01*** (0.00)
Time Since Last Crisis	−0.32*** (0.05)	−0.31*** (0.05)	−0.30*** (0.05)	−0.30*** (0.05)	−0.31*** (0.05)	−0.30*** (0.05)
CONSTANT	−0.92 (0.82)	−0.42 (0.89)	0.30 (0.94)	0.26 (0.93)	0.30 (0.93)	0.73 (0.93)
Observations	321,811	321,811	321,811	310,502	321,811	328,424
Pseudo R^2	0.248	0.261	0.258	0.255	0.261	0.255
log-likelihood	−1,768.55	−1,738.17	−1,744.99	−1,743.60	−1,736.56	−1,772.62

Standard errors in parentheses. Three temporal spline variables omitted from table.
† $p < 0.10$, * $p < 0.05$, ** $p < 0.01$, *** $p < 0.001$
−∞ indicates the variable was dropped because it predicted peace perfectly.

ALTERNATIVE CUT POINTS AND DENOMINATOR NEGLECT

MOUM misunderstand the purpose of a footnote in Dafoe (2011), to which they devote a page and a half in response. Mousseau (2009:53,68) writes that "not a single fatal conflict occurred among nations with contract-intensive economies." By contrast, "ten fatal militarized disputes took place between democratic nations [defined as polity≥7] that lacked contract-intensive economies." Dafoe argued that the finding of no fatal MIDs in contract-intensive economies is similar to the finding that the most democratic regimes (polity = 10) also experienced no fatal MIDs using Mousseau's data. This similarity is so for two reasons. First, 76% of countries coded as having a contract-intensive economy (CIE) also had polity = 10, so there was considerable overlap in these categories.

Second, comparing the frequency of fatal MIDs in dyads that both have CIE to the frequency of fatal MIDs under countries with polity≥7 is misleading due to denominator neglect: the comparison attempts to make an inference about the risk of fatal MIDs by comparing the absolute number of fatal MIDs for two groups of very different sizes. The inference neglects to consider that the denominators in the comparison are substantially different. There are 35,729 dyad years with DEMOCRACY (LOW)≥7, making up 12.4% of the sample; however, there are only 10,866 dyad years with *both*CIE = 1, making up 3.8% of the sample. It is thus not a surprise that there are fewer fatal MIDs under dyad years with *both*CIE = 1, than under dyad years with DEMOCRACY (LOW)≥7. On the other hand, there are 10,587 dyad years with DEMOCRACY (LOW) = 10, making up 3.7% of the sample; this suggests that DEMOCRACY (LOW) = 10 provides a better comparison group. Dafoe shows that a comparably exclusive sample of democracies also had a total absence of fatal MIDs.

MOUM are correct to worry about post-hoc adjustments to operationalizations of variables. However, they overstate the consequences. Even if scholars adopted a new operationalization of joint democracy, it is not the case that "all the previous research on the democratic peace [would be] automatically rendered inconsequential" (p.97). The polity≥7 threshold is not immutably deduced from confident theory; rather, most theories of democratic peace (e.g. Russett 2009:12) anticipate continuous effects with unspecified magnitudes and functional forms, perhaps with a positive quadratic curvature reflecting an autocratic peace and increasing marginal effects at the extremes. In most cases, the use of an indicator variable is an approximation to a more complex functional form; consequently, consideration of alternative cut points may provide insight and should not be ruled out. What matters is that modifications of functional forms are consistent with theory, that scholars are explicit about what they are doing, and that the activity is as principled as possible to avoid multiple comparisons bias.

CONCLUSION

The many contributors to this volume advance our understanding about the possible economic causes of the liberal peace. Many liberal political factors may play an important role in securing the liberal peace, such as regular and contested elections amongst political parties, civilian control of the military, freedom of the press, and transparent political decision making. Similarly, many liberal economic factors could be important in reducing the incentives and tendency for states to wage war against each other, including secure property rights, enforceable contracts, high human capital, gains from trade and labor mobility, economic freedom induced growth, capital openness, and greater mobility of capital. These factors also largely seem to be mutually reinforcing, and are deeply historically entwined in the formation of early institutions (Acemoglu et al. 2008; Robinson 2006). The theoretical and empirical study of how these factors might avert war is extremely valuable. However, it is naive to think that we can easily parse out and estimate the effects of these many potential causes of peace, especially using only cross-national regressions.

MOUM (2013) extend the interesting stream of scholarship by Mousseau, looking at the correlates of the contract-intensiveness of economies. As in the papers that have gone before, MOUM remind us of the strong and provocative empirical associations between peace and CIE, and they extend our understanding of these associations. However, contrary to the claims made by Mousseau (2009, 2012) and here, this scholarship has not provided persuasive evidence to make us doubt the empirical association between joint democracy and peace. Rather, their inferences lean on errors of interpretation, are sensitive to reasonable changes in the specification, and are generally overconfident in model-based causal inference. To echo Dafoe (2011), our understanding would likely advance more by testing more precise theoretical implications, by analysis of mechanisms on new empirical domains, and by the search for better research designs, rather than additional statistical horse races between the same imperfect measures of historically interwoven factors.

REFERENCES

Acemoglu, Daron, Simon Johnson, James A. Robinson, and Pierre Yared (2008) Income and Democracy. *American Economic Review* 98(3):808–842.

Angrist, Joshua D., and Jörn-Steffen Pischke (2010) The Credibility Revolution in Empirical Economics: How Better Research Design is Taking the Con out of Econometrics. *Journal of Economic Perspectives* 24(2):3–30.

Berk, Richard A. (2004) *Regression Analysis: A Constructive Critique*. London, UK: Sage Publications.

Choi, Seung-Whan (2011) Re-Evaluating Capitalist and Democratic Peace Models. *International Studies Quarterly* 55(3):759–769.

Dafoe, Allan (2011) Statistical Critiques of the Democratic Peace: Caveat Emptor. *American Journal of Political Science* 55(2):247–262.

Dafoe, Allan, and Bruce Russett (2013) Explorations and Challenges to the Democratic Peace: Weighing the Evidence and Cautious Inference. *International Studies Quarterly* (in press).

Dorn, H. F. (1953) Philosophy of Inference from Retrospective Studies. *American Journal of Public Health* 43:692–699.

Dunning, Thad (2010) Design-Based Inference: Beyond the Pitfalls of Regression Analysis? In *Rethinking Social Inquiry*, eds. Henry E. Brady and David Collier. New York: Rowman & Littlefield Publishers, Inc.

Freedman, David A. (2010) *Statistical Models and Causal Inference: A Dialogue with the Social Sciences*. Edited by David Collier, Jasjeet S. Sekhon and Philip B. Stark. Cambridge University Press.

Gelman, Andrew, and Hal Stern (2006) The Difference Between "Significant" and "Not Significant" is not Itself Statistically Significant. *The American Statistician* 60(4):328–331.

Geva, Nehemia, Karl R. DeRouen, and Alex Mintz (1993) The Political Incentive Explanation of "Democratic Peace": Evidence from Experimental Research. *International Interactions* 18(3):215–229.

Hayes, Jarrod (2012) Securitization, Social Identity, and Democratic Security: Nixon, India, and the Ties That Bind. *International Organization* 66(1):63–93.

Hegre, Håvard, Tanja Ellingsen, Scott Gates, and Nils Petter Gleditsch (2001) Toward a Democratic Civil Peace? Democracy, Political Change, and Civil War, 1816–1992. *American Political Science Review* 95(1):33–48.

Henderson, Errol A. (2002) *Democracy and War: The End of an Illusion*. Boulder: Lynne Rienner.

Huth, Paul, and Todd L. Allee (2002) Domestic Political Accountability and the Escalation and Settlement of International Disputes. *Journal of Conflict Resolution* 46(6):754–790.

Imai, Kosuke, Luke Keele, Dustin Tingley, and Teppei Yamamoto (2011) Unpacking the Black Box of Causality: Learning about Causal Mechanisms from Experimental and Observational Studies. *American Political Science Review* 105(4):765–789.

King, Gary, Michael Tomz, and Jason Wittenberg (2000) Making the Most of Statistical Analyses: Improving Interpretation and Presentation. *American Journal of Political Science* 44(2):341–355.

Maliniak, Daniel, Amy Oakes, Susan Peterson, and Michael J. Tierney (2007) *The View from the Ivory Tower: TRIP Survey of International Relations Faculty in the United States and Canada*. Williamsburg, VA: College of William and Mary.

Maoz, Zeev, and Bruce Russett (1993) Normative and Structural Causes of Democratic Peace, 1946–1986. *The American Political Science Review* 87(3):624–638.

Mintz, Alex, and Nehemia Geva (1993) Why Don't Democracies Fight Each Other? An Experimental Study. *The Journal of Conflict Resolution* 37(3):484–503.

Morgan, Stephen L., and Christopher Winship (2007) *Counterfactuals and Causal Inference: Methods and Principles for Social Research*. Cambridge University Press.

Mousseau, Michael (2009) The Social Market Roots of Democratic Peace. *International Security* 33(4):52–86.

Mousseau, Michael, Omer F. Orsun, Jameson Lee Ungerer, and Demet Yalcin Mousseau (2013) Capitalism and Peace: It's Keynes, not Hayek. In *Assessing the Capitalist Peace*, eds. Gerald Schneider and Nils Petter Gleditsch. Abingdon: Routledge, pp.80–109.

Oneal, John R (2006) Confirming the Liberal Peace with Analyses of Directed Dyads, 1885–2001. In *Approaches, Levels, and Methods of Analysis in International Politics*, ed. Harvey Star. New York: Palgrave Macmillan. 73–94.

Oneal, John R., and Bruce Russett (1997) The Classical Liberals Were Right: Democracy, Interdependence, and Conflict, 1950–1985. *International Studies Quarterly* 41(2):267–293.

Oneal, John R., and Bruce Russett (1999a) Assessing the Liberal Peace with Alternative Specifications: Trade Still Reduces Conflict. *Journal of Peace Research* 36(4):423–442.

Oneal, John R., and Bruce Russett (1999b) The Kantian Peace: The Pacific Benefits of Democracy, Interdependence, and International Organizations, 1885–1992. *World Politics* 52(1):1–37.

Oneal, John R., and Bruce Russett (2001) Clear and Clean: The Fixed Effects of the Liberal Peace. *International Organization* 55(2):469–485.

Reiter, Dan (2012) Democratic Peace Theory. Oxford Bibliographies Online: Political Science. http://oxfordbibliographiesonline.com

Robinson, James A (2006) Economic Development and Democracy. *Annual Review of Political Science* 9:503–557.

Russett, Bruce (1993) *Grasping the Democratic Peace: Principles for a Post-Cold War World.* Princeton, NJ: Princeton University Press.

Russett, Bruce (2009) Democracy, War and Expansion through Historical Lenses. *European Journal of International Relations* 15(1):9–36.

Russett, Bruce, and John Oneal (2001) *Triangulating Peace: Democracy, Interdependence, and International Organizations.* New York: W. W. Norton & Company.

Schafer, Mark, and Stephen G. Walker (2006) Democratic Leaders and the Democratic Peace: The Operational Codes of Tony Blair and Bill Clinton. *International Studies Quarterly* 50(3):561–583.

Sekhon, Jasjeet S (2009) Opiates for the Matches: Matching Methods for Causal Inference. *Annual Review of Political Science* 12(1):487–508.

Tomz, Michael (2007) Domestic Audience Costs in International Relations: An Experimental Approach. *International Organization* 61(4):821–840.

Tomz, Michael, and Jessica L. Weeks (2012) An Experimental Investigation of the Democratic Peace. Manuscript, Political Science Dept., Stanford University, and Political Science Dept., Cornell University.

Appendix A

TABLE A1

Table A1 is based on an analysis using exactly the same data and code as that used by MOUM (2013) in their Table 1, except that it substitutes the variable Democracy (High) for Regime Difference.

	(1) Crisis $t+1$	(2) Crisis $t+1$	(3) Crisis $t+1$	(4) Crisis $t+1$	(5) Crisis $t+1$	(6) Crisis $t+1$
CIE (Low)		−0.39*** (0.11)	−0.50*** (0.11)	−0.53*** (0.09)	−0.36** (0.12)	−0.52*** (0.08)
Democracy (Low)	−0.15*** (0.03)	−0.10** (0.03)				
Democracy$_{binary6}$			−1.08† (0.63)			
Democracy$_{binary10}$				−∞		
Democracy (Low)^2					−0.01** (0.00)	
Democracy (High)	0.05*** (0.01)	0.05*** (0.01)	0.04** (0.01)	0.04** (0.01)	0.05*** (0.01)	
Capability Ratio	−0.27** (0.09)	−0.30*** (0.09)	−0.32*** (0.09)	−0.31*** (0.09)	−0.30*** (0.09)	−0.32*** (0.09)
Major Power	2.36*** (0.30)	2.52*** (0.29)	2.55*** (0.29)	2.54*** (0.29)	2.54*** (0.29)	2.63*** (0.31)
Contiguity	2.12*** (0.28)	2.07*** (0.29)	2.02*** (0.29)	2.01*** (0.28)	2.05*** (0.29)	1.89*** (0.26)
log(Distance)	−0.61*** (0.09)	−0.66*** (0.09)	−0.67*** (0.09)	−0.67*** (0.09)	−0.67*** (0.09)	−0.68*** (0.09)
Number of States	−0.00 (0.00)	−0.01† (0.00)	−0.01** (0.00)	−0.01** (0.00)	−0.01* (0.00)	−0.01** (0.00)
Time since Last Crisis1	−0.32*** (0.05)	−0.31*** (0.05)	−0.31*** (0.05)	−0.31*** (0.05)	−0.31*** (0.05)	−0.32*** (0.05)
CONSTANT	−0.92 (0.82)	0.04 (0.85)	1.33 (0.86)	1.41 (0.88)	1.00 (0.84)	1.43 (0.90)
Observations	321,811	321,811	321,811	310,502	321,811	328,424
Pseudo R^2	0.248	0.254	0.248	0.244	0.254	0.243

Standard errors in parentheses. Three temporal spline variables omitted from table.
† $p < 0.10$, * $p < 0.05$, ** $p < 0.01$, *** $p < 0.001$ (all two-sided).
−∞ indicates the variable was dropped because it predicted peace perfectly.

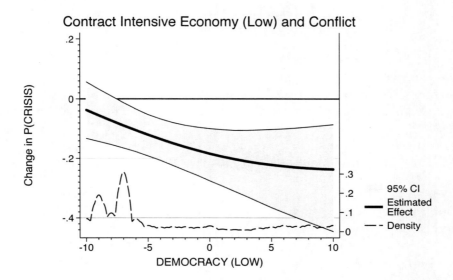

FIGURE A1 The estimated change in the probability of crisis from changing CIE (LOW) from the median value (0.85) to the 90th percentile value (2.38), for different values of DEMOCRACY (LOW), holding all other variables constant. Estimates based on MOUM's (2013) Model 2, with a DEMOCRACY (LOW) CIE (LOW) interaction added. The estimated association is insignificant when DEMOCRACY (LOW)<−7, which includes 32% of the sample.

Appendix B

Strong causal inference requires finding evidence (X) that is unlikely under a large subset of plausible causal theories (A), is likely under a small subset of theories (B), and, when really persuasive, gives us confidence that the truth is likely to be in this smaller subset (B); this can be expressed as $P(A|X) \ll P(A)$, $P(B|X) \gg P(B)$, and $P(B|X) > P(A|X)$, where $P(A|X)$ denotes the probability that the truth is in A given that we observed evidence X and $P(A)$ is the prior probability that the truth is in A. Given X, we can have much greater confidence that the truth is in B rather than A. MOUM argue that the evidence (X) they present in their chapter allows a rational observer to substantially reduce their beliefs that democracy is a cause of peace (denoted DP): $DP \in A$, $P(DP|X) \ll P(DP)$.

As can be seen through the application of Bayes formula, this requires that $P(X|DP) \ll P(X|\overline{DP})$: the probability of observing the evidence must be low if democracy is a cause of peace but relatively likely under one of the plausible alternatives.

Does the Market-Capitalist Peace Supersede the Democratic Peace? The Evidence Still Says Yes

MICHAEL MOUSSEAU
OMER F. ORSUN
JAMESON LEE UNGERER
Koç University, Turkey

We appreciate the chance to respond to Dafoe and Russett's (henceforth DR) reaction to our chapter and the challenge to the democratic peace (DP) causal hypothesis that the economic norms theory poses. DR have analysed our data and presented arguments that the best inference to draw from our chapter (Mousseau, Orsun, Ungerer, and Mousseau 2013, henceforth MOUM) and other works by Mousseau (2000, 2009) is that democracy remains at least one cause of the DP correlation. We would be perfectly content to reach this same conclusion, but cannot in light of the evidence.

Our main points are as follows. Foremost, we stress that DR are defending only the existence of the DP correlation: the inference of causation requires theory, which they take little heed of. Second, DR's results hold only with a specific erroneous measure of regime difference; we solve this issue by adopting a less-controversial measure, which shows the MOUM results are robust. Finally, we test DR's unsupported assertion that democracy is still significant in the MOUM regressions, showing that it is not. DR raise some important points to consider in the economic norms challenge to the DP, but close examination of them does not save the DP correlation, and by implication the DP causal hypothesis.

A CORRELATION, OBSERVED AGAIN AND AGAIN, IS STILL NOT CAUSATION

The heart of DR's argument that democracy causes peace is that it is supported in "hundreds of statistical" and other studies (Chapter 5b of this volume; see also Dafoe 2011:111). DR acknowledge, however, that there is no consensus on a causal explanation for the DP. So DR's resort to "hundreds" of studies is analogous to "hundreds" of studies reporting the correlation of ice cream consumption with shark attacks: just as the latter correlation is evidence that eating ice cream causes shark attacks, it cannot alone be compelling because (i) it lacks theory with substantial corroborating evidence; and (ii) there could be a third confounding variable that might cause both ice cream consumption and shark attacks, making the initial correlation spurious. A third variable might be summer season, which, by causing both ice cream consumption and swimming, may be the ultimate cause of shark attacks.

Similarly, the many studies of the DP correlation cannot, alone, be compelling evidence for democracy causing peace: not even millions of reports of the same correlation reduce the odds that at some future date a third variable can arrive offering an account of both variables. We understand that the idea that democracy causes peace might feel more intuitively correct than the idea that eating ice cream causes shark attacks, but the analogy fits because scientific knowledge derives from evidence, not intuition.[1]

Scientifically, the only way to infer causation in historical analyses is to compare competing theories for it (Bremer, Regan, and Clark 2003:8–9). Most agree that the most important factors in assessing theories are the generation of novel predictions, extent of corroborated novel predictions, the degree of novelty predicted, and the scope of anomalous evidence; the importance of a theory lies in its explanatory value.[2] The upshot is that to infer causation, we must consider the wider stream of evidence beyond the issue at hand.

As a causal explanation for the DP correlation, Mousseau (2000) introduced a third variable: CONTRACT-INTENSIVE ECONOMY (CIE). If a third variable (Z) fully accounts for the correlation of two variables (X and Y), evidence for this will be seen in a regression analysis, where inclusion of Z would remove the correlation of X and Y. In Mousseau (2000) direct data on CIE was lacking, but with Mousseau (2009) and MOUM direct data became available and the initial deduction was corroborated: CIE appears to account for the DP correlation. But merely rendering a variable (X) insignificant is not meaningful unless it is accompanied with theory. The Mousseau studies not only have theory, but by scientific standards economic norms theory is a comparatively strong one, having well surpassed any competing theory in the DP research program.[3]

---

[1]Philosophers of science agree that causation cannot be observed with direct evidence of the senses: we can only observe the indirect effects of causation. In historical (nonexperimental) research, such as large-N data analyses, coefficients can be interpreted in multiple ways, and thus cannot directly indicate causation. If one believes in a certain causation, however, such as the DP, it is human nature to perceive evidence for it as direct; it is precisely because of this human weakness that we seek scientific method. DR (p.134) mention experimental studies in the DP research program, but none of these are true experiments in that none can be said to have isolated the purported causation from democracy to peace.
[2]For a review, see Ungerer (2012).
[3]See MOUM 81; 101.

In their defense of democracy as a cause of the DP correlation, DR do not draw on any theory: they focus entirely on the DP correlation, defined narrowly as a dearth of militarized conflict among democracies, with most of their attention even more constricted to the specific regressions in MOUM, where they introduce two new variables that make some of the democracy coefficients significant: an interaction of CIE (LOW) × DEMOCRACY (LOW) (DR: Figures 1, 2, A1) and CIE (HIGH) (DR Table 1). Since DR offer no theoretical justification for the inclusion of these variables, their inclusion appears as an ad hoc and thus degenerating attempt to save a hypothesis (see Lakatos 1978:72).[4] DR know the importance of theory and evidence for it, as they repeatedly promote "testing more precise theoretical implications" (pp.121, see also Dafoe 2011:13–14) even as they disregard all the more precise testing of the theoretical implications of economic norms theory. Strangely, they describe our claim of the DP being spurious as based only on a "handful" of regressions (pp.111, 118). We do not understand this, as anyone can read MOUM and any number of the Mousseau studies and see that all this research is guided by theory and a solid record of "testing more precise theoretical implications." The stress on correlation as causation, selective neglect of the wider stream of evidence, and the peculiar thesis that we, not they, are ignoring the wider stream of evidence cannot serve as convincing foundations for democracy being a cause of the peace.

A CORRELATION CANNOT SURVIVE ON EPISTEMIC ERROR

In their effort to save the DP correlation, DR advocate controlling for the third factor regime difference, an established covariate of conflict related with democracy, using a specific measure, DEMOCRACY (HIGH) (meaning the *higher* democracy score in the dyad) over the one we used, REGIME DIFFERENCE (DEMOCRACY (HIGH) − DEMOCRACY (LOW), meaning the *lower* democracy score in the dyad). DR go to great lengths to describe the MOUM operationalization as "novel", "unconventional", and having "little precedent" (pp.112–114). This is odd, since REGIME DIFFERENCE has a long tradition in the literature (Werner 2000:345–49 especially), and we employed it because, to our knowledge, everyone who has compared DEMOCRACY (HIGH) and REGIME DIFFERENCE favors the latter: Henderson (2002:32–33) first observed that DEMOCRACY (HIGH) "conflates both the

---

[4]Furthermore, the statistically significant portion of the sample for DEMOCRACY (LOW) accounts for only 32% of the sample where CIE (LOW)>1.3, as reported by DR in Figure 1, a substantial limitation on the supposed peace-making powers of democracy. DR also draw from this interaction the empirical result that CIE is not significant for very low values of democracy, implying that CIE is conditioned by democracy (p.118), but this is an error: the reason CIE is insignificant at very low values of democracy is because there are *no cases in the data* of both nations being CIEs (defined by CIE_{binary}) with below-median values of DEMOCRACY (LOW), as predicted by economic norms theory.

allegedly conflict-dampening impact of joint democracy and the conflict-exacerbating impact of political distance ... making it difficult to distinguish between the competing processes" (see also Choi 2011).[5]

It is easy to demonstrate that to test the DP using DEMOCRACY (LOW), REGIME DIFFERENCE, and not DEMOCRACY (HIGH) is the better theoretically derived measure. Our operationalization model estimates:

INTERNATIONAL CRISIS =, where $z = b_0 + b_1$ DEMOCRACY (LOW) + b_2 REGIME DIFFERENCE + b_{3+k} Other Controls

Given REGIME DIFFERENCE = DEMOCRACY (HIGH) − DEMOCRACY (LOW), the operationalization defended by DR is

INTERNATIONAL CRISIS =, where $z = b_0 + b_1$ DEMOCRACY (LOW) + b_2 (REGIME DIFFERENCE + DEMOCRACY (LOW)) + b_{3+k} Other Controls

As we show in Table 1, the DEMOCRACY (HIGH) specification implies that, given regime difference is zero – democracy scores for states A and B are identical – countries will be more conflict prone as they democratize. This obviously contradicts the core hypothesis that the more democratic two countries, the more likely it is to observe a peace among them.

TABLE 1 Epistemic Implications of Democracy (High) and Regime Difference

Democracy$_A$	Democracy$_B$	Democracy (High)	Regime Difference
10	10	10	0
	−10		20
9	9	9	0
	−10		19
8	8	8	0
	−10		18
7	7	7	0
	−10		17
6	6	6	0
	−10		16
−10	−10	−10	0

DR (pp.113–116) are correct when they note the coincidental mathematical relation between REGIME DIFFERENCE and DEMOCRACY (LOW); however,

---

[5] DR claim DEMOCRACY (HIGH) is the standard measure on the grounds of their Google Scholar survey (pp.114–115). We could not replicate this survey, but it is not scientifically relevant anyway: ceteris paribus, older studies will have more citations than newer ones, and the whole idea of knowledge cumulation is that newer studies supersede older ones. As, an example, using Google Scholar citation numbers in the year 1500, we would continue to believe the world is flat.

as we demonstrated above, DEMOCRACY (HIGH) is also not immune to this mathematical relation. Given that the models are statistically identical, what matters is the theoretical motivation of the researcher: if we care mostly about the minimum and maximum levels of democracy in the dyad, and less so about the difference between them, we should use DR's DEMOCRACY (LOW) and DEMOCRACY (HIGH); if our aim is to assess regime difference and DEMOCRACY (LOW), the MOUM specification is the correct one. Since the issue at hand is the significance of the DP correlation controlling for regime difference, the MOUM specification is the correct one to follow. Furthermore, DEMOCRACY (HIGH) fails to measure regime difference *at all* when the DP correlation is tested using any other democracy measure than DEMOCRACY (LOW), which is precisely what DR are advocating (pp.113–116).

To be considered robust, correlates must hold using divergent reasonable measures, so another way to settle the controversy is to examine a new measure that is not mathematically related to DEMOCRACY (LOW). We thus turn to the operationalization introduced by Werner (2000), which has the advantage of coding institutional difference according to the component parts of the Polity2 measure in the Polity IV dataset, with the sound reasoning that there are in fact "multiple paths to the same value on the Democracy and Autocracy scales" (p.355).[6] As can be seen in Table 2, the robustness of the results using REGIME DIFFERENCE are confirmed using POLITICAL DISTANCE.[7] We have thus shown that the results of the original MOUM models are robust while controlling for regime difference in a way that is not mathematically related to DEMOCRACY (LOW).[8]

---

[6] The equation for computing this measure is: POLITICAL DISTANCE$_{ij}$ = [((xrcompi − xrcompj)/3)^2 + ((xropeni − xropenj)/4)^2 + ((xconsti − xconstj)/6)^2 + ((parcompi − parcompj)/5)$^{\wedge}$2)$^{\wedge}$0.5. Werner (2000) inverts the scale (multiplied by −1) in order to gauge political similarity; however, since we are measuring political distance we do not invert the scale and renamed it; thus, as the variable increases, so does POLITICAL DISTANCE.

[7] The results presented here are almost identical when following the Polity II imputation rules for missing data and thus are not reported.

[8] Due to space constraints other model specifications can be viewed in the online appendix at: http://home.ku.edu.tr/~mmousseau/.

TABLE 2 CIE, Democracy and ICB Crisis Onset 1961–2001

	Model I	Model II	Model III
CIE (Low)		−0.35***	−0.44***
		(0.11)	(0.11)
Democracy (Low)	−0.10***	−0.06	
	(0.03)	(0.04)	
Democracy$_{binary6}$			−0.37
			(0.68)
Political Distance	0.80***	0.83***	0.93***
	(0.15)	(0.14)	(0.15)
Capability Ratio	−0.28***	−0.31***	−0.31***
	(0.09)	(0.09)	(0.09)
Major Power	2.48***	2.63***	2.63***
	(0.31)	(0.29)	(0.29)
Contiguity	2.06***	1.98***	2.00***
	(0.27)	(0.27)	(0.27)
Distance	−0.65***	−0.70***	−0.70***
	(0.09)	(0.09)	(0.09)
Number of States	−0.00	−0.00*	−0.01**
	(0.00)	(0.00)	(0.00)
Intercept	−0.95	0.017	0.64
Pseudo R^2	0.255	0.260	0.258
Pseudo log-likelihood	−1649.1	−1637.8	−1643.1
Observations	301,291	301,291	301,291

±All independent variables lagged one year. Standard errors (in parantheses) corrected for clustering by dyad. Peace years and cubic spline variables not shown for reasons of space.
* $p<0.10$, ** $p<0.05$, *** $p<0.01$

THE INSIGNIFICANCE OF DEMOCRACY IS SIGNIFICANT

DR are correct to point out that the inability to reject the null hypothesis is not the same as the ability to accept the null hypothesis (pp.111–113); that to make this assertion one must "look at the statistical significance of the difference between variables rather than the difference between each variable's significance levels" (Gelman and Stern 2006:329). Rather than perform this test, however, DR just assumed that the differences between the DEMOCRACY (LOW) coefficients in MOUM Models 1 and 2 are insignificant. We carried out the test.

TABLE 3 Significance of Difference and Decomposition of the Democracy Variables

	Democracy (Low) Model I	Democracy$_{binary6}$ Model II	Democracy (Low)^2 Model III
Democracy^{ReducedModel}	−0.09***	−1.20**	−0.005***
	(0.03)	(0.59)	(0.01)
Democracy^{FullModel}	−0.05	−0.42	−0.003
	(0.04)	(0.69)	(0.002)
Democracy^{Difference}	−0.04***	−0.78***	−0.002***
	(0.01)	(0.19)	(0.00)
Observations	321,811	321,811	321,811
Pseudo R^2	0.25	0.25	0.25

Standard errors corrected for clustering by dyad are in parentheses. ** $p<0.05$, *** $p<0.01$. Decomposition of the total effect of the Democracy variables is performed through the KHB method (Karlson, Holm, and Breen 2010), which introduces CIE (Low) into baseline models of Democracy (Low) (Table 1, Model 1), Democracy$_{binary6}$ (Table A1, Model 1) and Democracy (Low)^2 (Table A1, Model 2) in MOUM 2013. As mentioned in MOUM 2013, Democracy$_{binary10}$ creates a problem of quasi-complete separation and is thus not decomposable.

As can be seen in Model I in Table 3, DEMOCRACY (LOW)^{ReducedModel}, negative (−0.09) and significant ($p<0.01$), is the total effect of DEMOCRACY (LOW). DEMOCRACY (LOW)^{FullModel}, negative (−0.05) but insignificant ($p = 0.165$) is the direct effect of DEMOCRACY (LOW).[9] The pivotal indicator proposed by Gelman and Stern (2006) would be DEMOCRACY (LOW)^{Difference}, the difference between DEMOCRACY (LOW)$^{Model\ 1}$ and DEMOCRACY (LOW)$^{Model\ 2}$, and we can see that it is highly significant ($p<0.001$), meaning that in the MOUM regressions the DP correlation is in fact insignificant. Table 3 also shows that the total effect of DEMOCRACY (LOW) is significant and negative (ß = −0.09, $p<0.01$). However, decomposition of this variable into direct and spurious effects shows that democracy does not have a direct effect on peace, whereas its spurious effect explained by CIE (LOW), (ß = −0.04), is starkly significant and negative. The measure DEMOCRACY$_{binary6}$ shows an even starker picture: DEMOCRACY$_{Reduced\ Model\ binary6}$ has a total effect of −1.20, whereas the direct effect DEMOCRACY$_{Full\ Model\ binary6}$ is again insignificant, and the spurious effect is −0.78 and significant, meaning that around 64.8% of this peace effect is significantly explained by CIE (LOW), thus spurious, and what remains—35.2%—is statistically indistinguishable from zero. We also see similar results for the variable DEMOCRACY (LOW)^2 in Model III.

---

[9]Gelman and Stern (2006:331) are primarily concerned with the 5% significance level. In our case, the significance levels associated with DEMOCRACY (LOW), DEMOCRACY$_{binary6}$, and DEMOCRACY (LOW)^2, respectively, are uncomparably high levels of 16.5%, 54.4%, and 17.7%.

THE PROGRESS OF KNOWLEDGE: THE ECONOMIC PEACE SUPERSEDES THE DEMOCRATIC PEACE

Dafoe and Russett have gone through the MOUM data and claim to have found "massive problems" in our results (p.10); but all they have shown is that it is possible to tweak the MOUM data and make the DP correlation significant with new variables that have no theoretical justification. They have thus made the grave error of equating correlation with causation, overlooking the wider stream of evidence that appears to favor the economic norms explanation over competing explanations for the democratic peace. They also sought to save the DP correlation by advocating a specific measure of a third factor, regime difference, that had previously been shown to artificially inflate the significance of democracy, and with the unsupported assertion that the insignificance of the DP in MOUM is not significant. But the democratic peace cannot stand on a specific and faulty measure of a third variable, and an unsupported assertion cannot override an empirical finding. Using an alternative and legitimate specification of regime difference, and employing the appropriate method for testing insignificance, we showed that the DP correlation is still insignificant across specifications, thereby overturning the primary evidence for the DP causal hypothesis.

Noting the "hundreds of statistical studies" reporting the DP correlation, DR assert that "until the contrary evidence at least partially approaches the supportive evidence, a reader should be wary about rejecting the various causal conjectures of the democratic peace" (p.112; see also Dafoe 2011:14). In fact, there is no scientific basis for being particularly "wary" of a challenging idea simply because a prior correlation has been observed again and again: like the correlation of ice cream consumption with shark attacks, even thousands of studies of the DP correlation would not reduce the odds that a previously untested third variable cannot explain the relationship. New ideas and new third variables *always* arrive without substantial bodies of research behind them, and the large number of studies in the DP research program are no more evidence for democracy causing the DP correlation than they are evidence for economic norms causing it, since the present evidence indicates that all the "hundreds" of prior studies, quantitative and quasi-experimental, were underspecified.

DR also assert, referring to numerous purposed variables in the DP research program, that "it is naive to think that we can easily parse out and estimate the effects of these many potential causes of peace" (p.121). We never said it was easy, but we must make something very clear: it is not any harder to parse out contract-intensive economy from democracy than it was parsing out other variables from democracy back in the day when "hundreds" of prior studies *supported* the democratic peace. Roughly half of all democratic nation-years lack contract-intensive economies, and these nations are not in peace (Mousseau 2012), and in Table 2 (MOUM: Chapter

5a this volume) we reported only moderate or low correlations of CIE with all the other economic variables in the DP research program.

The assertion that democracy must be a cause of peace because so many studies have said so, the selective neglect of the wider stream of counter-evidence, and the rhetorical labeling of anyone challenging the DP correlation as "naive" to think they can "easily" distinguish democracy from other factors, all remind us of Lakatos' description of how challenging ideas are often treated by defenders of defeated research programs:

> It's very difficult to defeat a research program supported by talented, imaginative scientists. Alternatively, defenders of the defeated program may offer *ad hoc* explanations of the experiments or a shrewd *ad hoc* "reduction" of the victorious program to the defeated one. But such efforts we should reject as unscientific. (Lakatos 1978:72)

The gravity of this exchange can hardly be overstated: once the heavy rhetoric is plowed aside, it is clear that the strongest effort to save the democratic peace causal hypothesis has not suceeded, and the democratic peace correlation has at long last an explanation that seems to prevail over all others. The economic norms peace now appears as the next progressive step in the democratic peace research program.

REFERENCES

Bremer, Stuart A., Patrick M. Regan, and David H. Clark (2003) Building a Science of World Politics. *Journal of Conflict Resolution* 47(1):3–13.

Choi, Seung-Whan (2011) Re-Evaluating Capitalist and Democratic Peace Models. *International Studies Quarterly* 55 (3):759–769.

Dafoe, Allan (2011) Statistical Critiques of the Democratic Peace: Caveat Emptor. *American Journal of Political Science* 55 (2):247–262.

Dafoe, Allan, and Bruce Russett (2013) Democracy and Capitalism: Interwoven Strands of the Liberal Peace. In *Assessing the Capitalist Peace*, eds. Gerald Schneider and Nils Petter Gleditsch. Abingdon: Routledge, pp.110–126.

Gelman, Andrew, and Hal Stern (2006) The Difference Between "Significant" and "Not Significant" Is not Itself Statistically Significant. *The American Statistician* 60 (4):328–331.

Henderson, Errol A. (2002) *Democracy and War: The End of an Illusion.* Boulder: Lynne Rienner.

Karlson, K. B., A. Holm, and R. Breen (2010) Comparing regression coefficients between models using logit and probit: A new method. Available at http://www.yale.edu/ciqle/Breen_Scaling%20effects.pdfLakatos, Imre (1978 [1970]) Falsification and the Methodology of Scientific Research Programs. In *Mathematics, Science and Epistemology: Philosophical Papers*, Volume 1, ed. John Worrall and Gregory Currie. Cambridge, UK: Cambridge University Press.

Maoz, Zeev, and Bruce Russett (1992) Alliances, Wealth, Contiguity and Political Stability: Is the Lack of Conflict between Democracies a Statistical Artifact? *International Interactions* 17(4):245–267.

Mousseau, Michael, Omer F. Orsun, Jameson Lee Ungerer, and Demet Yalcin Mousseau (2013) Capitalism and Peace: It's Keynes, not Hayek. In *Assessing the Capitalist Peace*, eds. Gerald Schneider and Nils Petter Gleditsch. Abingdon, Routledge, pp.80–109.

Mousseau, Michael (2000) Market Prosperity, Democratic Consolidation, and Democratic Peace. *Journal of Conflict Resolution* 44(4):472–507.

Mousseau, Michael (2009) The Social Market Roots of Democratic Peace. *International Security* 33(4):52–86.

Mousseau, Michael (2012) Market-Capitalist or Democratic Peace. In *What Do We Know About War? Second edition,* ed. John Vasquez. Rowan-Littlefield.

Oneal, John R., and Bruce Russett (1997) The Classical Liberals Were Right: Democracy, Interdependence, and Conflict, 1950–1985. *International Studies Quarterly* 41(2):267–293.

Ungerer, Jameson (2012) Assessing the Progress of the Democratic Peace Research Program. *International Studies Review* 14(1):1–31.

Werner, Suzanne (2000) The Effects of Political Similarity on the Onset of Militarized Disputes, 1816–1985. *Political Research Quarterly* 53(2):343–374.

COMMENTARIES

Coming to Terms with the Capitalist Peace

MICHAEL MOUSSEAU
Koç University

Capitalism has long been maligned as a cause of war, so when Stuart Bremer undertook what was probably the first systematic look at capitalism and war at the dyadic level he was surprised to find that nations with advanced economies were less likely than others to fight each other (1992:334–336). Most attention to Bremer's article, however, was placed on his observation that democracy was a more powerful force for peace than power preponderance—a result which quickly eclipsed his finding that capitalism was a more powerful force for peace than democracy. After a few more articles confirmed the democratic peace after controlling for development, consideration of development seemed to vanish from conflict studies. This disappearance was reasonable at the time, given the dearth of theory for a capitalist peace.

Now times have changed. By my count there exists at least four theories of capitalist peace, all backed with some evidence, and the capitalist peace may have overturned the democratic one. I believe the roots of the capitalist peace can be traced to Erich Weede's insights, built on classical economic theory, on how trade and free markets can cause development and peace (1996), which he dubbed the "capitalist peace" (2005). Separate from this research program, I developed a theory of how a market-intensive economy can cause peace and successfully predicted the economic conditionality to the democratic peace (Mousseau 2000). About the same time, Erik Gartzke, Quan Li, and Charles Boehmer (2001) linked financial openness with peace and, after that, Patrick McDonald (2007; 2009) linked size of government with peace.

In this essay, I seek to highlight what I think are important issues in the emerging capitalist peace research program. I begin by discussing the meaning of "capitalism" and its relationship with development, trade, and markets. I then review the relationship of the capitalist peace with the democratic peace, discuss various issues in research design, and assess the comparative efficacy of the competing capitalist peace theories. Along the way I identify what I think are promising steps in the road ahead.

A FREE MARKET CAPITALIST PEACE?

Several capitalist peace theories assume that "capitalism" means free markets, which in turn cause economic development. In this way, free markets or trade may account for the peace among nations with advanced economies. While these linkages are made explicit by some (Weede 1996), they are sometimes only implied by others. Gartzke and Hewitt in this issue (2010), for instance, use free markets to explain why "the most prosperous, developed nations appear largely satisfied with the global status quo" (p. 121).

I believe that only in classical economic theory are free markets thought to cause development. So I obtained the data and examined the hypothesis. It appears the classical liberals are wrong: measured with logged GDP per capita, development correlates with the proportion of GDP in foreign trade at only 0.08, with openness to foreign capital (Gartzke et al. 2001) at only 0.14, and with size of government (McDonald 2007) negatively at −0.13. At the dyadic level, trade correlates with development at only 0.26 (Mousseau, Hegre, and Oneal 2003:283).

It is hard to overstate the importance of these observations for grasping the capitalist peace. While the disjuncture of trade and free markets with development should not be construed as evidence against any of the free market models, it seems they are not equipped to account for the phenomenon many think they account: the apparent peace among nations with advanced economies.

A SOCIAL MARKET CAPITALIST PEACE?

By most definitions, "capitalism" is not about free markets but rather the degree to which an economy consists of actors linked in a market. In my work I give importance to the fact that actors linked in a market exchange their wares in free and voluntary contracts. Nations with poorer economies have fewer exchanges than others, and in some economies many exchanges occur that are not capitalistic but based instead on coercion or gift exchanges maintained with reciprocity (Polanyi 1957[1944]).

In a series of studies I have shown how capitalist nations can have common interests and be in a permanent peace (Mousseau 2000; 2009). This happens because citizens dependent on a market have greater opportunities in larger and wealthier markets compared with smaller and poorer ones. They thus have direct interests in their governments promoting growth in the market and in sustaining (or increasing) the size of the market by ardently protecting (or promoting abroad) free choice in contracting. Since markets can not function in anarchy and no one can automatically trust the contractual commitments of strangers, citizens also demand their governments competently enforce contracts and the rule of law—at home and abroad. War can not happen within or between capitalist nations because it requires the harming of others, and everyone is always better off when others in the market are richer, not poorer (even among states that do not directly trade). Thus, rather than fight, capitalist nations engage in intense levels of cooperation specifically aimed at promoting each other's markets. They also have common interests in preserving the sanctimony of international law as the vital backbone of the global marketplace. Empirical support for this thesis is robust: nations with contract intensive economies engage in high levels of mutual cooperation (Mousseau 2002), have common foreign policy preferences (Mousseau 2003) and, as far as the data inform us, have never had a single fatality in a militarized confrontation (Mousseau 2009).

Economic norms theory clearly predicts a capitalist peace, but it says nothing about free markets. A contract by definition must be voluntary without coercion, but this does not mean its terms can not be regulated by the state. A capitalist economy by definition consists of profit-maximizing actors, but this does not mean these actors can not demand their states promote market growth with heavy spending. In contrast to the free market capitalist peace variables discussed above, contract intensive economy correlates with development highly at 0.64.[1] It follows that a capitalist peace should not be automatically equated with interstate trade, free markets, or limited government.

DOES A CAPITALIST PEACE TRUMP THE DEMOCRATIC PEACE?

A capitalist peace and a democratic peace are not necessarily mutually exclusive, but to the extent that capitalism and democracy are related, a capitalist peace may supersede the democratic one. Gartzke (2007) reports that capital openness makes the democratic peace insignificant, but a subsequent reexamination of this claim shows it to be a consequence of several design errors (Dafoe 2009). My own work, however, indicates that the capitalist peace does overturn the democratic peace (Mousseau 2009). This means the tentative state of evidence today is that the capitalist peace effectively accounts for the democratic peace. Clearly, the imperative next task for scholars is to vigorously reexamine this challenge to the democratic peace.

NEED FOR MORE CUMULATIVE RESEARCH DESIGNS

Some analyses of the capitalist peace are not fully persuasive because they are not effectively integrated into the larger scientific venture or have relied

---

[1] Data on the contacting intensity of nations can be obtained at http://home.ku.edu.tr/~mmousseau/ under "Economic Norms Data."

on insufficient research designs. For instance, McDonald, in this issue (2010), failed to consider Gartzke et al.'s (2001) capital openness variable or my own contract intensive economy variable; Gartzke and Hewitt, in this issue (2010), failed to consider contract intensive economy or McDonald's size of government; and in a prior study I (2009) overlooked the size of government. To make progress we all must make greater efforts at testing our variables in the presence of their competitors—or explain why consideration of a competing variable does not fit the study at hand.

I also worry about analyses of militarized interstate disputes that make a distinction of initiators from targets. McDonald (2010) uses a directed-dyad design that appears to equate side A in a militarized dispute as the side making the demand or having started the conflict. But as the creators of these data made clear: "The state or states on Side A should not be interpreted to be the states that 'started' the conflict, or that are responsible for the conflict" (Ghosn, Palmer, and Bremer 2004:138–139). He also reports analyses at the monadic or country level. Monadic tests are greatly inferior to dyadic ones in controlling for external threats and opportunities to fight.

I am also weary of control variables that lack theory. I do not understand how a regression can have substantial meaning without guidance on whether each control variable is likely to be confounding (may partly explain the independent variable) or intervening (may be partly explained by the independent variable). Particularly worrisome is when a control variable that lacks a stated purpose correlates with the independent variable. Studies by Gartzke and colleagues (Gartzke 2007; Gartzke and Hewitt 2010) include a control for foreign policy agreement ("preferences") but offer no theory for it. There is theory and confirming evidence that predicts common preferences as well as peace as consequences of contract intensive economy (Mousseau 2003). It thus seems to me that controlling for preferences in an examination of peace among nations is similar to controlling for chemotherapy in an examination of deaths from cancer: the relationship will be significant and may cause other variables (democracy; smoking) to be insignificant, but without guidance the results can not be persuasive.

NEED TO COMPARE THE THEORIES

Ultimately, theory is needed to discern whether a third variable is confounding or intervening (Blalock 1979:474). We therefore must continuously integrate our empirical tests with updated assessments of our theories. There is a general consensus on several dimensions of consequence in comparing theories: predictive and explanatory power, strength and quantity of anomalies, and internal coherence. On internal coherence, the capital openness model (Gartzke et al. 2001) stands on comparatively solid ground because it has been worked through formally; though an absence of formalization does not mean a theory is incoherent.

Of the capitalist peace theories, the greatest distinction in explanatory power is between those that are generally limited to explaining militarized conflict and those that cast a wider net in modeling foreign policy interests. Two capitalist peace theories start with the bargaining model: the capital openness model (Gartzke et al. 2001) depends on successful signaling that reduces bluffing and thus the information problem; McDonald's model (2010) depends on size of government as solving the commitment problem. Bluffing does not occur, and commitments are not needed, among actors with common interests. These models thus apply only to situations where actors have competing interests and are not equipped to account for variance in interests or motives to fight among nations. Most arguments for how trade interdependence can cause peace rely on the assumption that trading is cheaper than fighting—nothing here that I can see about varying interests.

I believe only my own capitalist peace theory clearly explicates interests: leaders of states with contract intensive economies are constrained by voters to promote economic growth and secure markets abroad, and thus have common interests in protecting and enhancing the global market by maintaining the supremacy of international law and order. Beyond interests, this model offers novel accounts for Islamist terror (Mousseau 2002–2003), the origins of liberal democratic values and institutions, social trust, economic growth and development, the legitimacy of the rule of law, and the formation of the Westphalian interstate system (Mousseau 2009). I believe there are few clear-cut claims of added explanatory power by other capitalist peace theories, though I may be in error here. I encourage greater efforts to explicitly identify the explanatory scope of all theories, as knowledge of this power is vital in assessing their promise.

More important than explanation is an ability to predict, and all the models can claim some success in accounting for some variance in war and peace among nations—though a more-conclusive verdict must await a head-to-head contest where all variables confront each other directly. Beyond this, it seems most models have generated few nontrivial and novel predictions that have been subsequently confirmed. I believe the primary exception is my own economic norms model, which successfully predicted the economic conditionality to democratic peace (Mousseau 2000; Mousseau et al. 2003), cooperation (Mousseau 2002), and common interests (Mousseau 2003).

On critical anomalies, further work along the lines taken by John Mueller in this issue (2010) is sorely needed. Mueller is correct in pointing out that the Nazi occupation of most of Europe was profitable—suggesting a problem for liberal approaches that assume peace is always more profitable than war. He also points out that the advanced nations engaged in imperialism and fought each other in two world wars. But whether these conflicts pose a challenge to the capitalist peace depends on what we mean by "capitalism." Future studies should examine the size of government (McDonald 2009) and capital openness (Gartzke et al. 2001) of these nations at these times. There is no need to explore the contract intensity of these nations (my own thesis): while large portions of both Germany's and Japan's industrial economies were privately owned, the commanding heights of these economies were linked not by markets but by state bureaucrats, and most laborers were slaves in fact or practice; and during their periods of expansion the imperial nations did not have contract intensive economies as evidenced with emigration rates, which indicate weak opportunities in their domestic markets (Mousseau 2009:74).

John Mueller (2010) is also correct that any theory that depends on wealth being a universal dominant goal stands on weak grounds. In politics, actors often pursue goals other than wealth, the infamous case being Hitler's costly effort to exterminate Europe's Jews, who were also a very cheap source of labor. Nevertheless, I believe only two capitalist peace theories are stricken by this critique: the capital openness (Gartzke et al. 2001) and classical liberal (Weede 1996) models, as both seem to require wealth to be a dominant goal. The government size model (McDonald 2010) is based on credible commitments rather than signaling, and I believe only signaling requires actors to share the same goals so they can correctly read each other's intentions and costs through signals. My own economic norms model goes further and explicates variance in goals: nations with contract intensive economies are predicted to give more importance to market growth than other nations, and be more likely to have citizenries who believe that wealth is best achieved through trade rather than war. In this way, this theory identifies how popular ideas regarding war and peace can change over time, which Mueller rightly emphasizes, and how some countries can come to decide that trading is better than fighting (Rosecrance 1986).

THE CAPITALIST PEACE: A TANTALIZING RESEARCH BET

While the democratic peace has been in the spotlight over the past generation, the capitalist peace may prove to be the more powerful and useful observation. This is not only because the capitalist peace may supplant the democratic one: it is because the capitalist peace implies a more practical set of policy recommendations for achieving global peace and security. While the democratic peace suggests the amorphous and potentially conflict-inducing policy of promoting democratization abroad, the capitalist peace suggests—depending on which capitalist peace theory, if any, is the right one—the promotion of freer markets (Weede 1996; Gartzke et al. 2001;

MacDonald 2007) or increased regulation, redistribution, and spending to create full employment economies (Mousseau 2000; 2009). It is thus important to know the power of the capitalist peace, and which explanation for it is most persuasive. To do this correctly we must rely not on what feels right, but on the comparative predictive and explanatory power, and intensity of anomalies, of the competing theories. Whichever direction the evidence leads us, there seems little doubt that the capitalist peace offers a most tantalizing research bet.

REFERENCES

Blalock, Hubert M., Jr. (1979) *Social Statistics*, 2nd ed. New York: McGraw-Hill.

Bremer, Stuart A. (1992) Dangerous Dyads: Conditions Affecting the Likelihood of Interstate War, 1816–1965. *Journal of Conflict Resolution* 36(2):309–341.

Dafoe, Alan. (2009) Democracy Still Matters: The Risks of Sample Censoring, and Cross-Sectional and Temporal Controls. Available at: www.allandafoe.com/research.htm (Accessed February 25, 2009.)

Gartzke, Erik. (2007) The Capitalist Peace. *American Journal of Political Science* 51(1):166–191.

Gartzke, Erik and J. Joseph Hewitt. (2010) International Crises and the Capitalist Peace. *International Interactions* 36(2):115–145.

Gartzke, Erik, Quan Li, and Charles Boehmer. (2001) Investing in the Peace: Economic Interdependence and International Conflict. *International Organization* 55(2):391–438.

Ghosn, Faten, Glenn Palmer, and Stuart A. Bremer. (2004) The MID3 Data Set, 1993–2001: Procedures, Coding Rules, and Description. *Conflict Management and Peace Science* 21(2):133–154.

McDonald, Patrick J. (2007) The Purse Strings of Peace. *American Journal of Political Science* 51(3):569–582.

McDonald, Patrick J. (2009) *The Invisible Hand of Peace: Capitalism, the War Machine, and International Relations Theory*. New York: Cambridge University Press.

McDonald, Patrick J. (2010) Capitalism, Commitment, and Peace. *International Interactions* 36(2):146–168.

Mousseau, Michael (2000) Market Prosperity, Democratic Consolidation, and Democratic Peace. *Journal of Conflict Resolution* 44(4):472–507.

Mousseau, Michael. (2002) An Economic Limitation to the Zone of Democratic Peace and Cooperation. *International Interactions* 28(2):137–164.

Mousseau, Michael. (2002–2003) Market Civilization and its Clash with Terror. *International Security* 27(3):5–29.

Mousseau, Michael. (2003) The Nexus of Market Society, Liberal Preferences, and Democratic Peace: Interdisciplinary Theory and Evidence. *International Studies Quarterly* 47(4):483–510.

Mousseau, Michael. (2009) The Social Market Roots of Democratic Peace. *International Security* 33(4):52–86.

Mousseau, Michael, Håvard Hegre, and John R. Oneal. (2003) How the Wealth of Nations Conditions the Liberal Peace. *European Journal of International Relations* 9(2):277–314.

Mueller, John. (2010) Capitalism, Peace, and the Historical Movement of Ideas. *International Interactions* 36(2):169–184.

Polanyi, Karl. (1957[1944]) *The Great Transformation: The Political and Economic Origins of Our Time*. Boston: Beacon Press.

Rosecrance, Richard. (1986) *The Rise of the Trading State: Commerce and Conquest in the Modern World*. New York: Basic Books.

Weede, Erich. (2005) *Balance of Power, Globalization and the Capitalist Peace*. Potsdam: Liberal Verlag (for the Friedrich Naumann Foundation).

Weede, Erich. (1996) *Economic Development, Social Order, and World Politics*. Boulder, CO: Lynne Rienner.

Capitalist Influences and Peace

RICHARD ROSECRANCE
Harvard Kennedy School, Harvard University

Toynbee argues that the forces of industrialism should have prevented war in the nineteenth century (Toynbee 1939). Instead the universal forces of industrialism got poured into nationalistic bottles. Tariffs went up, imperial acquisition recommenced, and the stage was set for world war. Of course, Toynbee was not entirely correct about the analytical influence of industry. The Industrial Revolution made it possible to "make" things, rather than to "take" things. But if you take territory, you get a greater labor force and a greater ability to make things. You also get raw materials which industrialism needs. Finally, industrialism gives you weapons which, at least at first blush seem to make the waging of wars easier and more efficient, with quicker decision times. So machines alone do not prevent war. Industrialism does not in this sense increase interdependence between states, and it may even make states less dependent on one another.

Karl Deutsch contended that as previous agricultural states industrialized, they would import less and certainly would need fewer industrial products from the outside world. Thus trade over GDP ratios could be expected to fall, reducing overall interdependence. This was in fact true. In Europe, the ratios in 1914 were lower than the ratios for 1870. High ratios were not achieved again until the 1950s (Deutsch and Eckstein 1961). Another factor was the growth of intra-industrial trade. In the nineteenth century, commerce was largely between agricultural and industrial economies which traded food for manufactures. After 1950, trade was primarily in industrial products, and agricultural commodities lost their previous value in the terms of trade (Nurkse 1958). But rapidly developing industrial countries found a niche as differentiated manufactures products emerged, accounting for a rise in the FT/GDP ratio (Gould 1972).

But when ratios went up, political-economists might claim that they were involved with types of standardized industrial products like autos, TVs, electronics, cell phones, etc. in which all that the international market did was to give the potential purchaser an extended range of choice. Each major country (Great Power) could produce these items by itself, so it really did not need to trade to achieve availability. This already existed. Vulnerability interdependence did not exist in the sense of a deprivation of a whole line of goods if war intervened (Waltz 1979).

Beginning with Ray Vernon's "Sovereignty at Bay," however, one sees product life cycles that change this situation (Vernon 1971). They involve (1) U.S. development and production at home; (2) sale to export markets of the new product; (3) latecomer production abroad of the product; (4) export to the United States and finally (5) U.S. firms producing abroad in order to import (low labor cost) products to the United States. Production chains add vulnerability to the outcome (Brooks 2005). There are two possibilities: (1) an aggressor attacks and captures the home base of a major corporation; (2) the aggressor attacks and captures part of the production chain of one or more major corporations. In the first instance, the research and development facility is trapped, but the question arises: will the managers and technicians continue to perform for the conqueror? This question will be especially relevant if sanctions are placed on the aggressor, diminishing his ability to sell or buy abroad. In the second instance, segments of the production chain do not add up to a finished product. Would possession of automotive transmissions alone, say, aid an aggressor? Suppose that the home base firm before an attack enjoyed considerable economies of scale, industrially. These economies are likely to be lost to an aggressor who possesses only one link in the chain. And he may not be able to sell that segment to others at an appreciable return. As Jeff Frieden shows, fearing nationalization, in recent years MNCs have located only one or two links in the production process within the borders of developing societies. If they are seized, the new holder can do little with them, barring consent of the other international elements in the chain (Frieden 1994). As one example, consider the Hong Kong empire of Li & Fung.

> Li and Fung work with 10,000 suppliers in 48 countries to source materials and makers for clients. So a fabric from India that gets dyed in China will go to Thailand to be embroidered (with sequins made in Korea and rhinestones from Brazil) and then return to China to be cut into garments. The firm adheres to a '30/30' principle; it guarantees that it will purchase at least 30% of the business from each supplier, but will not exceed 70%. This ensures that no one in the network is captive [to the home office] . . . (Cukier 2007).

Seizure of a particular part of Li & Fung's production chain would do little to advantage an aggressor that was seeking the gains earned by the leaders of the corporation. It is even arguable that taking Hong Kong–unless it imprisoned and enlisted Li & Fung's managers themselves personally–would do little to advantage a conqueror. In the past, land could be captured. It was a fixed factor of production. But capital, labor, and technology cannot reliably be taken: they are intrinsically mobile and will leave. Thus MNC production chains link nations together in ways that military seizures of units of production will not fully sever. The gains achieved will be less than the costs endured to capture them. In which case, aggressors would be better off relying on free access to other markets rather than pursuing an evanescent attempt at imperial control.

The connections among markets are now very different from nineteenth century or early twentieth century counterparts. Trade was then the salient way of tying markets and production together. If trade were cut, countries would have to switch to autarchy and perhaps develop ersatz products or substitutes. That is why conflict is in these periods is linked to tariffs and financial restrictions on trade. By military expansion, one country seeks to substitute control for a failing access to markets.

In the twenty first century such strategies are anachronistic. This is because, as Robert Mundell proved, one can substitute the movement of factors of production for any deficiency in the movement of trade. If goods do not flow between markets, capital can (Mundell 1957). This permits a country to produce within the target market area the very products that it had originally sought to export to that market. In this way foreign direct investment—the ownership of 10–20 or more percent of a company (within the tariff area)—substitutes for the failure of trade. There were no such high FDI investments between Britain and Germany, Germany and France, or Austria and Russia in 1914. Such FDI as existed was largely devoted to ownership of firms in the colonies or agricultural countries overseas—Australian and Canadian railways or Argentine grain or cattle ranches. These FDI ties did not prevent World War I. Such ties were even weaker before World War II (Rosecrance and Thompson 2003). Where such ties exist reciprocally, however, recent data show that conflict among the parties significantly declines. It is important to note that there are many areas of the world that are presently linked together by such ties, making tariffs less worrisome: the U.S. and Europe; Japan and U.S.; U.S. and China: Japan and China: Japan and Europe. Thus the current Great Recession, even though it may raise tariffs, will not prevent one country from producing its goods inside the borders of another. The essential exchange and interdependence will not be measurably reduced or affected.

Erik Gartzke and Joe Hewitt contend usefully that military crisis is mitigated by the presence of nuclear weapons among major capitalist economies, giving rise to "Chicken" as the relevant game amongst them. But development also dampens conflict as middle classes prosper and gain power. It appears to be a fact that financially open nations experience fewer international crises. As we shall see below, however, much depends upon whether abundant or scarce factors of production are in political control at the time. Patrick McDonald claims that peace is strengthened as private property substitutes for previous government assets. Then the government (liberal or autocratic) has fewer resources of its own to command for use in war. John Mueller adds that the connection between peace and economic growth is mutually reinforcing. Trade is indeed better than conquest, but people have to acknowledge this. When they do, a world "sunk in bovine content" will develop even more rapidly. Erich Weede strives to apply such findings to China. Power transitions usually lead to war. Before these occur, China, thus, needs to be bound up in capitalist connections with the Western world and Japan. Mutual foreign direct investment, he says, strengthen such ties; so does economic openness.

In addition interdependence and reciprocity are strengthened in other ways. As Benn Stiehl and Bob Litan point out in their book, "Financial Statecraft," currencies are now more closely linked together than they were previously (Steihl and Litan 2008). The dollar the yen and the euro are the three dominant currencies in the world, and most others are tied to them. Except for the top three, few others are freely fluctuating. Members of the euro are drawn together fiscally as well as monetarily as a result of the European Stability Pact. Despite some past appreciation, China's renminbi is closely tied to the U.S. dollar. Most emerging countries have developed close links with one of the central or core currencies. This tends to suggest that both positive and negative interdependence subsist in such cases. If one major country's currency goes down, others will be drawn down with it, as the two currencies fall in tandem. Appreciation is also linked. In this way the communication of prosperity or recession takes place among economies tied together monetarily. Nor was it surprising that in 2008 China took a massive hit from the great recession as did European and American economies. Ultimately all three groups will recover together, though at different rates of growth.

In addition, preferential trade agreements have brought linked countries closer together. There is a huge literature on the effects of either customs unions or currency unions. Jeff Frankel and Andrew Rose have shown that GDP can rise appreciably if two countries tie their currencies to each other (Frankel and Rose 2002). Customs unions also result in marked increases in trade and GDP for the associated member countries (Rose and Honohan 2001). It is not surprising in this instance that countries are lining up to become members of the European Union and to join the euro currency. Those that are not involved in such large blocs have nonetheless sought bilateral Preferential Tariff Arrangements to gain benefits following the failure of the Doha Round of tariff cuts. Latin America and East Asia are offering new systems of tariff preferences. The U.S. has extended bilateral PTAs to 20 countries, and it will also benefit from East Asian arrangements to cut tariffs for its members.

Should countries then rest content that the development of capitalism, trade, and financial flows will prevent war among Great Powers? Not necessarily. We already know what happened in the nineteenth century when ecumenical influences were captured in nationalistic bottles. Nationalism is on the rise in Asia, the Middle East, Africa, and Latin America. It may be on the rise in China as it liberalizes and perhaps democratizes. Russia is already a burgeoning nationalistic power. Indian nationalism grows, but to this point in association with the United States. The mobilization and growing literacy of a people in the first instance stimulates national consciousness. This is already taking place in mainland China. In the longer term China, if left alone, will chart a nationalist, possibly anti-Japanese course. The Taiwan issue will become more important. How can this upwelling of nationalist fervor be channeled into progressive directions? Perhaps it is only through a greater migration, temporary if necessary, of rising elites. It is not possible to influence the Chinese population as a whole. But it is possible to try to socialize its leadership, more of which needs to study and work in Western countries and in the United States.

Finally, governance is important. This is not to endorse democrats in power as a solution to all problems. Germany was a democratizing country in 1914 and the Social Democratic Party was the largest in the Reichstag. But land and capital—"scarce" factors of production—dominated German politics at the end of the nineteenth century. For peace and openness to obtain, it is important that "abundant" factors of production—favoring openness—take the helm in national politics. Samuelson and Stolper showed that "abundant" factors of production—easily able to cope with foreign competition—favor low tariffs, while "scarce" factors need tariffs to protect themselves (Stolper and Samuelson 1941). Scarce factors were in fact in charge of every major power except England in 1914 (Rogowski 1991). Scarce capital and land ran Germany; scarce labor and capital preponderated in United States' politics; scarce capital and labor dominated Russia (as to opposed to abundant land). Austria-Hungary was controlled by scarce land and capital. Only in Great Britain did abundant capital and labor come to the political fore, and England was the last and most reluctant entrant into war.

Fortunately, abundant factors—particularly capital—have come to power in Europe and the United States in the years since. China's leaders have capitalized on abundant labor, initially sacrificing strengths in capital and land. In time, however, China too will move to abundant capital and the outcome will then revolve around industrial changes in Japan, the United States, and Europe. In relative terms, growing Chinese capital abundance will shift Western and Japanese economies toward reliance on labor which might then shift toward economic closure. American and Japanese capital will become less abundant, relatively speaking. Some, however, have claimed that a new factor of human capital might still remain abundant in Western countries and Japan. If so, future leadership in these countries might become less restrictionist than otherwise, and Western conflict with China could be moderated.

It is thus premature to claim that a "capitalist peace" has transpired or is waiting in the wings. Democratizing societies, capitalist or not, frequently conflict with one another. Autocratic countries may install scarce, not abundant, factors of production at the helm of state. As it did in the nineteenth century, nationalism still might press toward militarism if it is not thwarted in the next ten years. This can only be done by a greater association of elites of the major nations, educationally and culturally. Far more than was true of Germany in 1914, one of the great strengths of the Chinese leadership is its attention to and involvement with the outside world: the Chinese elite has reached an overarching conclusion that Beijing can learn and benefit from external influences. It may not emulate them, but it can study their successes as well as mistakes (Rosecrance and Guoliang 2009). So far, Social Darwinism, in the expansive military sense has few takers in China (Leonard 2008).

REFERENCES

Brooks, Stephen G. (2005) *Producing Security*. Princeton, NJ: Princeton University Press.
Cukier, Kenn. (2007) Rueschlikon Conference Report. Swiss Re, September.
Deutsch, Karl W. and Alexander Eckstein. (1961) National Industrialization and the Declining Share of the International Sector (1890–1959). *World Politics* 13(2):267–299.
Frankel, Jeffrey, and Andrew Rose (2002) An Estimate of the Effects of Common Currencies on Trade and Income. *Quarterly Journal of Economics* 117(2):430–466.
Frieden, Jeffry. (1994) International Investment and Colonial Control: A New Interpretation. *International Organization* Vol. 48(4):559–593.
Gould, John D. (1972) *Economic Growth in History*. London: Routledge.
Leonard, Mark. (2008) *What Does China Think?* New York: Public Affairs, Chapter Three.
Mundell, Robert. (1957) International Trade and Factor Mobility. *American Economic Review* 47(3):321–335.
Nurkse, Ragnar. (1958) *Problems of Capital Formation in Underdeveloped Countries*. London: Basil Blackwell.
Rogowski, Ronald. (1991) *Commerce and Coalitions*. Princeton, NJ: Princeton University Press.
Rose, Andrew K., and Patrick Honohan. (2001) Currency Unions and Trade: The Effect is Large *Economic Policy* 16(33):449–461.
Rosecrance, Richard, and Gu Guoliang. (2009) *Power and Restraint*. New York: Public Affairs.

Rosecrance, Richard, and Peter Thompson. (2003) Trade, Foreign Investment, and Security. *Annual Review of Political Science* 6:345–376.

Steihl, Benn, and Robert Litan. (2008) *Financial Statecraft*. New Haven, CT: Yale University Press.

Stolper, Wolfgang, and Paul Samuelson. (1941) Protection and Real Wages. *The Review of Economic Studies* 9(1):58–73.

Toynbee, Arnold J. (1939) *A Study of History, Volume IV*. London: Chatham House.

Vernon, Raymond. (1971) *Sovereignty at Bay*. New York: Basic Books.

Waltz, Kenneth N. (1979) *Theory of International Politics*. Reading, MA: Addison-Wesley.

Capitalism *or* Democracy? Not So Fast

BRUCE RUSSETT
Yale University

I welcome the request to comment on the three intriguing articles in this issue by Gartzke and Hewitt, McDonald, and Mueller.[1] Space and time constraints mean that much more theory and research will be needed to evaluate them properly. My basic message is to agree that elements of capitalism—meaning relatively free national and international markets for goods, services, labor, and capital—do help avoid conflict among states in the contemporary international system. But micro-level understanding of just why that happens for capitalism, as well as for democracy, remains contested in these articles as before.[2] So too does any claim that capitalism replaces some other widely accepted liberal or realist hypotheses rather than merely supplements them. The search for adequate causal explanations goes on, but is unlikely ever to produce a single explanation for what is probably an equifinal phenomenon. So both producers and consumers of this literature would be wise to refrain from early celebration or despair about the primacy of a capitalist peace. After some conceptual clarifications I discuss the three articles, in rough order of the degree to which they proclaim capitalism to

---

[1] I thank Allan Dafoe, Paul Huth, and John Oneal for valuable comments, and Joseph Hewitt and Patrick McDonald for sharing their replication files. My replication files are at http://dvn.iq.harvard.edu/dvn/dv/internationalinteractions.

[2] That rigorous DP or CP theory largely follows rather than motivates the first empirical observations disturbs some observers. Yet such efforts have a long history in science. While the idea of evolution was in the air of nineteenth century Britain, it remained for Charles Darwin to produce a good causal explanation. He spent his five-year voyage on the *Beagle* collecting thousands of specimens before conceiving the theory in *The Origin of Species by Means of Natural Selection*. Adequate micro-level understanding had to wait for Gregor Mendel's work on genetics and late twentieth century molecular biology.

be the prime influence. Only Gartzke and Hewitt claim that the effect of capitalism completely subsumes democracy.

On conceptual matters: The democratic peace (DP) is properly conceived as largely a dyadic phenomenon, with any monadic phenomenon generally weak and contingent (Russett 2009). Dyadically, it is a monotonic relationship (the more democracy, the less severe and frequent is violent conflict), but not necessarily a linear one; indeed the effect is especially strong at the ends of the dictatorship-democracy scale. It does not endorse the forcible imposition of democracy by outsiders (Russett 2005). It is a phenomenon of strategic interaction reflecting interests at both the domestic and international levels, and increasingly can be understood as extending beyond dyads to networks of triads, regions, and the whole globe (Maoz 2009, Kinne 2009, Dorussen and Ward 2010). Furthermore, this focus on interaction expands beyond the narrow DP to what Russett and Oneal (2001) called first the Liberal Peace and then the Kantian Peace (KP), involving commerce and IGOs. Our measure of capitalism has been restricted to trade by our effort to extend the temporal and spatial scope to times and states where dyadic measures of investment, communications, or labor markets have been unavailable. Nonetheless Oneal and I are comfortable with the Capitalist Peace (CP) enterprise if the analyses are properly specified and their limits are fully recognized.

We regard markets open to trade as a vital component of a capitalist peace. With proper controls for size, income, political regime, distance, etc., trade is somewhat correlated with other elements of the KP but still a strong and independent influence on conflict. Notably, trade openness has a monadic as well as dyadic effect on peace (Russett and Oneal 2001: chapter 4), which we attribute to political actors' interest in sustaining trade both dyadically and with the larger global system. We also concur that economic growth may contribute to peace, but do not label it as exclusively or inevitably a result of capitalism. (Soviet-style command economies grew rapidly for several decades; capitalist economies vary greatly in their growth rates.)

CAPITALISM, PEACE, AND THE HISTORICAL MOVEMENT OF IDEAS

In his article John Mueller extends his record of documenting the decline in large-scale political violence over the past century, and of addressing the ideas as well as the practices and institutions that probably contributed to that decline. Here he characterizes not just democracy and capitalism, but the widespread adoption of peace and economic prosperity, as desirable social goals, coupled with a somewhat lagging conviction that prosperity is better achieved by exchange than by conquest. Tracing the development of dominant ideas is a different and maybe more demanding enterprise than tracing the development of institutions and practices; certainly it has been less characterized by the manipulation of large data bases on "hard" variables like war, voting, and commerce. But it is refreshing to see the cultural dimension discussed here.

I would add something about the depth and spread of ideas about democracy and political equality. A corollary to his comments concerning the decline of colonialism is the fact that annual fatalities in colonial wars dropped from about 50,000 a year in the first wave of colonial rebellion after World War II, to 10,000 a year by the early 1960s and zero by the mid-1970s—no more colonies (Lacina and Gleditsch 2005). The failing ability and will to pay protracted high costs to suppress colonial people's aspirations for self-government owed much to the spread of egalitarian and democratic ideas to the colonies, and to the greater readiness among metropolitan populations to apply those principles to the peoples they had earlier colonized. So there is a similar and related spread of democracy as both a goal and a means to peace and prosperity.

Mueller is right to caution that the whole packet of liberal ideas (and institutions) need not go together. China, Singapore, and other authoritarian states embrace capitalism but not democracy. Despite its poverty, India was democratic decades before adopting more liberal policies toward domestic and global capitalism. In mature industrial countries some ideologies are liberal on civil liberties but not toward global capitalism, or vice versa. Just as it can be hard to distinguish between the effect of democratic and capitalist variables in quantitative studies, it may not be productive to unpack the whole "liberal" ideology too finely. The different elements share similar origins, and form a mutually reinforcing worldview.

CAPITALISM, COMMITMENT, AND PEACE

Patrick McDonald stakes a more modest claim than do Gartzke (2007) and Gartzke and Hewitt, which I discuss below. He contends that capitalism has more effect than democracy, but not that it washes democracy out. His argument about high ratios of public (i.e., government) to private property is a creative adaptation of some opportunity cost perspectives. So too his focus on internal political survival extends such analyses as Bueno de Mesquita et al. (2003) and Debs and Goemans (2010) of the structure of support on which a government depends.

In his book (McDonald 2009: chapter 9), democracy exerts an independent effect except in the 14 percent of cases with the highest public share. Democracy has a robust effect in the book's other dyadic analyses.[3] His

---

[3] Both in the book and article democracy's effect might be underestimated since he includes a measure of similar alliance portfolios to indicate shared interests. Alliance preferences may be endogenous to regime type, as the opposing cold war alliances each sought to defend political and economic interests shared across similar regimes. If so, alliance similarity could obscure the effect of democracy on conflict (Ray 2005, Russett and Oneal 2001: 236–37).

dyadic analysis here importantly distinguishes between initiator and target. For MIDs rather than wars (very rare events) democracy does not fare markedly worse than does his indicator of public/private property. He shows not only that the basic democratic peace proposition holds, but that democracies are more likely to be targets than initiators in disputes with mixed regimes. This fits with Oneal's (2006: 86–87) finding that autocracies are much more likely to target democracies than vice versa, and Huth and Allee's (2002: 255, 267) that in democratic/autocratic dyads it is usually the autocracies who escalate disputes.

Democracy works dyadically but not monadically. As indicated above, that is not surprising on either theoretical or empirical grounds. Of the contingent influences mentioned in Russett (2009), McDonald controls for great power status and number of states in the neighborhood (though not neighborhood quality; i.e., the proportion of nondemocratic states), but not the proportion of democracies in the system, or collective goods problems that impel big states to carry more of an alliance's collective defense effort, or differences among democratic institutions or top leaders. Even with all these in the equation (and the last ones are hard to measure), a robust monadic result may continue to evade us without close attention to democracies' bargaining with adversaries. Capitalism, however, works monadically as well as dyadically. So too does trade. These monadic results have promising implications for the spread of peace systemically, beyond similar dyads.

Both McDonald and Gartzke and Hewitt cite work on the pacifying effect of democracy as contingent on development. But Mousseau, Hegre, and Oneal (2003) find democracy not significant only in the poorest nine percent of democratic dyads over the years 1885–1992. Oneal and Russett (2005: 306) report that by 2000 only one percent of democratic dyads were below the threshold where democratic peacefulness was nullified. In Mousseau (2009) joint democracy would be significant throughout its range using the specification of either Mousseau et al. (2003) or Hegre, Oneal, and Russett (2010: Table 3). The latter includes the dyad's higher as well as lower democracy score, needed to identify the high probability of conflict between very democratic and very autocratic states (Oneal and Russett 1997). Even in Mousseau (2009), in 74 percent of democratic dyads (both states with a Polity score above +6) at least one member has a contract-intensive economy (CIE), and for them democracy's effect on conflict is significant. Most dyads where both states have CIE show both at a Polity score of +10 (Dafoe 2010). Neither can definitively be called the primary cause of peace.[4]

---

[4] Bayer and Bernhard (2010) raise a new specification issue in showing that analyses using the Polity scale rather than a simple regime dichotomy consistently *underestimate* the effect of democracy.

INTERNATIONAL CRISES AND THE CAPITALIST PEACE

Erik Gartzke and Joseph Hewitt continue here a long quest for a specification to show that evidence for a democratic peace is spurious. They offer hypotheses about capitalist signals, but unlike McDonald (2009) do not give micro case studies. Since they dismiss trade as not a proper capitalist variable, they are undisturbed by its failure to have any significant effect on conflict in Table 2 (p. 135), or in Table 3 (p. 137) after new variables are added to the first column. Interacting development (GDP per capita) with contiguity is a smart idea, but as cautioned above development is not necessarily a good measure of capitalism.

The scope and meaning of Gartzke and Hewitt's results showing that joint democracy does not inhibit crisis escalation is doubtful. That should be no surprise, since few democratic dyads ever escalate their conflicts into crises. They usually select themselves out by negotiations that prevent crises from arising. Only nine of Gartzke and Hewitt's 337 crisis dyads show both states with democracy scores above +5 (a low threshold). Five are ongoing conflicts of Cyprus or Greece with newly democratic regimes in *Turkey* (1963, 74, 76, 84, 87), and the other four are very recent and/or very unstable democratic regimes (Ecuador-*Peru* 1981, 1991; U.S.-*Syria* 1957; India-*Pakistan* 1990). Huth and Allee (2002: 251, 285–286; also Mitchell and Prins 1999) report that, even in dyads with enduring territorial disputes, only a few democratic dyads get involved in military confrontations and "there are no cases of mutual decisions to escalate to high levels!"

Their Appendix analysis of crisis onset is more central to the DP, and closely follows that by Gartzke (2007) for MIDs and wars. A verdict hangs on how persuasively they specify their equations. They still use interest (UN voting preferences), which is better conceptualized as endogenous: a consequence of regime type, trade patterns, and development rather than a truly independent variable (Russett and Oneal 2001: 228–237; Kim and Russett 1966), requiring a multi-equation system. This kind of endogeneity demands careful scrutiny.

Dafoe (2008, 2010; also Choi 2011) powerfully identifies three other research design flaws in Gartzke's 2007 claim to replace democracy with capitalism as driving the DP/KP. Correcting any one flaw vitiates that article's claim about MIDs. This analysis repeats the dubious practices of using atheoretic regional dummy variables, and of restricting the temporal domain. If the dummy for Middle East (which correlates quite negatively with democracy) is dropped from Model 1 in Table 4, the coefficient for DemLow becomes even more significant. If Model 1 without the Middle East dummy is applied only to the 1966–1992 period (cutting 16 years and shrinking the sample by 19 percent), DemLow remains significant, contra their note 6. Only with the Middle East dummy does DemLow become insignificant in this period. Then adding Financial Openness (Model 2) to those years just slightly reduces the effect of DemLow further. So the *combination* of the Middle East dummy and the restricted time frame—not Financial Openness—does the damage.

COMPLEXITY AND CAUTION

Democracy should not be subsumed as merely a correlate or consequence of capitalism. Capitalist peace theory can be expanded to consider a variety of possible direct and indirect effects. Indirect effects of capitalism on peace may operate not only through democracy, but through common IGO memberships, bringing IGOs into the orbit of capitalism as well as democracy. Ingram, Robinson, and Busch (2005) support this idea, finding not only that trade increases sharply in networks with greater IGO connection, but that the benefit comes from IGOs formed for social and cultural purposes as well as through economic IGOs. The complexity of causal patterns is a major theme of Russett and Oneal (2001). Our Kantian Triangle shows causal arrows for democracy, economic interdependence, and IGOs at each apex of the triangle contributing to peace at the center—but also three reverse arrows for peace contributing to democracy, interdependence, and the formation and effectiveness of IGOs. Then it adds six reverse causation arrows along the sides: between interdependence and democracy, interdependence and IGOs, and IGOs and democracy. There is some empirical support for all twelve, yielding a model of twelve simultaneous equations![5] The need to analyze networks as well as dyads imposes complexity far beyond anything yet achieved for international relations.

In the longer conference version of his comment here, Erich Weede cautioned that findings must be "replicated again and again" before discarding results that have so far withstood most challenges. "Liberals" should be cautious about exalting capitalism above democracy on weak evidence. Readers would do well to suspend judgment on some complex results until our research community has critiqued and replicated them, discovering just how the sausages were made. That is a necessary but not sufficient condition for creatively modeling complex causal relationships in an international system with endogeneities where liberal influences interact and strengthen one another. For example, Gat (2005) contends that representative institutions are best produced by the wealth and culture of modernity in republics of recent centuries. That culture assuredly includes capitalism and high

---

[5]This is a big problem even in two-stage models, for example the Keshk, Pollins, and Reuveny (2004) simultaneous model of the relations between trade and conflict. Hegre et al. (2011) show that a few theoretically-informed corrections produce the intuitively plausible two-way relationship: trade reduces conflict, and conflict reduces trade.

income, but also such elements as the control of debilitating disease, free expression, the sexual revolution and women's rights, property rights, and broader conceptions of human rights. While capitalism assuredly buttresses this culture, the culture in turn promotes both capitalism and representative government. We have a continually evolving system of liberal influences that adapt to one another and to changes in their institutional and ideational environment.

In such a system we may be able to identify certain variables as consistently important, but not fine-tuned stable results about the relative importance of one variable over another. These cautions are consistent with Mueller's admonitions. Still, they neither require despair of causal explanations nor impose an impossible standard on our complex quantitative analyses. Rather, they recognize our success in identifying various liberal ideas and institutions as both subjects and objects of international relations, and the need to respect that complexity as we embed our scientific research into our wider understanding.

REFERENCES

Bayer, Resat, and Michael Bernhard. (2010) The Operationalization of Democracy and the Strength of the Democratic Peace: A Test of the Relative Utility of Scalar and Dichotomous Measures. *Conflict Management and Peace Science* 27(1):85–101.

Bueno de Mesquita, Bruce, Alastair Smith, Randolph Siverson, and James Morrow. (2003) *The Logic of Political Survival*. Cambridge, MA: MIT Press.

Choi, Seung-Whan. (2011) Re-evaluating Capitalist and Democratic Peace Models. *International Studies Quarterly* 54:forthcoming.

Dafoe, Allan. (2008) Democracy Still Matters: The Risks of Sample-Censoring, and Cross-Sectional and Temporal Controls, at: http://www.allandafoe.com/research.htm

Dafoe, Allan. (2010) Statistical Critiques of the Democratic Peace: Caveat Emptor. *American Journal of Political Science* 54:forthcoming.

Debs, Alexandre, and Hein Goemans. (2010) Regime Type, the Fate of Leaders, and War. *American Political Science Review* 104:forthcoming.

Dorussen, Han, and Hugh Ward. (2010) Trade Networks and the Kantian Peace. *Journal of Peace Research* 47(1):29–42.

Gartzke, Erik. (2007) The Capitalist Peace. *American Journal of Political Science* 51(1):166–191.

Gat, Azar. (2005) The Democratic Peace Theory Reframed: The Impact of Modernity. *World Politics* 58(1): 73–100.

Hegre, Håvard, John R. Oneal, and Bruce Russett. (2010) Trade Does Promote Peace: New Simultaneous Estimates of the Reciprocal Effects of Trade and Conflict. *Journal of Peace Research* 47:forthcoming.

Huth, Paul, and Todd Allee. (2002) *The Democratic Peace and Territorial Conflict in the Twentieth Century*. Cambridge: Cambridge University Press.

Ingram, Paul, Jeffrey Robinson, and Marc Busch. (2005) The Intergovernmental Network of World Trade: IGO Connectedness, Governance, and Embeddedness. *American Journal of Sociology* 111(3): 824–858.

Keshk, Omar, Brian Pollins, and Rafael Reuveny. (2004) Trade Still Follows the Flag: The Primacy of Politics in a Simultaneous Model of Interdependence and Armed Conflict. *Journal of Politics* 66(4):1155–1179.

Kim, Soo Yeon, and Bruce Russett. (1996) The New Politics of Voting Alignments in the United Nations. *International Organization* 50(4): 629–652.

Kinne, Brandon. (2009) *Beyond the Dyad: How Networks of Economic Interdependence and Political Integration Reduce Interstate Conflict*. Unpublished Ph.D. Dissertation, Political Science Department, Yale University, New Haven, CT.

Lacina, Bethany, and Nils Petter Gleditsch. (2005) Monitoring Trends in Global Combat: A New Dataset of Battle Deaths. *European Journal of Population*. 21(2): 145–166. Update 2009 at: http://www.prio.no/CSCW/Datasets/Armed-Conflict/Battle-Deaths/

Maoz, Zeev. (2009) The Effects of Strategic and Economic Interdependence across Levels of Analysis. *American Journal of Political Science* 53(1): 223–240.

McDonald, Patrick. (2009) *The Invisible Hand of Peace: Capitalism, the War Machine, and International Relations Theory*. Cambridge: Cambridge University Press.

Mitchell, Sara McLaughlin, and Brandon Prins. (1999) Beyond Territorial Contiguity: Issues at Stake in Democratic Militarized International Disputes. *International Studies Quarterly* 43(1): 169–183.

Mousseau, Michael. (2009) The Social Market Roots of Democratic Peace, *International Security* 33(4): 52–86.

Mousseau, Michael, Håvard Hegre, and John R. Oneal. (2003) How the Wealth of Nations Conditions the Liberal Peace. *European Journal of International Relations* 9(2): 277–314.

Oneal, John R. (2006). Confirming the Liberal Peace with Directed Dyads, 1885–2001. In *Approaches, Levels, and Methods of Analysis in International Politics*, edited by Harvey Starr. New York: Palgrave Macmillan.

Oneal, John. R., and Bruce Russett. (1997) The Classical Liberals Were Right: Democracy, Interdependence, and Conflict, 1950–85. *International Studies Quarterly* 41(2): 267–293.

Oneal, John R., and Bruce Russett. (2005) Rule of Three, Let It Be: When More Is Better. *Conflict Management and Peace Science* 22(4): 293–310.

Ray, James Lee. (2005) Constructing Multivariate Analyses (of Dangerous Dyads). *Conflict Management and Peace Science* 22(4): 277–292.

Russett, Bruce. (2005). Bushwhacking the Democratic Peace. *International Studies Perspectives* 6(4): 395–408.

Russett, Bruce. (2009) Democracy, War, and Expansion through Historical Lenses. *European Journal of International Relations* 15(1): 9–36.

Russett, Bruce, and John R. Oneal. (2001) *Triangulating Peace: Democracy, Interdependence, and International Organizations*. New York: Norton.

The Capitalist Peace and the Rise of China: Establishing Global Harmony by Economic Interdependence

ERICH WEEDE
University of Bonn

Historically, the rise and fall of great powers has been related to great wars. Both world wars of the twentieth century would not have been possible without the previous industrialization and rise of Germany. World War II, which in Asia was a war between the Japanese on the one hand and the Western powers and China on the other hand, would not have been conceivable without the previous rise of Japan. The early phase of the Vietnam War has to be understood against the background of a declining France. If the rise and fall of great powers indicate great dangers, then one should question whether the world can peacefully accommodate a rising China. Here it is argued that the capitalist peace offers the best way to manage the coming power transition between China and the West.[1]

China is rising. In the thirty years after Deng Xiaoping began economic reforms the Chinese economy grew nearly by a factor of ten. Recently, the West suffered from negative growth rates whereas China grows by about 8 percent a year. The difference in growth rates between China and the West has been about 10 percent. A power transition of such speed is without historical precedent. Given its size China is a "natural" great power—unlike Britain, France, or Germany. Even the combined population of the United States and the European Union does not approach the population size of China. If China outgrows poverty, then it must become a world power.

Although war in the nuclear age threatens to be much worse than any previous world war, fear of nuclear war itself might exert some pacifying impact. Such fear, however, need not be our only protection against future wars. Economic interdependence itself makes war less likely. One finding of quantitative research is that military conflict becomes less likely if a pair of nations—say China and the United States, or China and India, or China and Japan—trade a lot with each other (Hegre 2009; Oneal and Russett 2005; Russett and Oneal 2001). Fortunately, all of them do. One may label this effect "peace by free trade". Foreign investment has some beneficial impact, too (Souva and Prins 2006). Moreover, economic freedom reduces

---

[1] Helpful comments by Nils Petter Gleditsch, Bruce Russett, Gerald Schneider, and Ekkart Zimmerman to the Potsdam ECPR conference paper (which is a forerunner of this one) are appreciated.

involvement in military conflict, and financial market openness reduces the risk of war, too (Gartzke 2005, 2007, 2009). Quantitative research has demonstrated that there is something like a capitalist peace.

Until a few years ago it looked as if the democratic peace were solid and robust whereas the capitalist peace between free traders was less so. Now, however, the democratic peace looks more conditional: It is not only restricted to relations between democracies, but might also be restricted to developed or market democracies (Mousseau 2005, 2009). It has been doubted whether it applies to the poorest democracies. Moreover, the less mature or perfect the democracies are, the weaker the democratic peace is. By contrast, peace by free trade or economic freedom looks more robust. Pacifying effects are not restricted to relationships between free traders on both sides of a dispute (Russett 2009:19). Moreover, the trade to GDP ratio is no longer the only or even the best way to document the pacifying effects of economic freedom or the invisible hand. By applying innovative measures of free markets, such as avoidance of too much public property ownership and protectionism, one may argue in favor of much more robustly pacifying effects of economic freedom than of political freedom (McDonald 2009).

The occurrence of World War I is the standard argument against peace by trade or economic interdependence because there was substantial economic interdependence between the Western powers and the Central European powers. Certainly, World War I serves as a useful reminder that commerce makes war less likely without making it impossible. But World War I is not as much of a problem for capitalist peace theory as frequently assumed. Moreover, there was no democratic contribution to pacification because the Central European powers were, at best, imperfect democracies. By contemporary standards, even the democratic character of the United Kingdom was not beyond suspicion because of franchise limitations. As far as trade linkages were concerned they were strongest where least needed—between Britain and France, between Britain and the United States, between Germany and Austria-Hungary. These pairs ended up on the same side in the war. Whereas strong trade links between Germany on the one hand and Britain or Russia on the other hand did not prevent them from fighting each other, Germany and France exemplify weak trade ties where strong ties were needed most in order to avoid hostilities (Russett and Oneal 2001:175).

Skeptics rightly observe that increasing trade did not prevent World War I, but they overlook that trade volumes rose not because of free trade policies, but in spite of mounting protectionism. Trade increased because of falling transportation costs, but *in spite of* protectionist policies. Finally, capitalist or commercial peace theory is an admittedly incomplete theory. It says only how risks of war may be reduced but it says nothing about what generates them in the first place. But commercial peace theory is certainly compatible with World War II, which was even bloodier than the previous world war as well as with the later reconciliation between the former Axis powers and the West. There was little trade between the Western powers and the Axis powers. Since the Axis powers were not democracies, the democratic peace could also not apply between the Axis and the West.

The different long-term effects of the settlements of both world wars may be explained by differences in application of a capitalist peace strategy toward the losers of the wars. After World War I France influenced the settlement more than anyone else. It did not even think of a commercial peace strategy. Misery and desperation within Germany contributed to Hitler's empowerment and indirectly to World War II. After World War II, the United States, however, pursued a capitalist peace strategy toward the vanquished. It promoted global free trade and subsidized even the recovery of the losers of the war. Germany and Japan became prosperous and allies of the United States.

By and large, there is a lot of agreement within the research community that democracies rarely fight each other. If all major countries, including China, were ever to become democracies, then the risk of major power war or global war could be dramatically reduced. But the risk of conflict and war seems to be highest between democracies and autocracies rather than between two autocracies. That is why the U.S.-China dyad looks at risk. Moreover, there remain some doubts concerning the effectiveness of the democratic peace where nascent, or poor or not yet "contract intensive," or unstable democracies are concerned. Since China is still poor, since China cannot avoid a period of transition, if it ever becomes a democracy, a democratic peace between China and other major powers looks more like a distant hope than like a pacifier that might become available in the near future when the Chinese economy might equal the American one in size, albeit not yet in per capita income.

Although few people in China expect a fast transition to democracy in the near future, the prospect for democracy in China is not hopeless. There is experimentation with elections at the local level. China is moving slowly toward the rule of law. Individual freedom has expanded. The press has become commercialized and investigative. For the sake of continuing economic growth and the achievement of a power status comparable to the United States, China has to become a knowledge society. The knowledge society requires liberalization. Those who criticize China for not moving faster toward democracy should remember some lessons from Western history. The sequence of establishing national identity, the rule of law, representative or accountable government, and mass franchise seems to matter. Establishing national identity first, the rule of law and accountable government second, and the mass franchise last is the best sequence to avoid political instability. China might need some time to institutionalize the rule of law and to move toward accountable government before it is ready for mass elections.

Economic cooperation and interdependence provide much more hope for the immediate future than democratization. The more countries trade with each other, the less likely military disputes between them become. Given the size of both economies and the distance between America and China, they already trade a lot with each other. As China is the first Asian giant to become capable of challenging the U.S., these pacifying ties happen to be in place where they are most needed. From a capitalist peace perspective there is another piece of good news. Although trade between India and China had been negligible for a long time, since 1999 it has grown. By 2009, China had become India's biggest trading partner. Economic interdependence or trade may exert some pacifying impact on the relationship between Asia's neighboring giants. Comparing the war-proneness of the Middle East with the avoidance of major military conflicts in the Far East over the past three decades, it is hard to avoid the conclusion that the East Asian focus on economic openness and interdependence, on commerce, exports and growth did contribute to the pacification of East Asia.

The qualifications which *might be* required to the peace by trade proposition do not negate these optimistic conclusions. Possibly, it is not trade but cross-border investment, capital market integration or even a commitment to economic freedom that pacifies most effectively. Or, it might even be the contract-intensity of economies (Mousseau 2009). Should future research confirm a shift of focus away from trade to other aspects of economic interdependence as the main pacifier, then optimism about Sino-American relations might still be based on some kind of capitalist peace. By contrast to Chinese hesitation to democratize, the seriousness of China's commitment to global economic integration deserves admiration. China is extremely open for such a big economy. Its share of world trade increased eightfold within 25 years after its economic reforms.

From an international trade perspective, all of East Asia has recently become a Chinese sphere of influence. China is the most important destination of Japanese, South Korean, and Taiwanese exports—ahead of the United States. Although Taiwanese politicians around the turn of the millennium rejected the idea of reunification *on the Mainland's terms*, and although *some* of them were attracted to the idea of declaring the legal independence of Taiwan, economic and social ties across the Taiwan Strait grew vigorously at the same time. Taiwanese companies employ millions of people on the mainland. About a million people from Taiwan live on the Chinese mainland. Mainland China has been the preferred destination of Taiwan's foreign investment. Since the lateral escalation of a military conflict between the People's Republic of China and Taiwan constitutes the most plausible scenario whereby the U.S. and China might get into a war, economic interdependence between China and Taiwan contributes to the preservation of peace. Recently, political relations between the People's Republic of China and the Republic of China on Taiwan have improved fast.

Given the record of Sino-Japanese wars in the past and the power of these neighboring states, the extent of Sino-Japanese economic cooperation provides another reason for optimism. The capitalist peace stands a chance to apply between China and its neighbors and competitors.

On the one hand, one may argue that the U.S. current account deficit and the U.S. bilateral trade deficit with China served the purpose of stabilizing China and integrating it into a U.S. dominated world order. Then, the economic relationship between the U.S. and China already served the national interests of both countries, at least until 2008. On the other hand, it has been argued that the global imbalance between Asian capital exports and American capital imports contributed to the crisis (Wolf 2009:100). Then the interdependence between China and the West explains not only how the Chinese economy can be affected by a crisis which began in the American housing market and banking system. The same interdependence, or more specifically, a division of labor, where China exports goods in return for American treasury bonds and where Americans consume too much, might be *one* of the determinants of the crisis. But this conceivable link between Chinese or Asian savings, American capital imports, and the current crisis is by no means generally accepted. The Fed and its monetary policy might be the main culprit. Had it followed the "Taylor rule" in setting interest rates in response to growth and inflation rates, then there would have been higher interest rates between 2002 and 2007, much less of a housing boom in the U.S., and at worst a minor recession instead of the descent into the depression from which the world has suffered (Taylor 2009). Or, the promotion of home ownership for everyone—without regard of credit worthiness—should have been avoided (Sowell 2009).

It is important to note that the capitalist peace is a less dangerous idea than the democratic peace. As the example of the American wars in Afghanistan and Iraq demonstrate, the idea of a democratic peace has been married to a crusading spirit in the recent past (Russett 2005). Moreover it was combined with an utter disregard of the meager prospects of success in bringing democracy to poor or oil-exporting societies with a long heritage of autocracy (Weede 2007). Legitimating current wars by hopes for regime change and future pacific benefits is dangerous. By contrast, the capitalist peace depends on decisions by private business. As the Sino-American dyad or even the PRC-Taiwan dyad demonstrate, strong and growing economic ties need not wait for regime similarity, democratization, or a lot of political agreement with each other. China's positive response to the opportunity of exploiting its comparative advantages within a global market, as well as its lack of readiness to reform its regime according to Western preferences, demonstrate that a capitalist peace between China and the West is feasible, whereas a democratic peace is not for a considerable time to come.

There are two reasons why the capitalist peace is more important than the democratic peace. First, the balance of empirical evidence has been shifting from supporting pacifying effects of democracy toward supporting pacifying effects of commerce and economic freedom, of trade and capitalism. Whereas early research investigated only pacifying effects of trade, more recent work also looks at capital market integration, protectionism, state ownership or economic freedom. It is too early to say which specific feature of market economies is most effective in underwriting peace. But one may dare to say that free markets promote peace. Second, the democratic peace—where its existence has rarely been called into question, i.e., among mature and prosperous market-oriented democracies themselves—is an effect of commerce and capitalism. Without capitalism and free trade, without economic development and prosperity, democracy is unlikely to be established and to survive (Inglehart and Welzel 2009; Lipset 1994). In this perspective, the democratic peace is little more than a component of the capitalist peace.

The promotion of peace by peaceful means is obviously preferable to the promotion of peace by war. The shining example of capitalist prosperity in the West, together with the demonstration by the early East Asian tiger economies that the West permits poor countries to catch up, sufficed to elicit home-grown reforms in China and elsewhere in Asia which improved the material conditions of life of hundreds of millions of people. There is an important difference between the promotion of peace by capitalism and commerce and its promotion by democratization. If one wants to enforce democratization by military means, then one may run into severe problems of implementation, as the United States has found out in Afghanistan and Iraq. The capitalist peace requires nothing more than the virtue of patience. It relies on limited government, whereas war easily expands the scope of government. Globalization promises to enlarge the market and therefore to increase the division of labor and to speed productivity gains and economic growth. By promoting economic freedom, trade, and prosperity, we simultaneously promote peace.

For the capitalist peace to apply, there are two requirements. First, capitalist peace theory has to be valid. In spite of some open issues, the research literature justifies some optimism in this regard. Second, global capitalism has to demonstrate good health and vitality. Since the financial and economic crisis of 2008, it is difficult to be optimistic in this regard. Open markets in rich countries for exports from poor countries generate credibility for free market institutions and policies. They complement export-oriented growth strategies in poor countries. Foreign direct investment by private enterprises and donations from private Western sources to poor countries are more likely to have a positive effect on the growth path of poor countries than official aid does. The more capitalist the rich countries become, the more they provide a model for emulation by poor countries as well as a market and a source of technology and investment for them. By resisting protectionism Western nations may simultaneously strengthen their own economies, improve the lot of the poor in the third world, and contribute to the avoidance of conflict and war. In a period of financial distress or during a global economic crisis, resistance to protectionism and other attempts to roll back capitalism are the most important tasks for those who prefer prosperity and peace over poverty and war.

In the first five months of 2009 global trade did decrease by as much as 30 percent. Globalization seems to be in retreat. When discussing the stimulus package, the American Congress had to be persuaded to include only a watered down "buy American" clause. It is still dubious whether the Obama administration is ready to lead the global fight against protectionism. During the depression of the 1930s the fight against protectionism was lost at the beginning when Smoot and Hawley succeeded in 1930 to raise American tariffs. Although the rise of Asia's demographic giants, China and India, makes a capitalist peace more urgent than ever, politicians do not fight hard enough for the Doha Round and global free trade.

REFERENCES

Gartzke, Erik. (2005) Freedom and Peace. In *Economic Freedom in the World*, edited by James D. Gwartney and Robert A. Lawson. Vancouver, BC: Fraser Institute, pp. 29–44.

Gartzke, Erik. (2007) The Capitalist Peace. *American Journal of Political Science* 51(1):166–191.

Gartzke, Erik. (2009) Production, Prosperity, Preferences, and Peace. In *Capitalism, Democracy and the Prevention of War and Poverty,* edited by Peter Graeff and Guido Mehlkop. Abingdon (UK): Routledge, pp. 31–60.

Hegre, Havard. (2009) Trade Dependence or Size Dependence? *Conflict Management and Peace Science* 26(1):26–45.

Inglehart, Ronald, and Christian Welzel. (2009) How Development Leads to Democracy. *Foreign Affairs* 88(2):33–48.

Lipset, Seymour M. (1994) The Social Requisites of Democracy Revisited. *American Sociological Review* 59(1):1–22.

McDonald, Patrick. (2009) *The Invisible Hand of Peace.* Cambridge: Cambridge University Press.

Mousseau, Michael. (2005) Comparing New Theory with Prior Beliefs: Market Civilization and the Liberal Peace. *Conflict Management and Peace Science* 22(1):63–77.

Mousseau, Michael. (2009) The Social Market Roots of the Democratic Peace. *International Security* 33(4):52–86.

Oneal, John R., and Bruce M. Russett. (2005) Rule of Three, Let It Be. When More Really is Better. *Conflict Management and Peace Science* 22(4):293–310.

Russett, Bruce M. (2005) Bushwacking the Democratic Peace. *International Studies Perspectives* 6(4):395–408.

Russett, Bruce M. (2009) Democracy, War and Expansion through Historical Lenses. *European Journal of International Relations* 15(1):9–36.

Russett, Bruce M., and John R. Oneal. (2001) *Triangulating Peace: Democracy, Interdependence and International Organizations*. New York: Norton.

Souva, Mark, and Brandon Prins. (2006) The Liberal Peace Revisited: The Role of Democracy, Dependence, and Development in Militarized Interstate Dispute Initiation, 1950–1999. *International Interactions* 32(2):183–200.

Sowell, Thomas. (2009) *The Housing Boom and Bust*. New York: Perseus (Basic Books).

Taylor, John B. (2009) *Getting Off Track. How Government Actions and Interventions Caused, Prolonged, and Worsened the Financial Crisis*. Stanford, CA: Hoover Institution Press.

Weede, Erich. (2007) Capitalism, Democracy, and the War in Iraq. *Global Society* 21(2):219–227.

Wolf, Martin. (2009) *Fixing Global Finance*. London: Yale University Press.

Index

Page numbers in *Italics* represent figures.
Page numbers in **Bold** represent tables.
Page numbers followed by 'n' represent footnotes.

abundant factors of production 147, 148–9
Adams, Henry 71
Afghanistan 162, 163
agenda control 5, 17–18, 19–20, **20**; *see also* policy affinity
AIC *see* Aike Information Criterion
Aike Information Criterion (AIC) 97–8
Allee, Todd 13, 112, 153, 154
alliance formation 25, 28–9, **30**, **32**, 40, 54, 55, 93, 152n
America *see* U.S.
analytic procedures *see* methodology/research design
Angell, Norman 2, 11, 16, 73
Aristotle 67
arms races/control agreements 44, 46, 47–51, 61
Austria-Hungary 146, 148, 159
autocracies 13, 38, 60n, 98, 120, 131, 149, 153, 160

Bairoch, Paul 68–9
bargaining: impeded by commitment problems 42, 44–5, 47, 48–9, 50, 60–1, 141; successful crisis diffusion 4, 12, 21, 27–8, 29, 141
Bayer, Resat 97, 153n
Bernhard, Michael 97, 153n
Bernhardi, General Friedrich von 71
Boehmer, Charles 4, 11n, 137
Bremer, Stuart 2, 54, 128, 137, 140
Britain 47, 49, 73, 146, 148, 158, 159
Buckle, Henry Thomas 72
Bueno de Mesquita, Bruce 13, 46, 90n, 152

capability ratio 25, 29, **30**, **32**, 40, 106, **107**, **108**, **109**, 119, 124, 132
capital openness/CAPITAL OPENNESS 3, 4, 21, 27–8, 100, **107**, **109**, 137, 138, 139, 140, 141, 142
capitalist peace: accommodating Asian economic growth 147, 148–9, 158, 161–4; contract theory *see* market capitalism/social-market capitalism; free-market capitalist peace *see* free-market capitalist peace; future security 148–9;
historical movement of ideas *see* historical movement of ideas; theoretical overview 1–6, 11–12, 16–20, 43, 59–60, 91–4, 137–43, 150–6; through predominance of private property ownership *see* public property ownership
China 57n, 147, 148, 149, 152, 158, 160–4
Choi, Seung-Whan 92, 95n, 115, 130, 154
CIE *see* CONTRACT-INTENSIVE ECONOMY (CIE)
civil war literature 5
classical liberalism 80, 83, 84, 138, 142
clientelist economies *see* personalist clientelism
climber metaphor for peace between democracies 14
cold war 2, 11, 15, 76
commitment problem 42, 44–5, 47–51, 60–1, 141
compatibility of interests 16, 17–21, **20**, 25, 27–8, **27**, 38, 40; voting preferences/INTERESTS (ICB measure) 25, 30, **30**, **32**, 33, 38, 154
constraint theories 14–16; *see also* cost/expense of war
contiguity *see* geographic contiguity
contract-intensive economies/impersonal markets 16, 43, 80–1, 84–9; causing market-capitalist peace 4, 84, 89–91, 92–3, 102; statistical variable *see* CONTRACT-INTENSIVE ECONOMY (CIE)
CONTRACT-INTENSIVE ECONOMY (CIE) 95, 153; results 95–101, **106**, **107**, **108**, **109**, 125, 133, **134**, **135**; specification issues 112, 116–21, 119, 128–9
cost/expense of war 14, 16–17, 18, 31, 44, 47–51, 72, 89, 141
Cramb, J. A. 67
crisis escalation *see* escalation
crisis intensity 4, 12, 22–3, 31–3, **32**
crisis onset: economic integration 26–7, **27**; escalation 28; interaction development with contiguity 22, 27, 28, 154; role of development 12, 17–20, **20**, 22, 23, 33, 38, 39, 40; testing market capitalist peace 93

166

INDEX

Cukier, Kenn 145
currency links 147
Cyprus 154

Dafoe, Allan 4, 6, 53, 82, 96, 97, 98, 114, 119–20, 121, 127, 134, 154; *see also* DR (Dafoe and Russett)
Dahl, Robert 64–5
Darwin, Charles 150n
data 55: 52–54, 94–5; *see also* Interstate Crisis Behavior (ICB) dataset; Militarized Interstate Dispute data set; polity score to measure democracy
democracy: cause of conflict 34, 43, 149, 151, 162, 163; in China 148, 160; in Gartzke's free market peace 21–4, 26, **27**, 29, **30**, 31, **32**, 33, 92, 139, 151, 154–5; in McDonald's capitalist peace 54, 55n, 56, **56**, 59–60, 80, 152–3; polity measures 24, 54, 94, 96, 120, 131, 153; rise of 75–6
democratic peace 12–13, 162–3; economic norms explanation 81–2, 95–9, **106**, **108**, 139, 163; economic norms explanation critiqued 82, 110–21, **124**, **129**; economic norms explanation defended 127–35; in liberal dyads 11, 14, 16, 21, 22, 33, 43, 60, 110, 151, 153, 154, 159, 160, 163; theoretical overview 3, 4, 11–16, 43, 59–60, 91–4, 150–6, 159, 162–3
Denzau, Arthur T. 86
Deutsch, Karl 80, 144
development 1, 2–3, 5, 10, 12, 138, 147, 154; causal relationship with peace 64, 70–1, 74, 75, 76; correlation with contract-intensiveness 139; *see also* contract-intensive economies/impersonal markets
crisis escalation 22, 29–30, **30**; crisis intensity 23, 31–3, **32**; and the democratic peace 33, 34, 43, 153, 159, 163; as a dominant goal 64, 65, 66–7, 67–70, **69**; interaction with contiguity 22, **27**, 28, 154; Middle East and North Africa 25; motive shift to policy differences 12, 16–20, 22, 23; statistical factor in crisis onset 38, 39, **40**; variable defined 25
DR (Dafoe and Russett) 127–32, 134
Drescher, Seymour 65

East Asia 147, 148, 161, 163; *see also* China; Singapore; Taiwan
economic crisis of 2008 1, 19, 146, 147, 162, 163, 164
economic growth *see* development
economic integration 21–2, 23, 26–7, **27**, 29, **30**, 31, **32**, 33
economic norms theory 81, 82, 84–9, 92, 101, 127, 128, 141, 142
economic openness 25, **27**, 29, **30**, 32, 38, **40**

Egypt 47
Engerman, Stanley 65
escalation: bargaining 4, 12, 21, 27–8, 29; between democracies 12, 21, 93, 154; during crisis onset 28, 44–5; hypotheses 12, 21–2, 28–30, **30**, 33; impact of market economy 93; use of Interstate Crisis Behavior (ICB) dataset 4, 11–12, 20
Eugene data generating program 55
Europe 69–70, **69**, 72, 76, 85, 141, 142, 144, 146, 147, 148, 159
European Union 147, 158
evolutionary theory 150n
expense/cost of war 14, 16–17, 18, 31, 44, 47–51, 72, 89, 141

Fearon, James D. 5, 12, 17, 18, 21, 44, 89
feudalism 85
financial openness 25, **27**, 29, **30**, 32, 38, **40**, 137, 147, 151, 155, 159
foreign investment 1, 83, 85, 92, 95, 146, 147, 158, 161, 163
France 47, 49, 72, 76n, 146, 158, 159, 160
Frankel, Jeffrey 147
free-market capitalism: caused by peace 64, 75; creating prosperity 83, 92; financial openness 25, **27**, 29, **30**, 32, 38, **40**, 137, 147, 151, 155, 159; pacifying effect 10, 12, 16–17, 34, 64, 137, 159, 162–3; *see also* prosperity/economic well-being; trade
free-market capitalist peace: contrasted with social market capitalist peace 80–1, 82, 83–4, 89, 92, 93–4, 102, 137, 138, 139; hypotheses 20–3; research context 1–6, 10–12, 16–17; research design 23–6; results 26–33, **30**, **32**, 38–9, **40**; theory 18–20
Frieden, Jeffry 145

Galtung, Johan 2
Gartzke, Erik 3, 4, 5, 6, 12, 26, 43, 59, 80, 83, 89, 92, 100, 102, 137, 138, 139, 140, 141, 142, 146, 150, 151, 152, 153, 154, 159
GDP: crisis escalation 29, **30**; crisis intensity 32–3, **32**; crisis onset 39, **40**; currency agreements 147; defining development 25, 26; linked to contiguity (development) 22, **27**, 28, 154; measure of wealth 99n; trade ratios 25, 56, 138, 144–5, 159
Gelman, Andrew 113, 133
geographic contiguity 22, 25, **27**, 28, **30**, 31, **32**, 33, 54, 55, **57**, **58**, 59, 72, 154
Germany 49–50, 72, 74, 142, 148, 149, 158, 159
Gleditsch, Kristian S. 53
Gleditsch, Nils Petter 2, 10n, 66, 92, 152
global markets 1, 12, 80; Chinese commitment to 161, 162; independence from democracy 152,

167

161; pacifying effects 16, 17–19, 22, 29, 31, 138, 151, 160, 163; personalist states 91; protection during economic recession 163–4; served by Market capitalism 90–1, 99, 139, 141, 142
government: military spending 44, 46, 47–51, 61; regime stability 45–7, 51–60; role in market economy 80, 81, 83–4, 139; size model (McDonald) 46–7, 137, 138, 140, 141, 142; *see also* public property ownership
Government Finance Statistics (IMF) 52–4
Great Britain *see* Britain
Great Recession/economic crisis of 2008 1, 19, 146, 147, 162, 163, 164
GREATPOWER 54, **56**

Hayek, Friedrich 80, 83, 102
Hegre, Håvard 16, 33, 112, 138, 153, 155n
Henderson, Errol A. 26, 115n, 129–30
Hewitt, Joseph 4, 6, 24, 80, 82, 83, 93, 94, 99, 100, 102, 138, 140, 146, 150, 151, 152, 153, 154
historical movement of ideas 4–66, 75, 151–2; democracy 75–6; peace promoting prosperity 64, 67, 70–1, 74; prosperity as a dominant goal 64, 66, 67–70, 74, 142, 151; prosperity through trade 64, 67, 71–4, 147, 151
Howard, Michael 69, 70
Hungary *see* Austria-Hungary
Huth, Paul 13, 112, 150, 153, 154

ICB dataset *see* Interstate Crisis Behavior (ICB) dataset
idea entrepreneurs 65, 66, 70, 73, 75
IGO membership 155
IMF *see Government Finance Statistics* (IMF)
imperialism 2, 17, 73–4, 80, 144–6
impersonal markets/contract-intensive economies 16, 43, 80–1, 84–9; causing market-capitalist peace 84, 89–91, 92–3, 102; statistical variable *see* CONTRACT-INTENSIVE ECONOMY (CIE)
India 145, 148, 152, 154, 158, 161, 164
industrialization/industry 12, 17–18, 26, 69–70, 142, 144–7, 148, 158
informational problems in bargaining 44–5
intensity of crisis 4, 12, 22–3, 31–3, **32**
interest compatibility 16, 17–21, **20**, 25, 27–8, **27**, 38, **40**; between contact-intensive/clietelist economies 87–8; voting preferences/INTERESTS (ICB measure) 25, 30, **30**, **32**, 33, 38, 154
intergovernment organizations (IGO) 155
Interstate Crisis Behavior (ICB) dataset 10, 11; crisis definition 24, 93, 101; crisis escalation/intensity analysis 20, 21, 24, 28–9, **30**, **32**;

crisis onset analysis 4, 26–8, **27**, 38–9, **40**, **132**; MIDs comparison 20–1, 24, 82, 93
Iraq 99, 162, 163
Israel 47

Japan 69, 72, 147, 148, 149, 158, 161, 162
Jones, Eric 69

Kant, Immanuel/Kantian peace 2, 3, 5, 11, 41, 43, 67–8, 71, 73, 74n, 151
Keynes, John Maynard 4, 81, 84, 102
Kuznets, Simon 67
Kydd, Andrew 48

Lakatos, Imre/Lakatosian standards 4, 97, 98, 129, 135
Latin America 147, 148
Lenin, Vladimir 2, 80
Li & Fung 145–6
liberal peace research agenda 1–6, 11–20, 59–60, 91–4, 150–6, 162–3
life insurance/LIFE INSURANCE PREMIUMS/CAPITA 85, 86, 94–5, *117*, 118
Lipson, Charles 11
Litan, Robert 147

McDonald, Patrick 3, 4, 5, 6, 17, 80, 83, 102, 137, 140, 143, 147, 152, 153
Mahan, Alfred Thayer 73
MAJOR POWER (social market peace analysis) 99, **106**, **107**, **108**, **109**, 116n
MAJORPOWER (public property analysis of peace) 55, **57**, **58**, 153
market capitalism/social-market capitalism 16, 43, 80–1, 84–9; statistical evidence for peace 95–101, **106**, **107**, **108**, **109**, 127–35, 139; theory of peace 81, 84, 89–91, 92–3, 101–2, 137, 138–9, 141; theory of peace critiqued 111, 112, 113–20
methodology/research design: capitalist peace through private property ownership 51–5; commentary 139–42, 153, 154; free market capitalist peace theory 11–12, 20, 23–6; market capitalist peace 94–5, **106**, **107**, 111–21, *117*, 119, **124**, 127–35, **130**, **132**, **133**; need for cumulative research design 139–40; trap of inductive theorizing 12–13, 140
Middle East 26, 38, 40, 47, 148, 154, 155, 161, 162
MIDs *see* Militarized Interstate Dispute dataset
Militarized Interstate Dispute dataset 54; evaluating the case for democratic peace 98, 99, 110–13, 116, 119–20, 153, 154; ICB dataset comparison 20–1, 24, 82, 93; targets in militarized interstate disputes (McDonald) 54, 59, 140
military spending 44, 46, 47–51, 61, 147

INDEX

Milward, Alan 65
Moltke, General Helmuth Von 67
MOUM (Mousseau, Orsun, Ungerer and Mousseau) 110–21, 124, 125, 127–35; *see also* market capitalism/social-market capitalism
Mousseau, Michael 3, 4, 5, 6, 7, 16, 33, 41, 42, 43, 81, 82, 84, 86, 87, 92, 93, 94, 96, 98, 99, 101, 110, 111, 112, 116, 118, 119, 120, 121, 128, 129, 134, 137, 138, 140, 141, 142, 143, 153, 159, 161; *see also* MOUM
Mueller, John 2, 4, 65, 66, 68, 70, 74, 141, 147, 151–2, 156
Mundell, Robert 146

nationalism 90, 148, 149
Nazi occupation of Western Europe 72, 141, 142
Nietzsche, Friedrich 67
North, Douglass 86
nuclear weapons 14–15, 18, 146–7, 158

Oneal, John R. 16, 26, 38, 60, 113, 115, 151, 152, 153, 158
Orsun, Omer F. 110; *see also* MOUM

Pearson, Karl 71
Perpetual Peace (Kant) 11, 67–8
personalist clientelism 84–8, 89–90, 99
Polanyi, Karl 16, 84, 138
policy affinity 12, 17–21, **20**, 22, 23, 27–8, 27, 39, **40**, 90, 139, 140
polity score to measure democracy 24, 54, 55n, 60n, 97, 131, 153n
Powell, Robert 42, 44n, 45, 47, 50
power status: free market peace analysis 25, 28, 29, **30**, 31, **32**; public property analysis of peace 54, 55, **56**, **57**, **58**, 59, 153; social market peace analysis 99, **106**, **107**, **108**, **109**, 116n
Preferential Tarrif Arrangements 147–8
private ownership 43, 46, 59, 60, 102; *see also* public property ownership
production 145–6, 147, 148, 149
property rights: domestic capacity for war 45–51, 89, 100, **107**, **109**, 147, 159; source of conflict *see* territorial conflict
prosperity/economic well-being: as a dominant goal 64, 66, 67–70, 74, 142, 151; in economic norms theory 99n, **107**, **109**; free-markets/trade 64, 67, 71–4, 83, 92, 137, 147, 151; removing motive for war 16, 18, 138
public property ownership: affecting a regime's ability/willingness for military action 45–51, 89, 100, **107**, **109**, 147, 159; in free market 80; in the impersonal economy model 100–1; indicator of likely military interstate disputes 152, 153; targeting in military conflict 4, 41, 42, 47, 50, 51–61, 153

Quan Li 137

regime difference 10, 11; justifying interventionism 153; leading to conflict (free market peace theory) 24, 28, 29, 38; use of DEMOCRACY (HIGH) 95n, 113–14, **117**, 119, 124, 127, 129–31, **130**, **132**, 134; use of REGIME DIFFERENCE to measure 82, 95, 99, **106**, **108**
regime stability 45–7, 51–60
Renan, Ernest 71
resources: conflict over *see* territorial conflict; domestic capacity for war 45–51, 89, 100, **107**, **109**, 147, 159
Rise of the Trading State, The (Rosecrance) 74
Rose, Andrew 147
Rosecrance, Richard 2, 6, 72, 73–4, 142, 146, 149
Rummel, Rudolph 2, 43
Russett, Bruce 2, 4, 6, 13, 18, 21, 26, 38, 55n, 60n, 82, 97, 110–21, 127, 134, 158, 159, 162; *see also* DR (Dafoe and Russett)
Russia 49, 49–50, 73, 99, 146, 148, 159

Samuelson, Paul 148
scarce factors of production 147, 148, 149
Schelling, Thomas 14–15
Schumpeter, Joseph 1, 2, 3, 5, 16
Selectorate theory 46–7, 90n
Seung-Whan Choi 92, 95n, 115, 130, 154
shark attack analogy 127–8, 134
Simon, Herbert 86
Singapore 92, 96, 98, 152
slavery 65, 66, 75, 80
Smith, Adam 72, 83
social market capitalism *see* market capitalism/ social-market capitalism
Stern, Hal 113, 132, 133
Stolper, Wolfgang 148
Stravinsky, Igor 71
Suez Crisis 47

Taiwan 75, 148, 161, 162
targeting public property regimes in military conflict 4, 41, 42, 47, 50, 51–61, 153
taxation 46, 47, 48, 49, 50, 52, 61, 84
territorial conflict: between contiguous states 25, 72, 154; development as a factor in reduced escalation/intensity 23; development as a reducing factor 12, 17–18, 19–20, **20**, 22, 38–9; Middle East 26; relationship to wealth 73; servicing industrialism 144
Toynbee, Arnold 144
trade: achievement of wealth 64, 67, 71–4, 76, 142; capital representativeness 11n, 138, 139; in capitalist peace research 2–3, 41, 137; contract-intensive economy analysis 93, 95, 99,

INDEX

100, **101**; cost of war 18, 141; and factors of production 144, 146; free-market capitalist peace analysis 24, 29, **30**, 31, **32**, 38, 40; military target likelihood analysis 54–5, 56, **56**, **57**, **58**; pacifying effects 1, 3, 43, 158–60; protection 146, 147–8, 163
Treitschke, Heinrich von 71
Turkey 154

Ungerer, Jameson Lee 81, 110; *see also* MOUM
United Kingdom 47, 49, 73, 146, 148, 158, 159
U.S. 34; and East Asia/China 146, 147, 160, 161, 162; economic growth 69, 69; Great Recession 147, 162, 164; production patterns 145; and Russia 15; slave emancipation 65; and Syria 154; territorial conflicts 72; trade 146, 147–8; war on terror 14, 162; World War I 1n

value-systems 67, 69, 70–1, 74n, 75
Vernon, Ray 145
Vietnam War 57n, 158

Wagner, R. Harrison 41n, 48
Wallerstein, Immanuel 80
war: absence between democracies/impersonal capitalist states 81, 92; bargaining model of 41, 42; between contiguous states 25, 72, 154; blamed on capitalism 80; civil war literature 5; cold war 2, 11, 15, 76; cost/expense of war 14, 16–17, 18, 31, 44, 47–51, 89; in democratic peace 13–14; desirability of 65, 67–8, 69; domestic capacity for war 45–51, 89, 100, **107**, 109, 147, 159; domestic constraints 47; economic after effects 65, 72–3, 160; motive shift territory to policy differences 12, 17–18, 19, 20, **20**, 22, 23, 39, **40**, 139; promoting innovation/civilization 70–1, 72; shadow of nuclear weapons 14–15, 18, 146–7, 158; World War I 48–50, 80, 146, 158, 159; World War II 72, 146, 158, 160
"war on terror" 14, 141, 162
wealth *see* prosperity/economic well-being
Weede, Eric 1, 3, 6, 16, 43, 83, 89, 92, 102, 137, 138, 142, 147, 155
Wells, H. G. 70
Werner, Suzanne 129, 131
Westernization 75
Wilkenfeld, Jonathan 29, 93
World Bank life assurance data 94–5
World War I 48–50, 80, 146, 158, 159
World War II 72, 146, 158, 160
Wright, Quincy 68
Wyatt, H. W. 71

Zola, Émile 71